809 STE ✓
loan

Understanding Metaphor in Literature

Studies in language and linguistics

General editors: GEOFFREY LEECH & MICK SHORT
Lancaster University

Already published:

A Dictionary of Stylistics
KATIE WALES

The Communicative Competence of Young Children
SUSAN H. FOSTER

Linguistic Purism
GEORGE THOMAS

Women, Men and Language
Second edition
JENNIFER COATES

Lexical Ambiguity in Poetry
SOON PENG SU

Understanding Metaphor in Literature
GERARD STEEN

UNDERSTANDING METAPHOR IN LITERATURE:

AN EMPIRICAL APPROACH

GERARD STEEN

Longman
London & New York

Longman Group Limited,
Longman House, Burnt Mill,
Harlow, Essex CM20 2JE, England
and Associated Companies throughout the world.

Published in the United States of America
by Longman Publishing, New York

First published 1994

808 GTE

ISBN 0 582 217156 CSD
ISBN 0 582 101182 PPR

British Library Cataloguing-in-Publication Data

A catalogue record for this book is
available from the British Library

Library of Congress Cataloging-in-Publication Data

Steen, Gerard,
    Understanding metaphor in literature: an empirical approach/
Gerard Steen.
        p. cm. — (Studies in language and linguistics)
    Based on research done for the author's thesis (doctoral) under
the title: Metaphor in literary reception
    Includes bibliographical references and index.
    ISBN 0–582–21715–6 (CSD). — ISBN 0–582–10118–2 (PPR)
    1. Metaphor–Psychological aspects.   2. Discourse analysis,
Literary.   3. Reader-response criticism.   I. Title.   II. Series:
Studies in language and linguistics (London, England)
PN228.M4S74   1994
808'.001–dc20   93–32427
                                                         CIP

Set in Palatino 9/11 pt by 15
Produced by Longman Singapore Publishers (pte) Ltd
Printed in Singapore

For Annemieke

Contents

CONTENTS

Preface

Metaphor has been the subject of such rich and varied investigation that it may be asked why it is necessary to add yet another publication to this stock. The reason is simple: although philosophical and theoretical speculation have been rife across the centuries, attributing a crucial function to metaphor for the way we make sense of all sorts of phenomena, such ideas have only recently been put to the test in empirical research on the actual usage of metaphor by people. This situation obtains even more for the particular aspect of metaphor that is the focus of the present book, understanding metaphor in literature.

Metaphor in literary reading involves psychological processes which have not received much attention from psychologists. It is true that psychologists have studied various aspects of metaphor processing in the recent past, but metaphor's specifically literary function, if it has one, has hardly been addressed. Nor have text-linguists and psycholinguists looked at literary text processing in much detail, so that there have not been many treatments of metaphor in literary reception from this quarter either. Finally, the few empirical researchers of literature with a psychological bent have produced interesting but scattered observations, mainly unconnected with mainstream psychological research on metaphor.

That metaphor in literary reception involves psychological processes is due to the fact that reception is a mental process taking place on the basis of individual acts of reading. If this seems a superfluous observation, it has been largely ignored by linguistics and literary theory, the other two disciplines that have a stake in the study of metaphor in literary reception. There is little informed attention to psychology in the writings of most linguists , who have mainly concerned themselves with the formal characteristics of metaphor. Linguists have been the originators of what has come to be known as the two-stage theory, which privileges literal meaning over other kinds of meaning, but this grammatical point of view does not translate directly into a two-stage psychological process. This difficulty, however, has not had a great effect upon the way most linguists have subsequently conceived of the role of literal and metaphorical meaning in actual usage.

Since Aristotle, literary critics and theorists have speculated on the aesthetic function of metaphor in literature. Metaphor, they have asserted, is especially suited to opening the eyes of the reader to previously unnoticed aspects of reality, and to expressing vehement or subtle emotions. To what extent these ideas about the cognitive and affective function of metaphor can be seen reflected in the actual processing of metaphor in literature by readers, however, has not been part of their concern. Although it is true that reading and interpretation have been at the centre of literary studies, literary scholars and critics have been largely interested in their own acts of reception, eventually to be laid down in professional publications. This kind of activity bears a very tenuous relationship with 'ordinary' literary reading.

How readers understand metaphors in literature is therefore still a very unclear matter. If the essential functions accorded to metaphor by a long tradition of thinking amounts to anything in the case of literature, it ought to be possible to collect evidence from the behaviour of readers which corroborates this view. It is the aim of this study to present aspects of an empirical theory of metaphor in literary reception and to show how evidence can be collected from readers' processing of metaphor in literary texts, in order to evaluate how that processing relates to the function of metaphor in literature.

The book is divided into three parts. Part One is called 'Reader, Text, Context'. It will provide an account of the empirical study of understanding metaphor in literature by discussing present-day developments in psychology and linguistics (Chapter 1) and literary theory (Chapter 2). I will argue that metaphor processing is affected by the three factors of text, reader, and context, and that understanding metaphor in literature can be conceptualized as embodying one specific type of configuration of these factors. In Chapter 3 I will make a first attempt at examining whether there is an observable and determinate relation between metaphor processing and literary reading by presenting two empirical studies on the relation between readers' experience of literariness and metaphors. Text, reader, and context variables were manipulated in order to investigate their effect on the experience of literariness through metaphors.

Part Two is concerned with 'Processes'. Understanding metaphor in literature is not a unitary process, and a number of processing distinctions are proposed in the context of the psychology of reading in Chapter 4. These distinctions are further developed by means of a series of pilot studies in thinking out loud about literary texts, which are presented in Chapter 5. This in turn leads on to a comparative study of the incidence of various kinds of metaphor processing in literary and journalistic reception in Chapter 6.

In Part Three, called 'Properties', I turn to the role of differences between metaphors. Chapter 7 presents a theoretical framework for the conceptualization and measurement of differences between metaphors. Literary and journalistic metaphors are then compared in Chapter 8 by means of two rating studies designed to tap five basic metaphor dimensions which can be presumed to be valid for all metaphors. Chapter 9 examines the effect of two of these dimensions, one cognitive and one affective, on the processing data reported in Chapters 3 and 6. In Chapter 10, I will discuss the bearings my findings have on linguistic, psychological, and literary approaches to metaphor.

The theories and hypotheses put forward in this book have been tested by means of a statistical analysis of data collected from readers of literature (Chapters 3, 6, 8, and 9). I have taken care not to bother the non-initiated reader with extensive discussions of technical points about figures. All necessary details regarding the test statistics have been moved to end notes, and I have attempted to explain the results of most tests in succinct and common language. Given the experimental nature of my research, though, it is unavoidable that students of language and literature with a more traditional training will have to deal with a partially unfamiliar type of academic discourse. I trust they will soon feel sufficiently at ease with cognitive psychology to appreciate its use as a fruitful approach to the study of understanding metaphor in literature.

Publisher's acknowledgements

The publishers are grateful to the following for permission to reproduce copyright material:

Wylie, Aitken & Stone Inc. and George Weidenfeld & Nicholson Limited for the excerpt from *Miami and the Siege of Chicago*, copyright © 1968 by Norman Mailer.

We have been unable to trace the copyright holder for Figure 4.1 and would appreciate any help that would enable us to do so.

Author's acknowledgements

This book is primarily based on research done for my doctorate dissertation 'Metaphor in literary reception: A theoretical and empirical study of understanding metaphor in literary discourse'. I am grateful to the Netherlands Organization for Scientific Research, NWO, for having financed that project under contract 301–180–023. I am also highly indebted to the supervisors and reading committee of my doctorate: Elrud Ibsch, Leo Noordman, Dick Schram, Lachlan Mackenzie, Jan Hoeksma, and Jean-Pierre van Noppen. Their comments, suggestions, and corrections have been essential for the completion of the first stage of this book.

Since then I have had discussions and correspondence with a number of other people. They have contributed to a further clarification of the purpose of my book, stimulating me to carry out extensive rewriting and reordering of the argument, and to collect new data. I would like to mention Richard Gerrig, Ray Gibbs, and Shaike Shen in particular. Without their response, this book would not have received its present focus and form. Other people whose comments have been helpful are Guillaume Beijers, Charles Forceville, Norbert Groeben, Mike Hannay, Hans Hoeken, and Wilbert Spooren.

Mick Short, one of the General Editors of the series in which this book appears, has been of invaluable assistance. Thanks are also due to Longman, whose help and advice have been exemplary.

Last but not least I wish to thank my life's companion, Annemieke Keunen, for everything. This book is for her.

Amsterdam, 1994

PART ONE
Reader, Text, Context

CHAPTER ONE

From metaphor as cognition to metaphor in discourse processing

1.1 The cognitive turn

Until quite recent times, metaphor was seen by most linguists, philosophers, and other researchers of language as a linguistic oddity, lying outside the centre of their daily occupations. Metaphor was 'deviant', *'impropre'*, *'uneigentlich'* (Mooij 1976: 8). It was regarded as 'fancy language' used by poets, politicians, or people otherwise mentally unbalanced. Statements like (1–3) were considered to lie outside the rules of language:

(1) Juliet is the sun (Shakespeare)
(2) Religion is the opium of the people (Karl Marx)
(3) Football is war (Rinus Michels)

As a consequence of its alleged odd status, metaphor was not deemed worthy of a place at the core of linguistics. Its study was hence mainly left to the literary critics.

At the end of the 1970s, however, landmark publications such as Ortony (1979a), Honeck and Hoffman (1980), and Lakoff and Johnson (1980) completed what may be called the 'cognitive turn' in metaphorology. From 'the resurgence of metaphor' (Sampson 1981), through its promotion to a position as 'the figure of figures' (Culler 1981c), we arrived at 'the ubiquity of metaphor' (Paprotté and Dirven 1985). Dirven and Paprotté (1985: *viii*), for instance, say that metaphor is now seen as 'being situated in the deepest and most general processes of human interaction with reality'. It is a cognitive mechanism, 'helping in the construction of a conceptual world with its own laws' (1985: *viii*). Metaphor has become intelligible as a highly revealing instance of the human capacity for making sense. This cognitive approach to metaphor has grown into one of the most exciting fields of research in the social sciences, with psychologists leading the way for cognitive linguists, anthropologists, and poeticians.

Illustrations of the cognitive power of metaphor are readily given. If Juliet is the sun, then she is the centre of the speaker's universe. If religion is the opium of the people, then it keeps them happy but incapable of independent judgement and action. And if football is war, then almost anything is allowable to attain the goal of victory. Other consequences of (1–3) may be imagined without difficulty. These examples show how common rules of inference also apply to metaphors, producing implications and entailments of varying validity (Lakoff and Johnson 1980).

Metaphor has thus become comparable to other instruments of conceptualization, like models and theories in folklore and science. This was foreseen before the current fashion in metaphor studies in such seminal philosophical publications on metaphor as Black (1962), Turbayne (1963), and Hesse (1966). Other important books developing the cognitive approach in more recent times are MacCormac (1985), Kittay (1987), Levin (1988), Soskice (1988), and Winner (1988). New collections have been edited by Haskell (1987), Van Noppen (1990), Fernandez (1991a), and Shen (1992). Moreover, Lakoff and Johnson's *Metaphors We Live By* has been followed by Lakoff (1987a), Turner (1987), Johnson (1988), Kövecses (1988), and Lakoff and Turner (1989). With the founding of the special journal *Metaphor and Symbolic Activity*, the institutionalization of metaphor as a specific domain of research in the social sciences was completed.

The revaluation of metaphor as an important topic for cognitive and social research has happened on a scale that does not have an equal in history: Van Noppen et al.'s (1985) recently published bibliography, covering the past fifteen years, contains more entries than the one by Shibles (1971), which deals with a previous period of more than fifteen centuries (also see the complement by Van Noppen and Hols, 1991). What is more, the subject of the above-mentioned collection of papers by Van Noppen (1990), *How to Do Things with Metaphor*, is of course not simply an allusion to one of the important approaches to metaphor in the twentieth century (the pragmatic tradition of speech act theory initiated by Austin); it also shows that the state of metaphor studies is regarded as mature enough for a consideration of its practical relevance and opportunities of application. We have come a long way from the traditional view of metaphor as a mere linguistic quirk.

The cognitive turn has had three significant consequences. First of all, metaphor has had its notorious stigma of abnormality or deviance removed. Note the recent well-known titles *The Rule of Metaphor* (Ricoeur 1979) and *Metaphors We Live By* (Lakoff and Johnson 1980). Metaphor has become the thing to be expected in cognition instead of the thing to be avoided in language. It is now much less the Aristotelian mark of genius, literary or scientific, and much more the property of all men, women and children. This makes metaphor an attractive object for interdisciplinary research into the relation between language and thought and related topics, such as the social construction of reality.

The second consequence of this new situation is less fortunate. For with metaphor's conquering of the social sciences, it has lost its comfortably clear character as an apparently well-defined problem within rhetoric and poetics. As noted above, modern metaphorology incorporates work by psychologists and other social scientists, besides both familiar and novel variants of semantic and pragmatic analysis. Dirven and Paprotté (1985: ix), representatives of one recent approach to metaphor within the framework of cognitive linguistics, go much further when they claim: 'One main result of metaphor research in linguistics and ·psychology has been that the disciplines now find themselves challenged to redefine their scope, their aims and their methods.' To what extent this is solely due to metaphor is a moot point, but it is true that changes are occurring both in the field of linguistics and in other disciplines involved with metaphor. This makes it more difficult to assess the results of modern metaphor research, for sometimes they come with their own novel scientific criteria for evaluation, as is the case in cognitive linguistics itself. Indeed, the tendency in cognitive linguistics to attribute a cognitive function to all metaphorical elements that can be detected in the language system is one which may be questioned from the angle of language behaviour. Some examples of metaphor as cognition as proposed by some cognitive linguists seem to be a product of the strong swing of the pendulum from metaphor as expression to metaphor as cognition. One aim of this book will be to redress the balance between research into the structure of metaphorical language on the one hand and the way it is processed in actual usage on the other. As will be argued in this chapter, there is no one-to-one relation between the results of linguistic analysis and those of empirical work on discourse processing. From this starting-point we may be able to make progress from the recently achieved theoretical perspective on metaphor as cognition to the development of a cognitive view of metaphor in discourse processing.

The third consequence of the revaluation of metaphor is the framing of a question which is a result of the other two consequences, and the main subject of this book. If people's use of metaphor has become part and parcel of our view of cognition, and its proverbial relation to literature has been undermined, what *is* the relation between metaphor and literature? Can we still speak of such a thing as 'literary metaphor'? And do metaphors in literature have a special cognitive function which can be differentiated from the cognitive function of metaphors elsewhere? Where do we have to look to find an answer to these questions: in language, in cognition, or still other areas related to literariness? To suggest answers to these questions will be my main concern in this book.

But first it is the goal of this chapter to trace some of the features of metaphor research in the new, cognitive paradigm. I will make an attempt in particular at restoring the equilibrium between metaphor as a kind of *expression* and metaphor as an *idea* in discourse. There is a distinction between *linguistic metaphor* and *conceptual metaphor*. Both can be regarded as *information structures*, but they have a basis of their own in the systems of language and knowledge. Both the linguistic and conceptual information structures of metaphors are processed by language users, including readers of literature, when they understand metaphors in discourse. In this chapter I will attempt to show how the linguistic and conceptual dimensions of metaphor can contribute in different ways to the on-going understanding process of metaphor in discourse.

I will begin by briefly introducing the important difference between linguistic and conceptual metaphor and place them in context. This structural view of metaphor is then complemented by a processing view in section 1.3, which will present the generally accepted cognitive approach to metaphor processing as a kind of analogizing. These sections form the preparation for section 1.4, which is concerned with the role of analogical mappings in discourse. The main points of this section will be two: (i) what may be *analysed as* an analogical mapping when we talk about linguistic metaphors *in texts* does not necessarily have to be *realized as* an analogical mapping *by readers* when we talk about their role in discourse processing; and (ii) when it *is* a matter of actual analogical mapping during discourse processing, this still does not require the postulation of pre-existing conceptual metaphors in the mind. These points go against the views of one of the most important metaphor theorists on the cognitive scene, George Lakoff. As a result, Lakoff's interesting proposal for a definition of linguistic metaphor will have to be amended – this will happen in section 1.5.

1.2 Conceptual and linguistic metaphor: A structural view

The most provocative linguistic account of metaphor that has emerged from the cognitive turn is that of George Lakoff and his colleagues. Theirs is a radical departure from the position that metaphor is a figure of speech. Instead, Lakoff (1986a) argues, metaphor is a figure of thought. Figures of speech are just a surface manifestation of such metaphorical figures of thought, and, indeed, figures of thought can be expressed by other means than language (Kennedy 1990). Lakoff and Johnson (1980) thus speak of *conceptual metaphor*, suggesting that metaphor is a matter of understanding one thing in terms of another. Lakoff (1987a) approaches understanding, one of the basic objects of study for psychology, in terms of gestalts, whence experience, perception, and categorization are linked. As a result, the linguistic study of metaphor needs to be informed by the psychological study of cognition.

Lakoff and Johnson have become famous for their proposal that we understand arguments as wars, love as a journey, or theories as buildings. To give a less familiar example, consider (4):

(4) LIFE IS A GAMBLING GAME
   I'll *take my chances*. The *odds are against me*. I've got an *ace up my sleeve*. He's *holding all the aces*. It's a *toss-up*. If you *play your cards right*, you can do it. He *won big*. He's a real *loser*. Where is he when the *chips are down*? That's my *ace in the hole*. He's *bluffing*. The president is *playing it close to his vest*. Let's *up the ante*. Maybe we need to *sweeten the pot*. I think we should *stand pat*. That's *the luck of the draw*. Those are *high stakes*.
   Lakoff and Johnson (1980: 51)

Lakoff and Johnson claim that many such conceptual metaphors (stand-ardly indicated by capitalization) have become highly conventionalized. There is nothing innovative or deviant about them, as can be seen from the plenitude of familiar linguistic expressions that are available to convey them. They argue that conventional conceptual metaphors belong to the common knowledge of the language user, and that they are stored as conceptual units in the mind. This is a structural view of metaphor as cognition or conceptualization: it is claimed that the available metaphorical structures in long-term memory are applied to the understanding of metaphors during discourse processing.

It follows that the verbal aspect of metaphor ought to be regarded as dependent on, or derived from, conceptual metaphor. Lakoff and Johnson have coined the term *linguistic metaphor* for the verbal manifestations of conceptual metaphor, and this is the term that I will also adopt here. It should be realized, however, that the relation of linguistic to conceptual metaphor is one of partial autonomy. There are various ways in which the linguistic expression of a conceptual metaphor can affect the appearance of the conceptual metaphor in question.

Grammar is one area in which this loose relationship between conceptual and linguistic metaphor can be noted. The cognitive approach to metaphor provides a sound explanation of the fact that one conceptual metaphor may manifest itself in many grammatical variations of linguistic organization (Dirven 1985). As can be seen from (4), the conceptual metaphor LIFE IS A GAMBLING GAME is realized by various grammatical means. 'He's

7

bluffing' expresses the conceptual metaphor by means of a verb, but 'He's a real loser' evokes the conceptual metaphor by a noun. Other expressions are relatively fixed and idiomatic wholes, such as 'when the chips are down'. In other words, cognition on the basis of conceptual metaphor is relatively independent of the way it is expressed grammatically in language: all of these different linguistic expressions can be said to relate to the same conceptualization of a situation. However, their individual grammatical structure is bound to have an effect on the processing of the metaphor in question: some of the above linguistic expressions can be connected to the conceptual metaphor by means of analytic links ('he's a real loser'), while others have to be connected in their entirety by some more abstract procedure ('when the chips are down').

Lexical structure is a second area of interest: verbal expressions containing different lexical items may also be derived from the same conceptual root metaphor. The previous example may serve to illustrate this phenomenon, too: being 'a loser' is much less specific an expression than 'playing it close to your vest'. According to Lakoff and Johnson, both are connected to the conceptual metaphor that LIFE IS A GAMBLING GAME, but their individual meanings still embody distinct lexical realizations of the same basic idea. Again, metaphor as linguistic (in this case, lexical) structure has a role of its own to play during processing.

Rhetoric is a third area in which there is room for play between metaphorical conceptualization and metaphorical expression. Idiom, 'dead' metaphor, simile, allegory, analogy, and extended comparisons are all commonly seen as related to linguistic metaphor. The conceptual view of metaphor now facilitates their treatment as varying verbal manifestations of related or perhaps identical underlying conceptual structures. One aspect of this position was argued by Ortony (1979b), who claimed that the explication of a metaphor in terms of a simile does not present a gain in psychological terms, because both are dependent on the process of non-literal comparison. However, from a linguistic point of view, it would be very surprising if there were no functional difference between the expression of a conceptual metaphor as a simile, a metaphor, or an analogy, for instance. Again, it is an open question how metaphor as conceptualization and metaphor as rhetorical expression affect the process of understanding metaphor.

These observations show that, despite the apparent underlying conceptual unity, there still is a good degree of linguistic variety which has to be taken into account when one studies the relation between linguistic metaphor and conceptual metaphor. Indeed, this variety is so large that it took the advent of cognitive linguistics as a modern form of semantics to discover the underlying unity in the first place. The structure of conceptual metaphor, as it is supposed to be stored in the mind of the language user, is of a different order to the structure of linguistic metaphor as it appears in the text. The interaction of these two kinds of information structure during processing is what constitutes the most interesting target for research.

As will be appreciated, the cognitive approach to conceptual and linguistic metaphor exemplified by Lakoff and Johnson has a good deal of power when it comes to handling central problems. A point I wish to emphasize here is that, in general, the recently developed cognitive view of metaphor is not identical with the approach taken by Lakoff and Johnson. There are two counts on which one has to distinguish between their position and the standpoint of other cognitive metaphorologists. They have to do with Lakoff and Johnson's philosophical assumptions about doing cognitive science, and with their methodology.

Lakoff and Johnson have proposed a number of fairly specific hypotheses about metaphor as cognition that are not endorsed by everyone working in the field. In particular, Lakoff and Johnson advocate a particular philosophical stand called experientialism, which transcends what they call objectivism and subjectivism; it would take us too far afield to explain the difference between these views, but, more importantly, this issue seems immaterial to much of the work carried out on metaphor by other researchers of cognition. Further, Lakoff and Johnson's experientialism is based on the psychological tradition of gestaltism, a kind of holism which seems a rather more restricted approach to understanding than is commonly accepted. These are fairly radical propositions that are interesting in their own right, but they do not characterize what is fundamental about work on metaphor as cognition. Most cognitive scientists working on metaphor have by-passed these issues and concentrated on the empirical value of the proposal that people live by conceptual metaphors. A recent example of this kind of empirical attention, the exchange between Glucksberg and Keysar (1990), Gibbs (1992), and Glucksberg et al. (1992), will be discussed in section 1.4.3.

The second reason why Lakoff and Johnson's approach to metaphor is not to be equated with the cognitive paradigm is methodological. The empirical evidence adduced for their views derives from the careful analysis of numerous linguistic examples. However, this analytic method is not generally representative of the cognitive approach in metaphorology. The reason is that, although the analysis of *language structure* is highly useful, it cannot serve as the sole basis for the study of *actual language use*. Language analysis may serve a function to derive all sorts of expectations and speculations about processing, but that is quite another matter, namely theory formation. Theories have to be tested, and the analysis of further language data cannot count as a serious test of predictions about individual language use.

The same kind of criticism has been voiced by the anthropologists

Alverson (1991), Quinn (1991), and Quinn and Holland (1987). Instead of using an analytic approach to metaphor as cognition, then, many cognitive scientists doing empirical research on metaphor usage conduct experiments. It is here that we find the most advanced discussions of methods and techniques for studying metaphor as on-going individual cognition. There have been reviews touching on methodology by Ortony et al. (1978), Hoffman and Kemper (1987), and Winner (1988), who says: 'The lesson to be learned is that there is no "pure" measure of metaphor comprehension' (Winner 1988: 47). However, this conclusion does not invalidate the need for pluriform empirical testing as a sequel to language analysis and theory formation.

Despite the philosophical and methodological points raised above, Lakoff's work is quite central to present-day metaphorology. His radical views have proved highly fruitful for developing the cognitive paradigm which takes metaphor as a form of thought. Psychologists such as Gibbs and Glucksberg are testing implications of his approach regarding the existence and function of conceptual metaphors, while anthropologists are redressing the 'overly philosophic or universalistic intent' by filling in contextual details (Fernandez 1991b: 10). One of the most important reasons for this situation is that Lakoff also appeals to metaphor as a form of analogy. This is the predominant view of metaphor in cognitive psychology, which we now also have to take on board.

1.3 Metaphor as non-literal analogical mapping: A processing view

1.3.1 The psychology of analogizing

Characteristic of the depth of the changes in metaphorology is the altered approach to the definition of metaphor. As noted above, in the traditional approach, metaphor was seen as a particular type of figure of speech, and had to be demarcated from simile, analogy, allegory, irony, indirect speech, and so on. Words were regarded as having been used inappropriately and sentences as containing meaningful falsehoods, as in other figurative language. The road to salvation from nonsense for metaphor went by similarity rather than, for instance, by contiguity (metonymy) or opposition (irony). However, the cognitive view of metaphor as 'a figure of thought' emphasizes that it is knowledge rather than meaning that is responsible for the construal of similarity which lies at the basis of the process of understanding one thing in terms of another (Lakoff 1986a).

Most cognitive scientists nowadays take 'understanding one thing in terms of another' to be guided by principles of analogy (for instance Sternberg et al. 1979; Gentner 1982; 1983; Holyoak 1982; Trick and Katz 1986; Lakoff 1987a). In analogy, a mapping takes place of the structure of one cognitive domain, often called the *source* or base domain, onto the structure of another, the *target* domain. The term *mapping* suggests a kind of projection of structure from A on to B. The result of such a mapping is the organization of our view of relevant categories in the target domain, B in terms of the source domain, A. Thus the solar system may be the source domain, the conceptual structure of which is mapped on to the target domain of atoms. Atoms can then be understood in terms of their having a nucleus around which revolve a number of electrons that are kept in position because of prevailing relations of mass and attraction (Gentner 1982).

What we are dealing with in this section is the nature of the *actual process* of understanding metaphor. The *information structure* of linguistic metaphor as it appears in the text triggers a *process* of analogizing, which in turn *may* have recourse to *information structures* in long-term memory called conceptual metaphor. If a conceptual metaphor is available, accessible, and retrieved, then there is an interaction between the metaphorical textual structures and the metaphorical knowledge structures during the on-going process of text comprehension. This interaction triggers the mapping process from one domain to another, using knowledge structures that have become activated by the structure of the text.

Let us consider this global picture of analogical mapping in a bit more detail. On the one hand, a certain degree of structural resemblance between the conceptual domains concerning, say, solar systems and atoms is presupposed in order to facilitate the mapping. On the other, the mapping itself may also create or affect the structure of the target domain. This is particularly salient in the case of scientific modelling. For instance, when the mind is seen as a computer, the analogy creates the notion of a general knowledge store in the mind (MacCormac 1985). Whether there really is a knowledge store in some part of the brain remains an unresolved question. This predictive, hypothesizing quality of metaphor is one of its fascinating cognitive functions in science (Hoffman 1985). Metaphors do not (only) exploit pre-existing similarities between categories and domains, they may also create them (Camac and Glucksberg 1984).

The novelty of the cognitive approach based on analogy does not rule out an important role for the traditional notions in metaphorology of 'resemblance', 'comparison', and 'interaction'. In this respect, the cognitive turn does not constitute a break, but an empiricization of the philosophical and analytic proposals of well-known writers on metaphor such as Richards (1936), Beardsley (1958), Black (1962), Mooij (1976), and Ricoeur (1979).

11

The cognitive view of these traditionally central aspects of metaphor is based on empirical, especially experimental research on how people solve analogies and process metaphors. The effect of this research has been to see metaphor as just one specific manner of establishing similarities between categories.

Similarities between categories may not only be metaphorical, but also literal (Gentner 1989). However, literal comparison need not be fundamentally different from metaphorical comparison, and analogical reasoning may be the process involved in grasping both. This view has received increasing support in the past few years. For instance, in their introduction to the recent volume on similarity and analogical reasoning, Vosniadou and Ortony (1989) characterized the difference between literal and metaphorical analogizing as one between within-domain comparison and between-domain comparison. Consider the following two analogies:

(5) a. Paris : France :: London : England
     b. Paris : France :: head : body

The similarity between the relations of Paris and France on the one hand and London and England on the other is located in one conceptual domain, geography. The comparison is therefore called literal. However, the similarity between Paris and France and head and body links up two domains. Indeed, the identification of the two domains depends on this very intermediate ground constructed for the non-literal, that is metaphorical, comparison. In the case of (5b), one could think of 'most important part', 'control centre', and so on as the grounds upon which the comparison may be based. Let me clarify the effect of selecting one of these perspectives, 'most important part'. It emphasizes that humans cannot survive without their head on their body, and could suggest that the French need their capital as a cultural and political precondition for survival. By contrast, 'control centre' suggests a view of man as a rational being rather than one driven by instincts, which could suggest that Paris wields a kind of repressive power over the rest of France. The 'most important part' ground defines the domain of 'head : body' as a biological one of organism, whereas the 'control centre' ground places it in a philosophical light of the struggle for dominance between mind and body. Similarly, when Paris is the most important cultural and political part of France, then we have a rather different angle on their relationship than when Paris is seen as a repressive power centre. Hence the conclusion in Vosniadou and Ortony that the important difference between literal and metaphorical comparison lies in the problem of accessing the appropriate domains when dealing with between-domain comparisons: it is an open question which domain both parts of the comparison belong to, whereas this is not the case in literal comparison.

Another distinction between literal and metaphorical comparison is the fact that the notion of 'distance' between domains is seminal for metaphorical comparisons, whereas there is no question of between-domain distance in literal comparison. Although there are many theoretical difficulties with modelling domains and the distances between them, for operational purposes these difficulties can often be resolved in practical and acceptable ways (Trick and Katz 1986). For instance, Ortony (1979b) used an attribute elicitation task to determine how far particular categories manifested an overlap between properties. He requested subjects to list the predicates of forty terms. By simple quantitative comparison, he then determined how many properties were shared between terms (categories) from a number of different conceptual domains and took these relative differences as a measure of the distances between the domains compared.

Ortony (1979b), Miller (1979), and Holyoak (1982) were among the first to propose that analogy may cover literal and non-literal, or metaphorical, similarity. I will follow their approach to analogy by saying that a comparison between categories is literal when the categories come from the same domain, and that it is non-literal or figurative when they come from different domains. By contrast, Gentner (1989) manifests a more restricted use of *analogy*, in the sense that it only refers to non-literal proportional comparison. There is thus a fair degree of conceptual consensus, although terminological usage regarding *literal, metaphorical, comparison,* and *analogy* may vary among writers.

It is unnecessary for our purposes to discuss the way analogies may arise in connectionist models of computation (Rumelhart 1989), or how analogical reasoning may be simulated in Artificial Intelligence (Holyoak and Thagard 1989; Gentner 1989). Instead, we may take a more superficial view of analogy, ignoring questions of hardware and implementation, and be satisfied with a higher-level, 'information-constrained' approach to analogizing: 'In a sense, the objective at this level is to capture only the input-output mapping of people's analogical thought processes without regard to just how they might be accomplished in more specific terms' (Palmer 1989: 333). In other words, we are concerned with analogical representations.

1.3.2 Beyond similarity?

In a recent series of publications, Sam Glucksberg and his associate Boaz Keysar have questioned the approach to metaphor as a kind of non-literal analogical comparison (see especially Glucksberg and Keysar 1990; forthcoming). They argue against the view that metaphors are implicit similes, in which one category is likened to another. Instead, they claim that similes are implicit metaphors and, more importantly, that metaphors are attempts to create *ad hoc* categories which are referred to by the prototypical exemplar of that *ad hoc* category, namely the vehicle. Thus, in:

(6) My job is a jail

the category of jobs is assigned to a novel category of unpleasant and confining situations which is referred to by the prototypical exemplar of that category, namely the vehicle jail. In other words, Glucksberg and Keysar claim that the term *jail* fulfils two functions at the same time: it is a classifier, just like the term *furniture* in (7):

(7) A table is a piece of furniture

But it also happens to be the most prototypical instance of the class in question. This approach has received a great deal of attention, as it seems able to account for a number of interesting phenomena, including the relation between simile and metaphor, in a novel and enlightening fashion. In particular, metaphors are not seen as (non-literal) identity statements (or comparisons), of the form 'A is like B', but they are approached as class-inclusion statements, of the form 'A belongs to the category B'.

However, my point here is that Glucksberg and Keysar's proposal does not make analogy and similarity irrelevant to a processing account of metaphor. If the vehicle has the dual function of classifying and instantiating the *ad hoc* class concerned, then there is at least similarity between the topic and vehicle terms at the basic level of categorization. In other words, jobs and jails do resemble each other in certain respects because they belong to the same class, and analogical processing may have to work out *how* they belong to the same class. For a good example of research on this kind of processing, see Gick and Holyoak (1980).

Glucksberg and Keysar (1990: 11) have made the following point about the role of similarity: 'The similarity that is thereby perceived among category members is thus a product of that categorization, not an antecedent of it. That is, the categorization produces the similarity, not the other way around.' Hence the title of their article, 'Beyond similarity'. This is a well-founded psychological explanation of the above-mentioned traditional view in metaphorology that some metaphors create similarities rather than formulate pre-existing ones (see especially Black 1979: 37–40). But if Glucksberg and Keysar's arguments for the conceptual status of metaphors as category inclusion statements are attractive, they do not exclude the possibility that processing such statements could often work by means of analogical strategies for comparison. When one attempts to understand the statement that 'Some jobs are jails', there is no reason why the *ad hoc* category could not arise *as a result* of comparing jobs to the prototypical member (jail) of the as yet unavailable class of 'unpleasant and confining situations'. Only for conventional metaphors, which may or may not include 'A job is a jail', could one presume that there may be an *ad hoc* category which is already there in the mind, ready for use by the listener. But for less familiar metaphors, the identity of the novel superordinate is precisely what is at issue, and similarity and analogy may play a crucial role in creating the *ad hoc* category. I conclude that it remains an empirical question how categorization, analogy, and similarity are related. The processing view of metaphor as mapping a non-literal analogical relation between two concepts may be retained for further inspection of its role in discourse processing.

1.4 Analogical mappings in discourse processing

The problem of understanding metaphor in discourse may now be cast in terms of analogical processing. Assuming for the moment an unproblematic notion of linguistic metaphor, how can we explain that readers are able to understand such metaphors in terms of a non-literal analogical mapping between one knowledge domain and another? How can the input of a linguistic metaphor into working memory lead to the output of a well-structured analogical representation? In particular, does the output always involve an analogical representation in the first place?

As we saw in section 1.2, Lakoff and Johnson (1980) have explained the phenomenon of analogical mapping in language use by postulating the existence of a whole range of ready-made conceptual metaphors (or non-literal analogies) in the mind. As Lakoff (1986a: 223) himself says: 'There is a big difference between having a metaphorical mapping exist as a unit in your conceptual system and putting together the same metaphor fresh the first time.' I will examine this difference below, arguing that Lakoff and Johnson's use of it is misleading, and consider some of the implications for discourse processing.

The grounds for postulating the existence of conceptual metaphors have been recapitulated by Lakoff (1986a: 218–19):

> The love-as-journey metaphor was the example that first convinced me that metaphor was not a figure of speech, but a mode of thought, defined by a systematic mapping from a source to a target domain. What convinced me were the three characteristics of metaphor that I have just discussed: (a) the systematicity in the linguistic correspondences, (b) the use of metaphor to govern reasoning and behavior based on that reasoning, and (c) the possibility for understanding novel extensions in terms of the conventional correspondences.

The critical question regarding conceptual metaphors is: do the conceptual metaphors postulated by Lakoff and Johnson really reside in the minds of individual human beings? And do people always understand all metaphors by means of analogical mapping? When Lakoff raised this question in his paper on metaphor as a figure of thought, he pointed out an important limitation of his approach, and provided a response that merits close attention:

> But do all competent speakers of a language have the same conventionalized metaphors? And how do we know, for any given individuals, whether the love-as-journey metaphor is conventionalized *for them*? The analytic methods devised by Johnson and myself (Lakoff and Johnson 1980) are not sufficient to answer such questions. All our methods permit is an analysis of conventional metaphors in the conceptual system underlying the speech of an *idealized* native speaker. (1986a: 223)

It is my claim that the recourse to the idealized native speaker implies a shifting of the theoretical basis of 'conceptual metaphor' from individual psychology to a supra-individual, that is a social or cultural, basis. Note the following comment from Lakoff and Turner (1989: 51): 'Basic conceptual metaphors are part of the *common conceptual apparatus shared* by members of a culture' (my emphasis). I believe that the 'common conceptual apparatus' is nothing but a series of abstractions from regularities of speech found among individual language users. These are social or cultural patterns. Individual psychology, by contrast, is the territory of actual metaphorical structures in real people's minds. As different people may share other parts of the postulated common conceptual apparatus, the relation of conceptual metaphor to discourse processing needs to be elucidated anew. Although this does not detract from the value of the work of Lakoff and Johnson (1980), it does suggest that it cannot be applied straightforwardly to individual behaviour without some difficulty. As Glucksberg et al. (1992: 580) have pointed out, we 'face the challenge of showing how speakers and hearers integrate linguistic, conceptual, and discourse knowledge to produce and comprehend metaphorical expressions'.

1.4.1 Highly conventional metaphors

It is doubtful whether many cases of conventional metaphorical expression in ordinary language use still require or trigger active analogical mapping by the individual language user. There is evidence that people understand such conventional metaphors directly and do not become aware of their non-literal nature (Gibbs 1984; Hoffman and Kemper 1987). George Lakoff has taken the evidence for direct understanding of metaphors as one important reason for the postulation of conceptual metaphors: 'Any concept that is part of the conventional conceptual system is used automatically, unconsciously, and effortlessly; that goes for metaphorical concepts [. . .] as well as for nonmetaphorical concepts' (1986a: 223). However, postulating conceptual metaphors is not the only way to account for the observation that people may understand conventional metaphors directly.

Do all of these *linguistic* metaphors require the retrieval of a *conceptual* analogical mapping from long-term memory, or the on-line construction of a novel analogical mapping during processing, by every individual in order to be understood? I believe that the answer to this question is 'No'. It should not be forgotten that the fact that there may be a general pattern of non-literal analogical structure behind such metaphorical ways of expression is a fact about a speech community: what is a metaphor from an analytic perspective upon the language as a generalized code does not have to be a metaphor in the language use of every individual. A logical analysis of general speech patterns does not correspond in a one-to-one manner with a theory of individual behaviour (Medin and Ortony 1989: 182). People may use metaphorical language patterns without needing a representation of the underlying structure of these patterns in terms of non-literal analogical correspondences (Langacker 1988). That is, people may 'understand conventional metaphors directly' because there is no question of metaphorical mapping during their own language processing. Hence, it does not follow from the observed automatic understanding of conventional metaphors that a category of conceptual metaphors has to be postulated for the individual mind.

Although the relevant linguistic metaphors may be analysed conceptually to characterize the knowledge structure of a speech community as a whole, such resulting conceptual metaphors at the cultural level do not have to carry over directly into the individual minds of participants in that culture. It is true that one may detect metaphorical relations between different senses of verbs like *to go* (in the context of travelling and dying), and that one may even find systematic extensions in related verbs such as *to pass away*. However, these conceptual metaphorical relations are located at the supra-individual level of language and culture as systems: the *idealized* native speaker. Systematic metaphorical relations may have become part of the systems of language and culture through motivated processes of extension of meaning by individuals in the past, but that is quite another matter. From the synchronic, empirical perspective on *individual* processing, many of the conceptual metaphors identified by Lakoff and Johnson (1980) may be regarded as instances of polysemy (Jongen 1985; Kittay 1987: 106–13). In other words, to the individual language user, the metaphorical meaning of some words and phrases has become just as directly accessible as their literal meaning. The analogical mapping originally motivating or maintaining the figurative connection between the two meanings may thus have lost its use in the mental lexicon of individual language users.

1.4.2 Non-literal analogy construction versus retrieval

My first point about Lakoff's application of metaphorical mappings was a denial of the relevance of metaphorical mapping to individual processing for many conventional metaphors. This denial hinges on the nature of the linguistic metaphors in question. Only dead and highly conventional metaphors can be used to forward this kind of argument. This is one place where the distinction between metaphor as linguistic versus metaphor as conceptual structure has paid off when it comes to describing their interaction during the process of understanding metaphor.

The next issue has to do with distinguishing between metaphorical mappings as activities versus metaphorical mappings as already available conceptual representations. When people have to solve riddles like (8), non-literal analogical processing takes the form of an active search for mappable relations between the domains of airplanes and insects (Trick and Katz 1986; Tourangeau and Sternberg 1981, 1982; Gick and Holyoak 1980; Johnson-Laird 1989):

(8) The Concorde is the mosquito among aircraft

In this kind of analogical reasoning, the individual produces new knowledge by on-line inferencing. Initially there is a search for two pertinent domains. Next they are connected. Then a mapping is attempted and conclusions are drawn from this mapping regarding the primary subject of the riddle. Finally these conclusions may be stored. Some metaphorical language processing may involve this kind of active analogizing and hence actually produce new knowledge.

This has to be opposed to the kind of knowledge (and potential for action) facilitated by the above-mentioned use of conventionalized metaphorical language, which was recast as a case of individual polysemy. Although linguistic metaphor is present in both cases, the example of actual analogical reasoning under (8) shows that it is the individual who establishes a metaphorical connection between two domains. By contrast, the case of polysemy implies that there is no metaphorical connection constructed or retrieved during processing. The process of understanding polysemous expressions only depends upon one's competence as a speaker of a language and it makes available the kind of knowledge already belonging to those conventionalized linguistic metaphors. The latter do not function as metaphors to the individual anymore. On-line inferencing about a metaphorical riddle such as (8), however, is based in the application of analogical reasoning abilities, leading to a novel metaphorical mapping by the individual. It produces metaphorical knowledge that is inferred from the juxtaposition of two concepts X and Y located in two domains A and B.

This process of on-line metaphorical mapping also has to be contrasted with another process, namely the use of models, or analogically organized knowledge that is readily available from long-term memory. When models are used during processing, concept X, for instance 'atoms', is part of an entire domain of knowledge, B, that is already structured analogically with regard to A, in this case solar systems. Thus, when people understand sentences like (9) many of them do not have to produce a new mapping between (X) atoms and (Y) solar systems in order to understand the meaning of *attracts*:

(9) The electron is attracted by the nucleus

Instead, they may use the relations already established between the two domains A and B for speedy understanding of the utterance. They may simply retrieve (part of) the analogical representation of X stored as a model. This is the kind of situation where metaphor as linguistic structure does relate to metaphor as conceptual structure, and where both are used during the on-line processing of discourse.

It seems to me that retrieval involves the only true psychological equivalent of Lakoff and Johnson's (1980) conceptual metaphor: it pertains to those metaphors which are already represented conceptually as such in the individual mind, and which can be accessed in a memory search as relatively complete units. And although it is imaginable that such individual conceptual metaphors also lie at the basis of the other two kinds of metaphorical mapping discussed above, this is not a necessary condition at all. People can use conventional metaphors in linguistic expressions about dying, and can solve riddles about atoms and solar systems, without requiring individual representations of such analogical mappings to be readily at their disposal: polysemy and instantaneous analogical reasoning, respectively, can plausibly account for these phenomena. Empirical research will have to determine which speakers process which kinds of metaphorical expressions in which manner.

In sum, all three variants of metaphorical mapping discussed above are to be seen as relatively self-contained manifestations of non-literal analogy. One question arising is whether dead and highly conventional metaphors still involve non-literal analogizing from the perspective of individual language processing. I have argued that they can also be regarded as part of a cultural pattern in language which does not bear a one-to-one relation with individual language use. From the angle of the individual, many of the dead and conventional linguistic metaphors may be nothing but instances of polysemy. By way of contrast, the process of on-line metaphorical mapping exemplified by (8) is related to individual analogical processing. It embodies a constructive view of analogizing. And finally, the kind of metaphorical mapping illustrated by (9) concerns the retrieval of already represented analogical models rather than their fresh construction by means of analogical reasoning. It is the closest psychological equivalent to what Lakoff and Johnson may mean when they speak of conceptual metaphors.

The point is that the same linguistic data may be connected in varying degrees to the postulated process of metaphorical mapping. As a result, there is no clear conclusion to be drawn from the analysis of the underlying conceptual organization of patterns of language use. Where the individual does not actually map love as a journey, but the language expresses love as a journey anyway, there is a different situation in terms of psychological processing than in the situation where the individual conceptually relates love to a journey. Many of the conceptual metaphors found by Lakoff and Johnson may be the conceptual repository of our cultural knowledge, but such knowledge is bound to have highly variable cognitive representations and effects at the level of individual minds.

1.4.3 Empirical beginnings

In a recent article Gibbs (1992) used polysemy to make the opposite point: 'there is much evidence that the meanings of polysemous words are related to one another in terms of family resemblances and that many of a polysemous word's meanings are motivated by the metaphorical projection of knowledge from one domain to another' (1992: 574). Gibbs makes a similar claim about what he calls the 'systematicity of literal expressions', referring to the kind of linguistic material used above to illustrate the conceptual metaphor LIFE IS A GAMBLING GAME (4). However, there Gibbs (1992: 573) does not use the term 'motivate', as he did with polysemy, but the much stronger term 'explain': 'The hypothesis that knowledge in long-term memory may be metaphorically structured makes it possible to explain what until now have been seen as unrelated literal expressions.' It is possible that the systematicity between diverse linguistic metaphors can be attributed to the metaphorical structure of knowledge in the mind of every individual. I do not wish to pronounce on this issue, preferring to remain agnostic. More to the point, however, I will now argue that the assumption of metaphorical long-term knowledge does not say much about the problem whether it also plays a role in the processing of polysemous expressions or dead and conventional metaphors.

Gibbs (1992: 576) believes that there is a connection between the assumed metaphorical structure of long-term knowledge and on-line processing, and adduces as evidence the fact that people can agree on the metaphorical meaning of expressions like (10):

(10)   Some marriages are iceboxes

He writes:

> In their descriptions, 84% of the participants reported some image of a large freezer (varying in size from a large refrigerator up to a walk-in freezer) with a married couple sitting or standing in a frozen position. When specifically asked, 88% of the participants stated that the couple did not enter the freezer voluntarily, 94% suggested that the couples were quite unhappy to be there, 74% suggested that each spouse was unhappy with the other person, and 79% claimed that the couple could not easily get out of the freezer. These specific descriptions of people's mental images for *Some marriages are iceboxes* reflect the constraining presence of the conceptual metaphor *relationships are containers*. (Gibbs 1992: 576)

However, I doubt whether any strong consequences follow from this evidence. The most these data could show is that people are able to *recognize* relations between marriages and iceboxes in terms of a more abstract idea that relationships are containers. Asking people to spell out the meaning of expressions like (10) gives them ample time to use ordinary strategies of reasoning, which, given the concrete clarity of the metaphors, can lead them straightaway to such features as reported by Gibbs (1992: 576). As Glucksberg et al. (1992) have also pointed out, this finding could have a bearing on the *availability* of such conceptual metaphors, but it does not relate to their *accessibility* during on-line processing. Moreover, the more abstract idea that relationships are containers could just as easily be a result, or an inference, of these data instead of a source. Gibbs's findings are too removed from on-line processing to be able to bear directly upon the potential activation of a conceptual metaphor.

This means that the systematicity in polysemy and dead and conventional metaphors may indeed *motivate* the postulation of long-term metaphorical knowledge, but it does not *explain* the role of such knowledge during the on-line processing of apparently metaphorical expressions by individuals. What is a metaphor in the system of a language may have a 'literal' representation in the mind of many individuals. As a result, whether or not there is a metaphorical motivation to the structure of long-term memory, it is not required for the processing of the expression in question, for the expression can be understood by looking up the 'literalized' meaning in the private mental lexicon directly.

Glucksberg and his associates have begun to investigate this issue empirically. They phrased their research question as follows:

> But what does it mean to 'have' such correspondences? It can mean that we can appreciate and understand the analogies between travelers and lovers when it is

pointed out to us. It can also, but not necessarily, mean that these systematic mappings between travelers and lovers, vehicles and relationships, and destinations and goals are prestored in semantic memory — that is, they are available when appropriate occasions arise. It can, but again not necessarily, mean that such conventional mappings are accessible in any given context and thus can serve as the conceptual basis for understanding. (Glucksberg et al. 1992: 579)

In another paper, results of two experiments are reported which demonstrate the difference between availability and accessibility (Glucksberg et al. 1992). People were given a story in which somebody is growing angry, her anger being described in terms of heated fluid under pressure. Subjects then had to select the best conclusion to the story out of two alternatives, one of which was phrased consistently with the conceptual metaphor of the story, namely *blew her top*, but the other of which was inconsistent, namely *bit his head off*. It turned out that the average choice for the consistent idiom was above chance for thirty-six different stories. Glucksberg et al. (1992: 13) concluded that 'conceptual analogical information thus seems to be available, at least when people make considered, non-speeded judgments or choices'.

However, the question whether such available knowledge is also accessible or accessed during on-line comprehension yielded a negative answer. An experiment measuring reading times used the same materials as the selection task described above. It was argued that the activation of the conceptual metaphor during the reading of the story would facilitate the comprehension of the final sentence of the story if it was consistent with the conceptual metaphor in question, but would not facilitate the comprehension of a metaphorically inconsistent ending. The results showed that there was no facilitation of the comprehension of the final sentence for those stories with a consistent conceptual metaphorical basis. Glucksberg et al. drew the following conclusion (1992: 21): 'Our failure to find an effect of analogical consistency does not, of course, mean that people (a) do not have conceptual metaphors available in semantic memory, or (b) do not access those metaphors under certain circumstances. Our conclusion pertains specifically to the claim for automaticity, which we feel is certainly wrong.' The role of conceptual metaphor during on-line comprehension therefore remains an undecided and important point for further research.

1.5 Linguistic metaphor

In the previous section we looked at the processing of metaphor in discourse in terms of analogical mapping. The main aim of the present book, however, is to account for the way readers understand metaphors when they come across them in literary texts. It is therefore necessary to derive a definition of metaphor as a linguistic entity from the cognitive discourse approach sketched above.

Lakoff and Johnson's phrase 'linguistic metaphor' is meant to capture that class of linguistic expressions, written or spoken, that can be related to conceptual metaphor as dealt with above. On their approach, the criterion for linguistic metaphor is the phenomenon of understanding one thing in terms of another: those linguistic expressions that can be understood directly, without recourse to another domain of cognition, are not meta-phorical, whereas the others are metaphorical (or otherwise figurative). (Rhetorical distinctions between metaphor, non-literal analogy, simile, and extended comparison are left out of consideration here.) This definition of metaphorical and literal expressions was elaborated in the provocative paper by Lakoff (1986b), where 'The meanings of literal' are analysed as four allegedly conjunctive assumptions characterizing the term:

Literal 1, or *conventional literality*: ordinary conventional language – contrasting with poetic language, exaggeration, approximation, embel-lishment, excessive politeness, indirectness, and so on.

Literal 2, or *subject matter literality*: language ordinarily used to talk about some domain of subject matter.

Literal 3, or *non-metaphorical literality*: directly meaningful language – not language that is understood, even partly, in terms of something else.

Literal 4, or *truth-conditional literality*: language capable of 'fitting the world' (i.e. of referring to objectively existing objects or of being objectively true or false). (Lakoff 1986b: 292)

Lakoff goes on to show that these assumptions are not conjunctive but disjunctive, and a choice has to be made as to which meaning is to characterize true 'literalness'. In order to achieve a consistent application of the term *literal*, Lakoff makes the following proposal: 'I suggest here that literal, in any technical discussion, be restricted to the meaning of Literal 3, in the sense of being directly meaningful, without the intervention of any mechanism of indirect understanding such as metaphor or metonymy' (1986b: 293). By implication, language that is indirectly meaningful and requires a mapping from one domain to another is metaphorical. As stated above, the basis of metaphor in analogical mapping is the psychological equivalent of the old criterion of similarity or resemblance, thus also making for a demarcation between metaphorical and metonymic language.

If this seems a fruitful starting-point, however, there now arises a problem that has to be solved in terms of the relation between conceptual metaphor and its role in discourse processing. For it seems that there are two ways of deciding if the following linguistic expressions for someone's death are based on 'indirect understanding':

(11) a. He's gone
      b. He's still with us
      c. He's left us
      d. He's passed away

From a generally conceptual point of view, (11a–d) may be claimed to be based on conceptual metaphor, as Lakoff and Johnson have done: DEATH IS A JOURNEY. But from a processing point of view, it is highly questionable whether 'any mechanism of indirect understanding' is involved, as was argued in the previous section with reference to polysemy. I believe that these expressions need not give rise to non-literal analogical processing, or depart from a conceptual metaphorical representation in the individual mind at all.

This observation has an important consequence. If it is correct, then not all expressions designated as metaphorical by Lakoff and Johnson are *in fact* understood indirectly by all individual language users. However, this is what the definition called 'Literal 3' above suggests. Therefore, the negative part of that definition has to be changed from its current state (see above) to:

> Literal 3, or *nonmetaphorical literality*: directly meaningful language – not language that is *potentially* understandable, even partly, in terms of something else.

As a result, the positive definition of linguistic metaphor also has to be phrased in terms of *the potential for indirect understanding*. Linguistic metaphors are hence those expressions *that may be analysed* as involving a supporting domain of reference for describing their meaning: they do not actually need to be *realized* as such by language users.

What is at stake here is the relation between language as an abstract system, individual language users, and cultural knowledge. Linguistic metaphors may be studied as the verbal repository of a cultural store of conceptual metaphors, but their cognitive realization in discourse by individuals can still vary in the manners illustrated in the previous section. If both the cultural and the individual processing aspects of this issue are to be accounted for, the more encompassing view needs to be taken. Therefore, linguistic metaphors are those expressions that *can* be analysed on formal grounds as involving two semantic domains. The criterion for linguistic metaphor hence lies in the domain of semantics. It includes polysemy, dead metaphors, and highly conventional metaphors, but raises the question whether these are understood 'literally' or metaphorically', that is, directly or indirectly (see also Lakoff 1987b). This starting-point highlights the need for research on the use of metaphor from both a cultural and a processing perspective. As to the latter, the criterion for the psychological realization of linguistic metaphor as non-literal analogy is the empirical observation of the individual's activation of two cognitive domains.

1.6 Conclusion

This chapter has introduced three essential aspects of the study of metaphor since the cognitive turn. They are metaphor as conceptual structure, metaphor as linguistic structure, and metaphor as analogical processing. Conceptual and linguistic metaphor can be regarded as two kinds of information structures which affect the triggering and shape of the on-going process of metaphor understanding by means of analogizing. However, the main point of this chapter has been that we still do not know very much about the precise interaction of these two factors during processing.

I have argued that Lakoff and Johnson's assumption of a metaphorical structure for long-term memory may be wrong, and that their findings may have to be recast as dealing with the structure of knowledge at a *cultural* level instead of an individual level. At any rate, even if there is such a thing as a metaphorical basis to the knowledge structure of individuals, then it still is an open question whether this kind of conceptual metaphor plays an important role in the on-going understanding of metaphors during language use, including reading. Empirical evidence has suggested that metaphorical structures may be *available* to people when they think about texts, but this does not imply that they are *accessible* and *actually accessed* during on-line comprehension. This means that the effect of conceptual metaphor as cognitive structure on the actual understanding process of metaphor remains to be determined by future research.

A similar point can be made about the other factor, linguistic metaphor. What Lakoff and Johnson regard as linguistic metaphor is a motley affair. Included are idioms, polysemy, dead metaphors, highly conventional metaphors, conventional metaphors, novel extensions of conventional metaphors, and novel metaphors. It is highly dubious whether all of these expression types always trigger 'indirect understanding'. Although they can be *analysed* as involving two semantic domains, this does not mean that every language user will also *activate* two conceptual domains when he or she comes across these varied metaphor types. Therefore I have argued that we should maintain a strict theoretical distinction between what can be analysed as a linguistic metaphor, what can be postulated as a related conceptual metaphor, and the analogizing which can sometimes be observed in the understanding process related to these different kinds of information structures.

This approach to understanding metaphor in terms of three aspects (language structure, knowledge structure, and on-going process) has ignored another factor which is fundamental to this book. I am speaking of the factor of literature as a discourse context for the actual process of understanding metaphor. Discourse context can affect the use of both language structures and knowledge structures during processing. The language user may look for different aspects of the text, and for different aspects of knowledge, in order to process metaphors in literature in the contextually appropriate way. What is more, context may have affected the structure of the text and the metaphors it contains during the stage of text production. Hence, metaphors in literary texts may have contextually appropriate properties which distinguish them from other metaphors and which may have a typical effect on the nature of the process of understanding them. Therefore we will have to consider the nature of literature as a contextual factor which can affect the understanding process of metaphors. This will be the task of the next chapter.

CHAPTER TWO

Metaphor in literary discourse processing

2.1 Literary criticism and the psychology of reading

The relation between metaphor and literature has always been seen as quite intimate. This may be due to the influence of Aristotle's treatment of metaphor in his *Poetics* rather than in *Rhetoric*. He wrote that 'to be good at metaphor [. . .] is a sign of natural genius'; and it is natural, because it 'cannot be learnt from anyone else' (*Poetics* IIID, 4; in Russell and Winterbottom 1972: 122). The poet can surprise the reader with unexpected metaphoric comparisons, and thereby provide pleasure and insight at the same time. It has since been the concern of many literary scholars to point out the subtleties of metaphoric meaning and effect in literary texts.

From our present vantage-point, these interpretative activities of literary critics are not incompatible with the analytic approach of cognitive linguists such as George Lakoff. He, too, sees it as his main project to describe and motivate the meaning and effect of metaphors. One result of this research, however, has been to undermine the close relation between metaphor and literature. If we live by metaphors, what is so special about their occurrence in literature? Having said that, another result has been to make more exact the relation between literature and metaphor. Indeed, the special nature of many literary metaphors can now be traced to two different origins: first, they may involve new linguistic expressions of familiar conceptual metaphors, or, second, they may reveal newly constructed conceptual metaphors, exhibiting the poet's eye for resemblances at its most original (Lakoff and Johnson 1980; Turner 1987; Lakoff and Turner 1989). Literary scholars now have at their disposal an approach to language and its cognitive basis which can increase the validity of their own discussion of the origin, effect, and value of particular metaphors (compare the first chapter of Turner 1987). There appears to be sufficient common ground for establishing a link between the metaphor studies in cognitive linguistics discussed in the previous chapter and mainstream research on literature.

However, I will use my critique on the cognitive-linguistic approach to metaphor in Chapter 1 to place the relation between metaphor and literature on a slightly different footing. My main critical point in this connection was that, from the angle of discourse processing, what can be *analysed* as a linguistic metaphor in texts is not always *realized* as a conceptual metaphor – by retrieval or construction – in discourse processing. This applies to all kinds of discourse processing, including literary text comprehension. What is more, the same argument also goes for the realization in literary reading of presumably 'special' metaphors. To return to Aristotle, poets may express as many original non-literal insights as they can, but if readers do not pick them up as metaphors, then they do not count as such in their literary reading process. If a cognitive theory of understanding metaphor in literature wishes to include this variegated realization of metaphor by individuals, then it will have to be a theory of reader behaviour, or of discourse processing. There are two important implications that follow from this statement, which will be dealt with in the next subsections.

2.1.1 From text to reading

First, most of the traditional publications about metaphor in literature are to be regarded as dealing with the text rather than with reading behaviour. Literary text interpretation is a rich and many-sided activity which also includes references to the role of the reader, but it is still *text* interpretation. Literary scholars do not systematically investigate the processing behaviour of readers, but at best speculate, on the basis of their own reading, about the potential effect of textual structure on postulated readers. These are referred to by various names, as the following list from Freund (1987: 7) may illustrate: 'the mock reader (Gibson), the implied reader (Booth, Iser), the model reader (Eco), the super-reader (Riffaterre), the inscribed or encoded reader (Brooke-Rose), the narratee (Prince), the ideal reader (Culler), the literent (Holland), the actual reader (Jauss), the informed reader or the interpretive community (Fish)'. But the point is that they are idealized constructs, not real readers – 'personifications', in Freund's words. As has been pointed out by Groeben (1977), non-empirical variants of reception theory thus fail to achieve their own goal of describing the on-going process of reception. These publications do not even amount to a series of self-reports on the reading process, each based on just one case, namely that of the critic himself or herself. For this would amount to making the assumption that literary criticism can count as a valid reflection of spontaneous literary reception. But criticism is much too indirect and institution-ally constrained a type of discourse for that (*contra* Culler 1981b; see Culler 1988). As a result, I take most of literary criticism to contain analyses and interpretations of certain aspects of literary texts and, at best, hints and hypotheses for empirical research into their cognitive function in reading processes.

By contrast, the task of describing and explaining how people understand metaphors in literature is not concerned with the text, but with people's on-going acts of reading. It involves a consideration of text, reader, and context variables in the attempt to explain the process of how individual readers actually deal with metaphors in literature. If text interpretation focuses on attributed meanings and potential effects, empirical studies of discourse focus on cognitive processes.

Historically, these different objects of research have also become associ-ated with distinct methodologies. Text-oriented research is mainly analytic, interpretative, or hermeneutic, while behavioural research is empirical. However, I would like to emphasize that all research into literary reading can be perfectly empirical, including that part of reading research which temporarily concentrates on the factor of text properties. Empirical text research is called content analysis in the social sciences, and there are explicit methodological guidelines for going about it (see Van Assche 1991). Text research can serve two quite different functions in the empirical study of literature. Text properties can be used as an approach to text production, of which they are the result; or they can be used as an approach to text reception and post-processing, which they can affect in predictable ways. Both of these uses are functionalist or pragmatic, in that they refer to the relation between the text and the user of the text. For more extended theoretical discussion of these issues, I refer the reader to the debate on the empirical nature of literary studies (for instance Groeben 1977; Schmidt 1980; Ibsch and Schram 1987; Ibsch, et al. 1991).

Thus, when I use the phrase 'understanding metaphor in literature', it does not refer to my own process of how I might, or actually do, understand metaphors in literature, or my own view of how a student should do so. This is what traditional literary interpretation would entail. Rather, what I refer to is the mental processing by individual readers of the (linguistic) metaphors occurring in particular literary texts. Note that I mean *all* linguistic metaphors, defined as such in the first chapter. That is, I do not focus on allegedly 'poetic' or 'literary' metaphors, for I do not know what they are. I only know of metaphors occurring in literary texts, and I wish to examine their properties and use by real readers. Although there are many interesting and useful claims about the nature, function, or effect of metaphors in literature in the interpretative tradition, they may be valid only for the texts and reading processes of a few readers. These speculations will have to be recast in terms of a cognitive discourse theory about the way many people understand metaphors in literary texts, and predictions deriving from that theory will have to be tested empirically. To a literary scholar, this is an intimidating project, and I can only hope to clear the ground in these first chapters in order to make a beginning with this endeavour in the rest of the book.

2.1.2 From interpretation to reception

The observation that not all linguistic metaphors activate conceptual metaphors raises the question which metaphors are conceptually realized by which readers under which conditions. The difference between text interpretation and a behaviour-oriented discourse theory discussed above has a bearing on this issue. In text interpretation, the reader is likely to maximize the number of metaphors involving metaphorical concepts. It is therefore quite likely that literary text interpretation is a rather different kind of 'reading' from ordinary literary reception, for there readers have no business paying special attention to metaphorical concepts. This difference is due, of course, to the different roles that readers adopt during literary text interpretation and the ordinary reading of literature: in interpretation, they devote maximum and professional attention to the text as text, while in reception, they pursue their own private goals for reading literature. Thus the difference between my discourse approach and traditional literary studies not only involves a shift of attention from text to reading; it also redirects the focus from reading as critical interpretation to reading as everyday reception. By implication, in this book 'understanding metaphor in literature' does not refer to the professional explication of metaphor in literature, but to the processing of metaphor in literature in private reading, or reception.

For most readers by far, reception is the kind of reading in which literary metaphors exert their ordinary or special function. Although such functioning may still involve a good deal of variety, it is constrained by the fact that readers consume literary texts for private as opposed to public and professional ends. Psychological constraints on reception can be found for instance in the more limited time resources of the private reader. Another example is constituted by the greater need in private reading for personal relevance of the literary text. If reception is the area where we want to look for the general function of metaphor in literature, it is quite a different terrain from critical interpretation.

The difference between the role of metaphor in professional interpretation as opposed to private reading is increased by the fact that critics have often adopted an overall interpretative practice that is variously referred to as symbolic, metaphoric, allegorical, or analogical interpretation. The basis for this practice lies in the idea that literary texts often *say* one thing while they *mean* other, or additional things. This is a conventional expectation about literary texts as instantiating a particular type of discourse. The point is that this situation also suggests that, in professional literary interpretation, many linguistic metaphors are typically attributed with a conceptual function *because of* this general strategy of additional interpretation. The non-literal realization of metaphors adds the layer of figurative meaning to the activity of text processing, one which is left aside when metaphors are not realized by means of non-literal analogy but remain 'conventionally literal' in Lakoff's terminology. In other words, the general interpretative strategy of additional processing in literary criticism may affect the local phenomenon of metaphor processing in literature in that it raises the number of metaphors interpreted non-literally. The incidence of such metaphor processing in literary reception may hence be boosted by the variable of context, in this case the professional interpretation of literary discourse. In a nutshell, the figurative understanding of metaphor may be more frequent in literature *because* it takes place in literature.

An example of this situation is provided by Wellek and Warren in their *Theory of Literature*:

> Ignorance, to be sure, can confer an illegitimate originality upon the first examples of an unfamiliar convention. Indeed, the etymological metaphors of a language, not 'realized' by those whose native language it is, are constantly taken, by analytically sensitive foreigners, as individual poetic achievements. One has to know intimately both language and literary convention to be able to feel and measure the metaphoric intention of a specific poet. (Wellek and Warren 1949: 196)

What is noted here is that some readers may process what Lakoff and Johnson have called conventional linguistic metaphors in a conceptual manner instead of by-passing their figurative potential. All conventional linguistic metaphors can be processed by means of analogizing, and sometimes they are. Wellek and Warren call literary readers exhibiting this bias 'analytically sensitive', and this fits well with my proposal at the end of the previous chapter to regard as linguistic metaphors those structures which *may* be *analysed* as involving indirect understanding. However, over-zealous conceptual processing of metaphors in the literary context is denounced as 'illegitimate' by Wellek and Warren, because the imaginative potential of these linguistic metaphors was not intended to be realized by the poet — at least, in the eyes of Wellek and Warren. Apparently, the 'whole imaginative function of literature' (Wellek and Warren 1949: 197) may induce a mode of reading which stimulates conceptual processing of all textual elements that lend themselves to such treatment, regardless of whether they are 'genuine' poetic metaphors or not.

It is a moot point whether Wellek and Warren are dealing with reading as critical interpretation or everyday reception here. In any event, critical practice may be linked to the ordinary reading process in such a way that we cannot exclude the possibility that in private reading, too, context may induce another kind of attention to metaphors. This is a distinct theoretical possibility, for which circumstantial evidence exists in the work of Meutsch (1987), Vipond and Hunt (1989), and Zwaan (1993). They used different measures to show that texts were processed differently when they were offered as literary than when they were presented as non-literary texts. These are instances of contextual effects on text processing, and there is no reason to think that metaphors are exempt from such an influence. The nature of this contextual effect is what we will have to attend to in the next section.

2.2 Metaphor in literary discourse

2.2.1 The psychology of literary reception

At this point the question arises how the effect of literature as a particular type of discourse context on the processing of metaphors during reception can be theoretically framed. This question amounts to the requirement of a psychological definition of literature as a type of discourse. As hinted at the end of the previous chapter, I presume that literature as a type of discourse may affect the processing strategies readers use for integrating conceptual and linguistic information structures within their current text representation. But this is not the whole story: in most cases, literature as a type of discourse has also functioned as a context during the production of the text by a writer. Hence it may also have affected the resulting text structures of literary texts. Therefore we need to have a clearer view of this factor of context, so that we may derive hypotheses about the ways readers make use of metaphors during literary text comprehension, and about the discourse-typical nature of metaphors in literary texts.

The work by Meutsch, Vipond and Hunt, and Zwaan on literary reading belongs to a broader range of empirical research on literature, which takes literature as one socially distinct type of discourse that has to be demarcated from others, like religion or science (Ibsch et al. 1991; Kreuz and MacNealy 1993). In this kind of research, it is generally assumed that the communicative conventions for literary discourse are different from those prevailing elsewhere, and it is the task of literary theory to describe how they are different. There have been numerous discussions of the distinct nature of literature as a special kind of discourse. However, most if not all of them have their roots in the interpretative tradition referred to in section 2.1, because the call for going beyond interpretation has only been a fairly recent development in literary studies (Culler 1981a). The conspicuous exception is formed by Schmidt (1980), who has developed a theory of literature with the explicit goal of subjecting it to empirical testing. This theory has served as an inspiration for my definition of literature as a type of discourse.

With Schmidt (1980), literature can be defined as a social domain of discourse displaying certain regularities. In that domain, individuals produce, mediate, receive, and post-process texts as literary. According to Schmidt, the regularities that are manifest in their individual actions can be explained as deriving from two social macro-conventions for behaviour, called the aesthetic convention and the polyvalence convention. This is to be opposed to non-literary discourse behaviour, which exhibits a factual and monovalent character. Social regularities in the domain of literary discourse are assumed to be the result of acting according to internalized forms of the two conventions. Empirical evidence for the existence of the conventions as shared forms of knowledge about literature is presented by Hintzenberg et al. (1980). A review of the evidence collected so far in support of the effect of the polyvalence convention on text processing can be found in Groeben and Schreier (1992), who also present an extensive theoretical sophistication of the idea of polyvalence.

In order to avoid misunderstandings, let me make one comment on literature as a type of discourse that is governed by conventions. Conventionalism is no big thing. I do not use it as a philosophical position on the nature of the world. It is just a handy way to explain particular regularities in people's behaviour. If these regularities are subject to historical, social, and cultural variation, conventionalism is an attractive way to deal with this kind of phenomenon. However, since we have hardly any data about these regularities regarding literature in the first place, I take a pragmatic position about conventionalism and use it as a working hypothesis for collecting evidence regarding the existence of regularities. To what extent they are truly explicable by conventions can be decided at a later stage.

The concrete form of Schmidt's social conventions of aestheticity and polyvalence, and their effect on the psychological process of literary reception, is a complex affair. I will not go into extensive theoretical elaboration here, but summarize my position straightaway. More extensive discussion and further developments are presented in Schram and Steen (1992) and Steen and Schram (1993).

In literary reception, as a result of abiding by the aesthetic and polyvalence conventions or some form thereof,

(1) Readers take maximal freedom for the subjective realization of literary texts because they are not aiming at achieving practically important functions.
(2) Readers treat literary texts as fictional because they do not take them as directly tied to factually relevant circumstances.
(3) Readers realize literary texts in more than one way without thereby raising consequential interpersonal or social conflicts of interpretation.
(4) Readers realize literary texts with special attention to form as contributing to, and indeed partly determining, content.

Actually, 1–4 can be seen as more concrete statements deriving from the general premise (1), which captures the gist of Schmidt's opposition between the aesthetic and the fact convention. Subjective realization has to do with the aim of the reader of literature. My point about subjective realization is that it is the basis for all reading processes, but that it is constrained outside literature by a greater need for intersubjective communication than within literature.

The other three statements make explicit how the aim of subjective realization can be achieved by the reader. They deal with the traditional, basically semiotic, areas of reference (2), meaning (3), and form (4). In particular, factual circumstances might facilitate reference assignment in non-literary reading, but they do not guide the reading of those texts which are not aimed at practical functions. This allows more freedom to readers of literary texts for filling in their own view of possible situations. And (3) can be seen as a consequence of both (1) and (2): freedom from practical functions and factual circumstances relaxes constraints upon processes of meaning attribution. This increases the chance of divergence of processing within or between readers. In the same light, one may extrapolate towards (4) and say that readers of literature can take more time than readers of other texts to pay attention to form and style, as opposed to the message and content of the text; indeed, this kind of attention often leads to a realization of form-as-meaning. In sum, I regard literary reception as generally characterized by *subjectivity, fictionality, polyvalence,* and *form orientation.* Empirical evidence for the role of polyvalence and form orientation have been presented by Meutsch (1987) and Hoffstaedter (1986), respectively.

Note that this approach does not demand that all of these features have to be present before one can speak of literary reception. On the contrary, (1–4) are hypotheses which may turn out to be false, or which may have limited and varied validity. The point is that they characterize literary reading as it is generally conceived of in literary theory – they are variants of the proposal by Schmidt (1980), which is a summative discussion of the literary-theoretical tradition from an empirical point of view. They need not be complete nor correct, but they are intended as a testable summary of a good deal of thinking about literature as a distinct type of discourse. Their testability lies in the comparison of frequencies of incidences of subjectivity, fictionality, polyvalence, and form-orientation within and outside (parts of) literary discourse. Their value lies in facilitating this kind of empirical research, and in providing a basis for a further theoretical discussion of understanding metaphor in literature.

2.2.2 Metaphor in literary reception

The contextualist notion of literariness developed above will now have to be applied to the situation of understanding metaphor in literature. This means that we will have to trace the potential role of the literary-discourse features of subjectivity, fictionality, polyvalence, and orientation to form in metaphor processing. It will be intuitively clear that each of them can be related to understanding metaphor as conceived of in the previous chapter, namely as non-literal analogical mapping.

Subjectivity provides us with an unproblematic link between literariness and metaphor processing. The analogical basis underlying metaphor process-ing allows for various developments of the analogy, and each of them can be more or less subjective. By (inter)subjective analogy development I mean the varying degree of acceptability of the resulting meaning construc-tion. Although this raises all sorts of tricky questions, I believe that one may call certain products of analogizing more acceptable than others, given the particular context in which the analogy in question is developed. This issue could be investigated by having subjects rate concrete alternative solutions of an analogy as to their acceptability. I will not follow up this suggestion in this book, but am putting it forward as an indication of the testability of my proposal.

Polyvalence can come in here, too. Often there are more ways than one of setting up an analogical comparison, because many suggestions may arise from one metaphorical statement. Moreover, as we saw in Chapter 1, more than one target domain may be accessed for the same metaphor to establish the full range of analogical richness. Hence I do not find it surprising that metaphorical analogy allows for both a literary and a non-literary use when they are approached in terms of subjectivity and polyvalence. As a result, part of the literary nature of metaphor processing resides in the incidence of subjective and polyvalent realization.[1]

As to *fictionality*, it can be argued that metaphor is a form of fictionality itself. It works by identifying two concepts which cannot be identified if one adheres to the canons of literal truth and reference. There is a *pretence* that one concept is identical to the other. In other words, metaphor is an impossible fiction. (Compare this with literature itself, which ranges over the entire gamut of possible and impossible fictions.) If literature stimulates the creation of fictions, then metaphors are an excellent opportunity for manifesting this tendency.

Finally, there is the issue of *orientation to form* in literature. Whatever its conceptual basis, metaphor also remains a figure of speech, which is semantically different from other language. It has been recognized as such for centuries, and the literary orientation to form will include an attention to metaphors as an interesting formal feature of the text. Note that metaphor's semantic deviance is related to the creation of an impossible fiction, so that these two aspects may be closely related in actual reading.

In short, metaphors turn out to be excellent opportunities for readers to experience subjectivity, fictionality, polyvalence, and orientation to form during literary reading. Their function in literary reception may be to facilitate or stimulate these experiences, so that the reader's awareness of literariness is enhanced. In literary reading, metaphors may function as important crystallization points for the feeling of subjectivity, polyvalence, fictionality, and form-as-meaning. This is the general theoretical proposition which I will develop for empirical research.[2]

The success of metaphors in inducing these effects is dependent on three factors. First there is the role of common text structures and reader knowledge as discussed in Chapter 1. As to text structures, it is clear that there will be an effect on readers' realization of literariness as defined above of the difference between dead and highly conventional metaphors on the one hand and novel metaphors on the other. It seems to me that the latter are much more suitable for a literary function in the above terms than the former. Novel metaphors allow for new associations (subjectivity), which need not be limited to one area (polyvalence), and they embody new impossible fictions (fictionality) which may be all the more noticeable for that very reason (attention to form).

Second, there is the general factor of reader knowledge. As we saw in Chapter 1, the availability and accessibility of underlying conceptual metaphors differs from one reader to another. Even if two readers do possess the same conceptual metaphors in their mental encyclopedia, other factors may influence their activation of this knowledge from one text to another. As these kinds of text structures and reader knowledge affect all metaphor processing, they will also influence metaphor processing in literature.

The third factor is the role of context. It figures first of all in the activation of literature as a discourse context in different readers' usages of the above-mentioned text and knowledge structures. When readers know that they are reading literature, I expect that they will be more alert to the experience of subjectivity, fictionality, polyvalence, and form-as-meaning than others who are not reading literature. This mobilization of knowledge about literature as a type of discourse clearly has a bearing on the realization of metaphors in these respects. This is vividly dramatized in the practice of literary critics, but the interesting question is whether this effect extends into reader behaviour during ordinary reception. A more detailed discussion of the role of literature as context on metaphor processing will be offered in section 2.4 below.

But literature as a type of discourse also has an indirect influence on metaphor processing, through its prior role as context during text production. Literature as context during production affects the nature of the resulting texts in many ways. On top of the difference between metaphors which are dead and alive, other differences which are due to this influence may arise between linguistic metaphors. For instance, literary metaphors may be more suitable for polyvalent use than non-literary metaphors, either in themselves or through their position in the literary co-text. This is a textual factor which cannot be explained without reference to literature as context during production.

2.3 Typically literary metaphors

What is the special nature of metaphor in literature when we concentrate on the text as an object independent of the reception process? This question involves the relation between metaphor and literature during text production. It should be observed that subjectivity, fictionality, polyvalence, and an orientation to form-as-meaning are not only regarded as characteristic of literary discourse, but that they are also discerned to be inherent in one way or another in all metaphors, be they literary or non-literary. The approach to the nature of metaphors in literary texts thus focuses on the discourse-typical frequency of ubiquitous features of metaphors. In other words, we depart from a general theory of metaphor as non-literal analogy which includes as basic elements the parameters of (inter)subjective acceptability, (im)possible fictional reference, mono- or polyvalent content, and (in)significant form. The expectation is that, on average, metaphors in literary texts tend to exhibit properties related to the literary sides of these oppositions. What kind of properties could these be?

A general, more or less systematic, foundation for a theory of the cognitive nature of metaphors in literature has been developed in the publications by Lakoff and Johnson (1980), Turner (1987), and Lakoff and Turner (1989). Interesting applications of this view in the area of literary text studies can be found in, for instance, Freeman (1993) and Black (1993).

There are other cognitively inspired studies of the nature of metaphor in literature, such as Thompson and Thompson (1987), Tsur (1987), and Friedrich (1991), but they do not cover as extensive an area of literary and non-literary cognition as Lakoff and his co-authors have done. The same can be said about the handful of empirical studies involving metaphors in literature by psychologists like Gentner (1982) and Katz et al. (1985). Therefore my discussion of potentially interesting cognitive properties of literary metaphors will concentrate on Lakoff and Turner (1989).

Lakoff and Turner are concerned with a demonstration of the thesis that even metaphors in literature – and poetry in particular – are guided by general principles of cognition. Their aim is well illustrated by the following quotation:

> There exist basic conceptual metaphors for understanding life and death that are part of our culture and that we routinely use to make sense of the poetry of our culture. We might have used any of these poems as an introduction to these basic metaphors. We chose the Dickinson poem not to point out what is unusual about it but rather to introduce the range of common, unconscious, automatic basic metaphors which are part of our cultural knowledge and which allow us to communicate with each other, whether in ordinary conversation or in poetry. (Lakoff and Turner 1989: 15)

My present goal is to move in the opposite direction and to answer the question how can metaphors in literary texts, despite their general cognitive basis, still have the special 'literary' appeal which has been attributed to them for centuries.

Lakoff and Turner (1989: 215) have taken the following functional view of how writers use metaphors in poetry to achieve a special effect: 'Poets can appeal to the ordinary metaphors we live by in order to take us beyond them, to make us more insightful than we would be if we thought only in the standard ways.' This is the standard view of literary language as defamiliarizing experience and drawing attention to itself as a means of expression (foregrounding), which has been with us since Russian Formalism. Poets do this by means of four strategies, called the extension, elaboration, questioning, and composing of conceptual metaphors (1989: 67–69). Before we go on to consider the structural, or textual, implications of this functional approach to metaphor in literature, I will first discuss these four strategies in some more detail.

Extension is illustrated with reference to Shakespeare's *Hamlet*, where DEATH IS SLEEP is extended to include the aspect of dreaming:

(1) To sleep? Perchance to dream! Ay, there's the rub;
       For in that sleep of death what dreams may come?

(Quoted by Lakoff and Turner 1989: 67)

Extension involves the inclusion of those parts of a conceptual metaphor which are conventionally omitted from consideration when the non-literal analogy is used in discourse. Non-literal analogies usually involve a partial mapping from one domain to another, and poets can explore the opportunities for further extension of the metaphor to yield relatively new insights.

Elaboration, by comparison, takes place when a poet uses those parts of a metaphor that are conventionally included, but in a more specific and special manner than is customary. For instance, Lakoff and Turner argue that Emily Dickinson elaborates DEATH IS DEPARTURE by including the destination and filling it in as 'home':

(2) Afraid? Of whom am I afraid?
    Not Death, for who is he?
    The porter of my father's lodge
    As much abasheth me.

(Quoted by Lakoff and Turner 1989: 68)

I doubt whether Lakoff and Turner's analysis is quite correct, for, strictly speaking, in this passage the destination of the departure is not home itself. The destination of the departure which is death is *compared* with home, by means of an implied comparison ('*as much* abasheth me') between Death as the doorman of that destination and 'the porter of my father's lodge'. This comparison invokes a consideration of the destination of death as departure in terms of home, but in a more indirect manner than is suggested by Lakoff and Turner. The situation is more complex, I believe, for another metaphor seems to be involved in this passage, namely the metaphorical concept of HEAVEN IS MY FATHER'S HOUSE. In other words, what Lakoff and Turner classify as an elaboration, involving the 'special' filling in of the conventional metaphor DEATH IS DEPARTURE, can also be analysed as a composition of two conventional metaphors, in which the destination of DEATH IS DEPARTURE is 'filled in' as HEAVEN IS MY FATHER'S HOUSE. One question which arises here is how we can assess whether this composition also produces 'special filling in', or elaboration; and another is how to recognize that two rather than one of the above four operations are involved, that is, elaboration and composition. However, these questions are too intricate to disentangle here; but it should be clear that I believe this part of Lakoff and Turner's theory is still problematic.

Turning to the third operation poets can apply to conventional metaphors, we encounter a similar problem as we have noted just now. *Questioning* involves the poet's concentration on the boundaries and inadequacies of the conventional conceptual metaphor. Since every non-literal analogy is bound to break down at some point, this operation can be applied to any metaphor in an almost mechanical fashion. An example of this kind of use of metaphors was present in (1), where Shakespeare not only extends the metaphor DEATH IS SLEEP into unused realms, but simultaneously raises questions about the utility of the metaphor in those extensions. Again, the boundary between the two cognitive operations is unclear, and what Lakoff and Turner saw as extension above may just as easily be regarded as questioning. Although there may be an intuitive distinction between unused parts of a metaphor which do and which do not work, there may be a good deal of overlap between the operations of extension and questioning in practical analysis.

Finally, there is the operation of *composition*. We had occasion to refer to composition above when discussing (2). The formation of composite metaphors is taken as the most characteristic feature of poetic thought (Lakoff and Turner 1989: 70). Some of the metaphors in literary texts are shown to be highly complex, involving the joint use of more than one conventional metaphor. An important methodological problem in this area is the identification of the number and nature of the conventional metaphors involved. It seems to me that there is room for a good deal of ambiguity in the examples and analyses adduced by Lakoff and Turner. However, I will not press this point any further, and move on to the more important questions of this section: (*i*) how do these four allegedly typically literary or poetic operations relate to literariness as defined in section 2.2? and (*ii*) how can we develop this functional approach in terms of pertinent textual properties of metaphors in literature?

Lakoff and Turner's view of the way poets use metaphors can be related to my definition of literariness in terms of subjectivity, fictionality, polyvalence, and form-as-meaning with the help of the following passages:

> in using one's natural capacity for metaphorical understanding, one will necessarily be engaging in an activity of construal. All reading involves construal. . . . Literary works, and poems in particular, are open to widely varying construals. For any given person, some construals will seem more natural than others, and those are the ones that are often ascribed to the intention of the poet. (1989: 109–10)

The possibility for more than one construal per metaphor and the ranking of such construals on a scale of naturalness are what I mean by polyvalence and subjectivity, respectively. Another passage relates the feature of polyvalence to the operations of composition and elaboration: 'This shows not only that we can arrive at alternative readings of a passage by bringing to bear different basic metaphors but also that we can arrive at alternative readings by bringing to bear different parts of the same basic metaphor' (1989: 41). Therefore, metaphors can invite the subjective and polyvalent use of reader knowledge. The typically literary feature of attention to meaning-as-form and form-as-meaning is triggered by 'the special, non-automatic use to which ordinary, automatic modes of thought are put' (1989: 72), which causes what Lakoff and Turner call 'noticeability'. Poetic metaphors are thus noticeable as figures of speech and as impossible fictions. Lakoff and Turner (1989: 215) discuss the latter aspect in terms of metaphoric truth. All four features of literariness can hence be shown to be involved in the functional side of metaphors in literature.

The above considerations also have a number of implications for the structure of poetic metaphors. It may be concluded that literary metaphors are *novel* (by way of extension and elaboration), *critical* (by way of questioning), and *complex* (by way of composing). Note that all of these cognitive operations and their related structural features are not limited to cognition in literary discourse. It follows that we can only expect that metaphors exhibit the above or related properties more frequently in literary texts than in other kinds of texts. We are dealing with an average distinction between literary and non-literary metaphors, which is measurable in terms of distributional tendencies. How these and related metaphor properties can be observed empirically will be addressed in Part Three of this book.

One final note. Lakoff and Turner (1989) are concerned with the use of poetic metaphor. In this section I have tacitly generalized their ideas towards all literary metaphors. This does not mean that I am diminishing the differences between poetry and other kinds of literary texts. However, from the point of view of a social theory of literature as a type of discourse, poetry and non poetic, but otherwise aesthetic, text types should be approached as falling under one overall heading, literature. I believe that the cognitive operations and textual structures discussed above are valid for non-poetic literary discourse as well as for poetry. The differences between poetry and other kinds of literature may provisionally be approached in terms of a distribution of typical features again: if poetic metaphors are novel, critical, and complex, this may also be true of other literary metaphors outside poetry, if perhaps to a lesser degree. These are empirical issues which have to be researched.

2.4 Typically literary use of metaphors

2.4.1 Focus processing and vehicle construction

Having discussed the role of literature as a context for production with effects on the structure of metaphors in literary texts, we now turn to the potential effect of literary context on reception. The general expectation is that literary reception induces subjective, fictional, polyvalent, and form-oriented modes of reading. We have seen before that each of these features can also have a bearing on the processing of metaphors in literary texts. I will now examine one central thesis about metaphor processing in literature from this angle.

One aspect of analogizing which can give rise to subjectivity and polyvalence is the use of a non-literal analogy to communicate about the vehicle domain in addition to communicating about the topic domain. This possibility is extensively discussed by Reinhart (1976), who connects it with the traditional view of literary metaphor as producing double vision. Double vision is the activation by metaphor of two ideas at the same time, which normally would not be associated with each other; their co-ordinate activation leads to an interaction of images which may produce a double vision. Metaphors draw attention to parts of the literal and non-literal domains involved in order to have these parts incorporated in a figurative manner in the text representation of the reader. For instance, suppose one ends a discussion about human behaviour with:

(3) Man is a wolf

Integration of (3) within the discourse is brought about by linking 'man' to the current topic of discussion, and by adapting one's picture of man in such a way that a whole range of literal and non-literal attributes of man, suggested by the domain of wolves, may be attached to the mental model resulting from the previous discussion. That range may begin with a simple and unspecific negative picture of man, but it may also extend into associations with animals, predators, fierceness, and so on, quite possibly even evoking an actual picture of wolves in some people's minds. This is the process which Mooij (1976) has in mind when he speaks of dualistic theories of metaphor, Ricoeur (1974) when he elevates metaphor to the main problem of hermeneutics, and Friedrich (1991) when he equates poetic metaphor with the imaginative potential of language. Double vision is explained by Reinhart (1976) in terms of a process called vehicle interpretation. It can be fruitfully explained and developed as a form of additional communication about the vehicle domain from the angle of analogizing.

Reinhart (1976) presents a synthesis of the proposals by Richards (1936), Beardsley (1958), and Black (1962). After a careful discussion of such terms as *tenor* and *vehicle*, and *focus* and *frame*, she puts forward a novel distinction between 'focus interpretation' and 'vehicle interpretation'. I will slightly amend these terms by making use of 'focus processing' and 'vehicle construction', respectively, in order to be able to discuss these processes in terms of aspects of analogizing. Focus processing is understanding the entire metaphor in terms of the domain of the topic, tenor, or the target domain; it involves a reading of the focus (the non-literal word of a metaphor) in terms of the current domain of discourse. Thus T.S. Eliot's metaphor:

(4) I have seen the mermaids riding seawards on the waves

may receive a reading for *riding* (the focus) as *floating* ('focus processing'). Vehicle construction, by contrast, pertains to a relatively independent activation of the domain associated with the focus of the metaphor, or the source (vehicle) domain. For instance, *waves* may be read as *horse* ('vehicle construction'). From the point of view of analogizing, we see a two-way use of the non-literal proportional comparison:

(5) floating: waves :: riding: horse

Focus processing uses the analogy for deriving information about the current domain of discourse, while vehicle construction uses the analogy to enrich our view of the focus in relatively independent terms. Reinhart (1976: 392) claims that vehicle construction is especially necessary if 'the "image" aspect of the metaphor' is to be invoked. That is the way to a full *imaginative* understanding of the metaphor: a double vision of floating on the waves and riding a horse.

The theory of analogical processing can now explain double vision as involving an exploitation of a possibility which is inherent in all analogy, namely that of concentrating upon both source and target domain instead of focusing only on the latter. As these two acts of activation are not likely to occur simultaneously, it seems to be a matter of co-ordinative but serial processing with reference to two distinct cognitive domains. To be more precise, the following scenario is quite plausible. First, readers construct a schematic non-literal comparison on the basis of the text, to the effect that:

(6) X : waves :: riding : Y

It is of the highest priority that readers solve the first part of the equation, for that is the domain the text is about. If coherence is the guideline for building text representations, then the identity of the X is the main concern of the reader. Hence, 'riding' as a form of movement can be applied to the domain of waves by coming up with a typical form of movement in that context, for instance floating. As soon as this part of the puzzle is solved, there is no need for further analogizing when we look at the main drive for reading, the development of a coherent text representation.

This changes if the reader wants to explain or motivate the use of the contextually odd verb, that is, *riding*. This would be the case when readers are engaged in 'point-driven reading' (Vipond and Hunt 1984). As soon as this becomes a goal for processing, then a new equation is processed, namely:

(7) floating : waves :: riding : X

This shows that we may have to do with additional *and* serial processing, rather than actual *double* vision. The two processes lead to two distinct representations of the linguistic metaphor, even though the one (vehicle construction) will often be subsidiary to the other (focus processing). Processing a linguistic metaphor in two manners, however, is tantamount to local polyvalence: during focus processing, the reader is busy with the general topic of the text, but during vehicle construction, he or she is attending to the nature of an image. Hence 'double vision' is a good example of the polyvalent use of analogy construction. I will refer to it as two-way analogizing, as it involves the use of analogies in two directions. It may generally lead to an imaginative understanding of a metaphor.

Reinhart (1976) makes a case for the position that processing metaphor in poetry is characterized by vehicle construction, while ordinary metaphor processing is restricted to focus processing only. Thus metaphor offers a highly characteristic opportunity for reading according to the polyvalence convention: when focus processing and vehicle construction are co-present, two meanings of the metaphor are realized rather than one. We can now see that the basis for this possibility lies in the binary nature of (non-literal) analogy. This state of affairs is managed monovalently in ordinary discourse by 'weighting' the topic side of the analogy and subordinating the vehicle domain to it. It is a moot point whether it is the nature of metaphors in literature, or the 'literary' attitude of reading which is predominantly responsible for these tendencies. Reinhart (1976: 395) asserts that 'Experienced readers of poetry often emphasize the procedure of vehicle interpretation, while inexperienced readers tend to overlook this aspect of the metaphor and attempt a "literal substitution" or interpretation of the focus.' If this proves to be correct, then it may be partly explained by the prediction that experienced readers follow the aesthetic and polyvalence conventions more carefully: opportunities for the construction of multiple meaning as offered by vehicle construction would then be realized more frequently.

2.4.2 Metaphor processing and metaphoric processing

Because I am not sure whether two-way analogizing will always cause double vision or imaginative metaphor realization, I propose to make a distinction between *metaphor* processing and *metaphoric* processing. Metaphor processing refers to any psychological process relating to linguistic metaphors. It may be based on polysemy (no analogizing), conceptual metaphor realization (one-way analogizing), or metaphoric processing (two-way analogizing). By contrast, metaphoric processing is a particular *mode* of processing, which is dependent on the occurrence of two-way analogizing. I call this metaphoric processing, because it is usually singled out as the typical example of metaphor realization in literary studies: it involves the most extensive non-literal, or metaphoric, treatment of metaphors.

I wish to stress that metaphor processing and metaphoric processing constitute two viewpoints on metaphor in literature, which are seldom distinguished in literary criticism. In the various discussions, metaphoric processing of linguistic metaphors is given total priority, for it is attributed a typically literary function as it involves the exercise of the imagination. Metaphor processing, by comparison, is usually discussed only to the extent that it overlaps with metaphoric processing. From the standpoint of a cognitive discourse theory of metaphor in literature, however, this is giving short shrift to the object of research, which is metaphor processing in whatever mode. Hence the conjunction between the two viewpoints in the title of this section, which indicates a further move away from traditional literary studies to cognitive and social science.

An example of what I mean can be found in Wellek and Warren's *Theory of Literature*:

> Our own view ... sees the meaning and function of literature as centrally present in metaphor and myth. There are such activities as metaphoric and mythic thinking, a thinking by means of metaphors, a thinking in poetic narrative or vision. (Wellek and Warren 1949: 193)

The second half of this quotation refers to metaphoric processing. As a result of the common limitation of metaphor processing to metaphoric processing, the function of literary, in particular poetic metaphor, is explained as follows:

> If we pass from the motivation of linguistic and ritual metaphor to the teleology of poetic metaphor, we have to invoke something far more inclusive – the whole function of imaginative literature. The four basic elements in our whole conception of metaphor would appear to be that of analogy; that of double vision; that of the sensuous image, revelatory of the imperceptible; that of animistic projection. (Wellek and Warren 1949: 197)

The function of poetic metaphor is identified with 'the whole function of imaginative literature'. In a more recent treatment of this relation between metaphor and literature, Ricoeur (1974) provides a philosophical analysis of the preconditions for treating metaphor as the main problem of hermeneutics, showing that it still embodies the 'whole function of imaginative literature'.

On this view, then, poetic or literary metaphor is pre-eminently based in the reader's active conceptualization of two distinct, incompatible ideas, combined into a complex, interactive whole by means of non-literal, two-way analogical comparison. Ordinary analogizing is one-way analogical processing: conceptual metaphors are used in ordinary discourse to communicate about the target domain. Although there is a possibility that people use the non-literal analogy to think about the source domain by itself as well, this hardly ever happens. On pragmatic grounds alone, there would be a preferential interpretation for what is the topic and what is the figurative statement about the topic, leading to a concentration on the topic domain. This condition prevents a frequent two-way use of analogies, because the reader will usually begin by constructing an interpretation of the non-literal focus appropriate to the frame, or topic, and be satisfied. By contrast, when the imaginative potential of a metaphor is realized, readers pay separate attention to both cognitive domains. Not only do readers integrate the figurative part of the metaphor within the domain of discourse of the topic, but they will also pay attention to the domain of discourse activated by the focus itself, starting with the process of vehicle construction.

It is commonly felt that to neglect such imaginative features of metaphor in literature as analogy, double vision, sensuous image and animistic projection would be to miss its fundamental aesthetic function. But it is important to observe that this view leads to an unwarranted narrowing of the multi-modal phenomenon of *metaphor* processing in literature to the single mode of *metaphoric* processing. It was pointed out in the previous chapter that, in principle, processing metaphor need not involve the reader's activation of conceptual metaphors, either by means of retrieval or construction. What was said for ordinary discourse in Chapter 1 also holds for literature and the imaginative function of metaphor. During private literary reading, many metaphors in literature are processed without in the first place activating conceptual metaphors. Moreover, when readers do activate conceptual metaphors, they do not have to use them in two ways. They do not have to engage in focus processing *and* vehicle construction. In short, metaphors in literature do not *necessarily* require either one-way or two-way analogizing. These 'non-metaphoric' modes of processing metaphor are allegedly less typical of literary reading than metaphoric processing, and have accordingly — and in my view unjustifiably — been largely ignored in most literary theory. Yet such instances of metaphor processing also have to be accounted for when we consider 'understanding metaphor in literature'.

Linguistic metaphors may also play an important role in literary text processing that is *not* dependent on the mode of metaphoric processing.

(1) Linguistic metaphors may be present more often in literary than in

other types of discourse. Thus, readers may become aware that they have to process disproportionately many linguistic metaphors, when they feel they are reading 'flowery language'. It is unnecessary for them to realize the conceptual or imaginative content of such flowery language for them to be able to have such a feeling.

(2) Metaphors in literature may manifest particular properties more frequently than elsewhere, properties which need not depend on metaphoric processing for their effect. For example, readers may be aware that metaphors have particular emotive overtones, even though they need not realize the specific content or effect of such emotive aspects of metaphors as part of their conceptual representation.

(3) Readers may also have to think hard to work out what a figurative expression refers to in the fictional situation, without thereby realizing the imaginative potential of the figure *qua* figure. This is one-way analogizing, which requires the exertion of considerable energy to establish what the metaphor is trying to say about the topic, and it happens quite often in literary reception. Against the view of Reinhart (1976), then, it may be held that some focus processing is also typical of literary reception.

Therefore, even though linguistic metaphors need not be realized conceptually, in one-way or two-way manners, all of the time, they may still exert special effects on the reading experience, some of which qualify as 'typically literary'. In other words, processing linguistic metaphor is not the same as metaphoric processing, and metaphoric processing is not the sole basis for the special relationship between metaphor and literature.

2.5 Conclusion

Understanding metaphor in literature is a process which is not only affected by the factors of reader knowledge and text structure (Chapter 1), but also by the factor of context. Literature may exert a contextual effect on metaphor processing in various ways. When readers know they are reading a literary text, and this is usually the case, they mobilize specific reading strategies and knowledge about literary discourse which guide their reception process. I have argued that there are four features which are conventionally taken as typical of literary discourse: subjectivity, fictionality, polyvalence, and form orientation. Each of these aspects can be seen to figure in literary reception, and can be expected to affect readers' understanding processes of metaphor. Metaphors in literature are excellent candidates for facilitating or increasing the typically literary reading experiences indicated by these notions.

There are two sides to this relation between metaphor and the experience of literariness during reception. First, the literary context in which reception takes place may alter the way readers deal with the metaphors they encounter. This means that readers will realize relatively more metaphors in a literary fashion on account of their attitude towards the text. Hence they will realize their subjective, fictional, polyvalent, and formal potential relatively frequently. I have introduced a new term for one highly typical form of literary metaphor understanding, namely metaphoric processing. It involves a concentration on the domain of the vehicle which may cause double vision and polyvalence. However, non-metaphoric modes of metaphor processing such as focus processing may also lead to all typically literary features (subjectivity, polyvalence, fictionality, and form-orientation) when readers have to spend considerable energy on understanding the metaphor in question.

However, there may also be an effect in the other direction. It may be the metaphors themselves that cause subjective, fictional, polyvalent, and form-oriented reading processes. In other words, the degree of literariness of the general reading process, as measured by the incidence of these pertinent features, does not have to be caused by a literary attitude of reading, but may also be due to the processing of typically literary metaphors. This can be explained by the fact that literary metaphors are the result of a production process in which literature acted as a discourse-typical context. Thus, metaphors in literary texts may invite literary reception by means of subjective, fictional, polyvalent and formal processing much more insistently than metaphors outside literary discourse.

This leads to the following view of understanding metaphor in literature. Understanding metaphor in literature is a mental process which is part of literary reception. In comparison with metaphor processing outside literature, it is probably characterized by the more frequent occurrence of subjective, fictional, polyvalent, and form-oriented processing features. The incidence of these features is expected to differ in accordance with a number of variables: ordinary text structures (dead versus live metaphors), ordinary reader knowledge (availability of conceptual metaphors), discourse context during reception (activation of literary reading strategies, including metaphoric processing), typically literary text structures as an effect of discourse context during production (many novel, critical, and complex metaphors). Selected aspects of this framework will be developed further in the theoretical and empirical chapters of the rest of this book. The next chapter will begin by an empirical exploration of the relation between metaphor processing and the experience of literariness.

Notes

1. Pilkington (1991a) has made a related point in a lucid account of metaphor from the perspective of 'relevance theory', first put forward in Sperber and Wilson (1986). He argues that metaphors permit the listing of many different implicatures, and that this is the basis for their poetic effect (if they are realized, I would insist on adding). To allow for a range of implicatures is, moreover, another way of saying that 'no claim is made . . . that only one possible analogy underlies any given metaphor. Obviously, . . . various insertions of terms left implicit in one or the other format [are possible]' (Sternberg and Nigro 1983: 19n.). In addition, as pointed out in Chapter 1, it is not only a matter of filling in the analogical terms, but also of identifying the relevant domains from which the terms are to be derived. In general there are differences between the ease with which people can find source or target domains. As Johnson-Laird has noted, 'with an increase in the number of potential sources, however, any search algorithm runs into intractable difficulties' (1989: 330). For all forms of analogy this means that accessing source domains and target domains and their pertinent categories is highly subject-bound. My point is that, in non-literary discourse, readers have to remain within the limits of intersubjectively acceptable solutions for analogy construction, but in literary discourse there is explicit room for accessing subjective knowledge and associations.

2. The fact that metaphor in literature can be described with reference to all four traits of literariness distinguished in section 2.2.1 is no coincidence. Metaphor is often regarded as a miniature work of verbal art, embodying 'the whole function of imaginative literature' (Wellek and Warren 1949: 197; see also Ricoeur 1974). Making explicit the parameters on which metaphor and literature may be related in empirical research can help to test this view and throw other, neglected, dimensions of both metaphor and literature into relief.

CHAPTER THREE

Metaphor and literariness

3.1 Attention to metaphor

In this chapter I will enquire into the degree of association between metaphor and readers' experiences of literariness. The relation between metaphor and literariness can be investigated by addressing the question: Is there a relation between readers' attention to metaphor and literary versus non-literary reception? I will present two empirical studies in which data were collected and analysed in order to provide first insights into this issue.

That readers do pay attention to metaphors as literary text features is suggested indirectly by at least three studies. Van Peer (1986) included metaphor in his study of foregrounded language. Foregrounding being taken as a typical attribute of literary texts, the question was raised by Van Peer whether foregrounded language was indeed attended to by readers. An underlining task for strikingness showed that subjects did pay more attention to language analysed as foregrounded by the researcher than to backgrounded language. However, separate statistics for the role of metaphors within foregrounded language were not calculated. The same holds for Hoffstaedter (1986). She had forty subjects underline stretches of text they deemed poetic in twenty-eight poems, and reported that metaphors figured prominently in the underlinings. Unfortunately, she did not produce statistical evidence in this connection, because her main interest did not lie in metaphor by itself. Vipond and Hunt (1989) were concerned with 'discourse evaluations', which include a good number of metaphors. Discourse evaluations are instantiated by a variety of stylistic devices by which writers express certain attitudes about their subject-matter. To see if readers found discourse evaluations more striking than other parts of a prose text, Vipond and Hunt used a phrase selection task that contained both discourse evaluations and neutral, control items. At the end of every page, subjects had to select five phrases from a list of ten they had found remarkable during their reading of that page. By way of comparison, a paraphrased text version with neutral equivalents for the discourse evaluations was given to a second group of subjects. There was a significant effect of the discourse evaluation factor: in the original text condition, discourse evaluations were chosen more often as striking than the control items, whereas their literal equivalents in the paraphrased text version were not.

However, it may be wondered whether the use of a set list of phrases is the right measuring instrument: subjects may quickly notice the difference between the two kinds of phrases, especially because of the high frequency of metaphoric items among the discourse evaluations and their total absence from the neutral items. Moreover, the additional comparison between the two textual conditions is questionable, because the replacement of discourse evaluations by neutral equivalents may affect the text in other ways than just the aspect under consideration (see Van Assche 1991). For instance, the neutral equivalents may contain words which have a higher frequency in comparison with the discourse evaluations, which would make the discourse evaluations more striking anyway. In other words, none of these studies offers firm evidence for a positive relation between literary reception and attention to metaphors, although they are all highly suggestive.

Two further points need to be made. First, if there is a suggestion that literary reception and attention to metaphors are indeed related, this still needs to be ascertained in comparison with the relation between non-literary reading and attention to metaphor. For literary reception and attention to metaphor may be said to be typically related only if attention to metaphor is not similarly related to other types of discourse, such as journalism. None of the above studies has used this method of comparison to validate their conclusions, but the second half of this chapter will report the results of such an approach.

Another respect in which the above studies are unclear is whether metaphors are experienced as literary in some kind of conscious way rather than unawares. Are metaphors just 'felt' to be literary? Or are they indeed experienced as typically literary because they are recognized consciously for what they are? This chapter will also address this issue of explicit metaphor identification, and examine to what extent it is related to literature.

3.2 Effects of literary socialization and degree of metaphoricity

3.2.1 Introduction

This study is an exploration of the effect on metaphor processing in literary texts of the two factors of reader knowledge and text structure. We start from the central assumption formulated in Chapter 2, that metaphors in literature afford readers an opportunity for having literary experiences. The question is whether both of the above factors of reader knowledge and text structure, including linguistic structure, can be shown to have an influence on the experience of metaphors as literary. Let me briefly recapitulate the main reasons for this expectation.

To begin with the role of reader knowledge, the findings of both Hoffstaedter (1986) and of Vipond and Hunt (1989) strongly indicate that literary socialization is an important factor determining readers' realizations of let us say 'special language'. Therefore there may turn out to be a relationship between attention to metaphor and literary experiences for some, but not for all groups of readers. This point is addressed in the present study by comparing two distinct groups of readers, one having a greater degree of literary socialization than the other. The group having the greater literary socialization was predicted to realize more metaphors as literary than the other group.

As to textual structures, it is well-known that some metaphors are more deviant, striking, unclear, and so on than others. I will use a provisional short-cut, and say that metaphors may be more or less metaphorical. If metaphors can be assumed to be related to the experience of literariness, then this should hold more clearly for metaphors with a high degree of metaphoricity than for metaphors with a low degree of metaphoricity. The present study investigated whether this was the case by comparing readers' experiences of literariness related to two groups of metaphors, one group with a high degree of metaphoricity and one with a low degree of metaphoricity.

The relation between metaphor realization and experience of literariness was investigated in two steps, each measuring the amount of attention readers paid to metaphors as literary in distinct ways. First, subjects were asked to *underline* stretches as typically literary. And second, subjects were requested to *explain* their reasons for underlining stretches as typically literary. Such explanations were asked for in the form of a written assignment. This enabled us to test the following hypotheses:

H1 Literary socialization determines attention to metaphors as typically literary (underlining task) and explicit identification of metaphors as metaphors (explanation task).

H2 Degree of metaphoricity determines attention to metaphors as typically literary (underlining task) and explicit identification of metaphors as metaphors (explanation task).

Literary socialization was operationalized by means of a difference in literary education. The two groups of subjects used in the experiment were two university classes of arts students. One group consisted of second-year students who had received a class on the language of literature, including the role of metaphor, a week before the test. No explicit connection had been made between the two events, either by myself or the teachers. The other group was a class of first-year students who had entered university six weeks before the time of data collection. They had had no special training on the language of literature as part of their course. The difference in literary socialization should affect not just the underlining, but also the explanation data.

Degree of metaphoricity was operationalized by requesting two professors of English language and literature to order the metaphors of the experimental text in descending degree of metaphoricity. The resulting average rank order could then be used as a means to distinguish a group of high-metaphorical and a group of low-metaphorical metaphors. Underlining and explanation performance by the subjects was then split according to the two metaphor categories, and compared.

What sort of written response can be said to constitute 'explicit identifications' of metaphor? Much of this depends on one's definition of metaphor itself. Traditionally, metaphors are expressions which involve the transgression of literal meaning while establishing a semantic connection between literal meaning and intended meaning that is based on resemblance of some kind. However, the definition of linguistic metaphor put forward in Chapter 1 also includes those linguistic structures which are usually called similes, as it has been argued that they require the same processing operations as metaphor (Ortony 1979b). The examples of metaphor illustrating the work of Lakoff and Johnson (1980) do not discriminate between metaphor and simile either. As a result, subjects may give various responses by way of explanation for their underlining, which may all count as explicit identification of the overall notion of metaphor, even though the label *metaphor* itself need not be used. If the most obvious responses qualifying for explicit identification are *metaphor, trope, image, figurative,* and *non-literal,* then the above argument would also include *simile, comparison, analogy* and the like. In other words, there may be many terms for metaphor identification depending on the context and the tradition of critical (meta)language involved, and these terms need not function as such in other languages or, indeed, for other readers in the same language. This problem was resolved by consulting the above-mentioned professors of English when formulating criteria for analysing the explanation data — see section 3.2.3 below for further details.

3.2.2 Method

SUBJECTS

Two groups of undergraduates in linguistics and literature at the University College of York and Ripon St John (total N = 28) took the test as part of their classes in the autumn of 1989. Actually, the group at York was larger than fourteen (N = 25), but eleven subjects failed to complete and return the test on account of an additional task which is not discussed here. The group at York was the second-year group with prior instruction, but they were naïve as to the purpose of the experiment (average age: 29.9 years). They will be referred to as having an 'advanced' degree of literary socialization. The group at Ripon, who were freshmen, were regarded as 'beginners' (average age: 22.2 years).

MATERIALS

A fragment from Norman Mailer's *Miami and the Siege of Chicago* was used as the experimental text. After consultation with 5 native speakers who were academic researchers of language and literature at the Free University of Amsterdam, 19 metaphors were identified in the text (see Table 3.1).[1] Two native speakers of English, one Professor of linguistics and one Professor of literature, were requested to order the metaphors in descending order of degree of metaphoricity. Statistical analysis showed that the reliability of their combined score was sufficient.[2] Hence it was possible to use their individual scores for determining an average rank order of the degree of metaphoricity of the metaphors involved. The resulting order of the averaged ranking is displayed by Table 3.2. The first nine metaphors were grouped together, and will be referred to as 'high-metaphorical'; the last ten metaphors were also taken together and constitute the 'low-metaphorical' group.

PROCEDURE

The test was administered separately to the two groups of subjects. The text was offered without revealing its source, and its discourse type was left undetermined. First, subjects had to underline ten stretches of maximally five words each which seemed to them to be 'typically literary'; and

Table 3.1: Materials (metaphors are underlined)

At length, the moment came for Humphrey's acceptance speech. [...] He had a large audience, and his actor's gifts for believing a role. Tonight he was the bachelor uncle who would take over a family and through kindness, simple courtesy, funds of true emotional compassion, and fatherly dictatorial sternness upon occasion (of the sort only a bachelor uncle could comprehend – '... rioting, burning, sniping, mugging, traffic in narcotics, and disregard for law are the advance guard of anarchy, and they must and they will be stopped ...') he would bring back that old-fashioned harmony to his ravaged folks. Since he was now up on the podium, the crowd was cheering, and the gallery on signal from Daley roared like a touchdown just scored. Hubert Humphrey was warm; he could believe in victory in the fall. He smiled and waved his hands and beamed, and the delegates, loosened by the film on Bobby Kennedy now demonstrated for Humphrey. The twenty years in Washington had become this night property to harvest; politicians who didn't even like him, could think fondly of Hubert at this instant, he was part of their memory of genteel glamor at Washington parties, part of the dividend of having done their exercise in politics with him for twenty years, for having talked to him ten times, shaken his hand forty, corresponded personally twice, drunk with him once – small property glows in memory, our burning glass! [...] So they rose to cheer Humphrey. He was the end of the line, a sweet guy in personal relations so far as he was able – and besides the acceptance speech at a convention was pure rite. In such ceremonies you were required to feel love even if you didn't like him. Politicians, being property holders, could feel requisite emotions at proper ceremonies. Now they gave proper love to Humphrey, two-thirds of them did. They would only have to give it for an hour. Everybody knew he would lose. The poor abstract bugger.

From Norman Mailer (1968) *Miami and the Siege of Chicago: An Informal History of the American Political Conventions of 1968.* Penguin, Harmondsworth, pp. 201–3.

(*Note:* [...] indicate deletions of passages from the original, but [...] were not part of the text as presented to the subjects.)

---

second, they had to say in writing why they had underlined each of the ten stretches as precisely as possible. There was no time-limit, and in practice forty-five to sixty minutes was sufficient for every subject.

3.2.3 Results

UNDERLINING TASK

For every subject, I counted all metaphors listed in Table 3.2 which appeared in his or her underlinings. These data were cross-classified by the distinction between metaphors with a high rank and those with a low rank in the average rank order of degree of metaphoricity, and then summed. I

Table 3.2: Average rank order of metaphors by descending degree of metaphoricity

(a) *High degree of metaphoricity*
1. the bachelor uncle who would take over a family
2. the dividend of
4. like a touchdown just scored
4. warm
4. our burning glass
6. the advance guard of
6. property to harvest
8. glows in memory
9. loosened

(b) *Low degree of metaphoricity*
10. property holders
11. fatherly
12. dictatorial
13. funds of
14. his actor's gifts for believing a role
15. their exercise
16. ravaged
17. rite
18. the end of the line
19. abstract

Table 3.3: Average proportion of high- and low-metaphorical items underlined as typically literary by two groups of students (standard deviations in brackets)

	Degree of metaphoricity	
Literary socialization	*High*	*Low*
Beginners	0.37 (0.13)	0.36 (0.19)
Advanced	0.49 (0.10)	0.37 (0.14)

then averaged across subjects, keeping the data of the two groups of subjects apart. The resulting average number of underlinings for the high- and low-metaphorical metaphors was then divided by nine and ten, respectively, in order to obtain proportions of underlinings of high- and low-metaphorical items. The average proportions of underlinings of both groups of subjects are shown in Table 3.3. It can be seen from this table that the advanced group underlined more metaphors with a high degree of metaphoricity than metaphors with a low degree of metaphoricity, but that this is hardly the case for the beginners. Another way of looking at these data is to observe that the high-metaphorical metaphors were underlined more often than the low-metaphorical items, but that this difference is due only to the performance of the group with an advanced degree of literary socialization. What is the meaning of these data?

In order to determine whether the data of Table 3.3 support our predictions, we have to test whether the differences found in these data are due to chance variations in sampling, or whether they can be attributed to the effect of the factors under investigation, namely 'literary socialization' and 'degree of metaphoricity'. This can be done by means of a statistical test called analysis of variance. I will not explain how this test works, but simply report the results of the test in common language. The technical details can be found in note 3.[3]

The first part of the test concerns the magnitude of the overall or main effect of the factor 'literary socialization'. It turned out that this factor produced a statistically significant effect on the means of the two groups. Looking at the means displayed in Table 3.3, this finding suggests that the advanced group underlined more metaphors (high-metaphorical *plus* low-metaphorical) as typically literary than the group of beginners. This is in agreement with our hypothesis, which predicted that literary socialization determines attention to metaphors as typically literary (H1). However, further analysis of these data shows that this finding cannot be generalized towards other materials, and is restricted to the text used here (see note 3, Table IIIA *ii*).

Second, there is the question whether subjects underlined high-metaphorical items significantly more often than low-metaphorical items. The analysis of variance showed that the effect of 'degree of metaphoricity' on the underlinings of stretches as typically literary did not attain statistical significance. This result shows that subjects did not underline highly metaphorical metaphors more often as typically literary than low-metaphorical metaphors when we take chance variation between collecting data into account. In other words, the different mean scores of the two columns of Table 3.3 are not reliable, but due to chance. As a consequence, the underlining data do not support the hypothesis that degree of metaphoricity determines attention to metaphors as typically literary (H2).

It should be realized that the above results relate to the *main* effects of literary socialization and degree of metaphoricity. This means that the effect of literary socialization is calculated without discriminating between the high- and low-metaphorical metaphors; the analysis works with an average of these two means. Similarly, the main effect of degree of metaphoricity ignores any differences between the two groups of subjects on this score. However, it is also possible to do precisely that, namely to look at the interaction between these two factors. An interaction effect indicates whether there is a statistically significant difference between means for a particular combination of the two factors only. Thus the question arises whether the interaction between the factor of literary socialization and only one of the types of metaphors, namely either the high- or the low-metaphorical items, produces a significant difference between the means of the advanced group and the beginners. The analysis of variance showed that the effect of the interaction between literary socialization and degree of metaphoricity was not statistically significant either. This indicates that the groups of subjects did not perform differently from each other when we are looking at only one of the two degrees of metaphoricity, high or low. In other words, the difference between the two groups of subjects regarding the average proportion of either high-metaphorical or low-metaphorical metaphors which they underlined for literariness is not so large as to be attributable to the factor of literary socialization. It is again explained by chance variation in sampling between groups.

In sum:

(1) The difference between the two rows of Table 3.3 is statistically significant. This finding indicates that the two groups of subjects differ regarding the average proportion of both kinds of metaphors which they underline as typically literary. In particular, it can be seen that the advanced group underlined more metaphors than the group without prior instruction. This constitutes support for H1.

(2) The difference between the two columns of Table 3.3 is not statistically significant. This means that degree of metaphoricity did not affect readers' average proportion of underlinings of metaphors as typically literary. In particular, subjects did not select metaphors with a high degree of metaphoricity more frequently than metaphors with a low degree of metaphoricity. These data do not support H2.

(3) The difference between the two groups in either the left-hand or the right-hand column is not reliable either. This suggests that there is no effect of literary socialization on readers' choices of either high-metaphorical or low-metaphorical metaphors as typically literary.

EXPLANATION TASK: CODING AND SCORING

'Explicit identifiers of metaphor' were operationalized as follows. All distinct phrases from the subjects' responses qualifying as potential explicit identifiers of metaphors were listed and submitted for discussion to the two professors of English who had previously carried out the metaphor ranking. They were familiar with the linguistic and literary parlance concerning metaphor in English. Their task was to comment on the dangers inherent in accepting as explicit identifiers of metaphor those terms which were less clear or familiar. The idea was that these comments could be used as conservative guidelines in coding the data. As a result, the following terms (and their grammatical variants) were accepted as 'explicit identifiers of metaphor': *metaphor, comparison, likening, non-literal, image, simile, analogy, connotation.* An automatic computer search of the explanation protocols identified all occurrences of these terms. Upon visual inspection, one specific occurrence of each of the following terms, *image, comparing, like, connotation,* was not deemed pertinent for metaphor identification and ignored.

Examples of written explanations of underlinings of one selected metaphor are provided in Table 3.4. The example in question is a metaphor with a high degree of metaphoricity. No fewer than fifteen subjects out of the twenty who had underlined this metaphor as typically literary also explicitly identified it in their explanations. These examples will be discussed in the next section.

Table 3.5 presents the average percentage per subject of explicit metaphor identifications in the explanation data. We are dealing with the proportion of metaphors which subjects explicitly identified in the explanation task in relation to those metaphors they had previously underlined as typically literary. The means are again classified by the factors of literary socialization and degree of metaphoricity.

It can be observed from Table 3.5 that the beginners explicitly identified 45 per cent of the metaphors they had underlined as typically literary. But the advanced group explicitly identified about 55 per cent of their previously underlined metaphors. In addition, there seems to be a large difference between the explicit identification of metaphors with a high degree of metaphoricity as opposed to metaphors with a low degree of metaphoricity. Analysis of variance was used again to test the statistical reliability of these differences between means. In reporting the results of this analysis, I will use the format of the summary related to the previous data analysis (see the text following Table 3.3 above). Readers wishing to refresh their understanding of terms like 'main effect' can refer to the more detailed discussion preceding that summary.

There was no significant main effect for literary socialization.[4] The advanced group did not explicitly identify more metaphors than the beginners. This finding does not tally with H1, which predicted that literary socialization should affect the identification of metaphors as metaphors.

However, degree of metaphoricity did yield a significant main effect. Highly metaphorical metaphors were explicitly identified more often than low-metaphorical ones. H2 is thus supported by these data. Subsequent analysis showed that this finding is also valid for other metaphors than the ones used here (see Table IIIB *ii* and *iii* in note 4).

Third, the interaction between literary socialization and degree of

Table 3.4: Explanations of underlinings by two groups of students regarding one selected metaphor, i.e. *property to harvest* (criteria for explicit identification are capitalized)

S1. This phrase is literary because it, once more, uses ANALOGY, the ANALOGY of experience being LIKE corn . . . there to be collected and put to use at the correct time . . . a good ANALOGY but not one to be found in non-literary texts.

S2. choice of words used in description. 'property' refers back to his 20 yrs in Washington, and the use of 'harvest' is descriptive in the sense that he's reaping what he sowed 20 yrs ago.

S3. very unnatural expression, almost out of context

S4. again use of METAPHOR, suggest a more literary style

S5. METAPHORical use of words

S6. this is again a strong IMAGE (the IMAGEry in the passage is probably the single most powerful incentive to take it as 'literature'.

S7. is a type of saying rather than factual language. In my opinion, this kind of phrase is too vague to be non-literary.

S8. refers to 'twenty years in Washington' – abstract being referred to in concrete terms

S9. METAPHOR. twenty years cannot be property, nor can it be harvested

S10. a METAPHOR/which is a literary device

S11. a METAPHOR creating the IMAGE that H has served 20 yrs in politics and only has a very small bundle (the size of hay) to show for it once it has been reaped + harvested. negative IMAGE. shows what will come later

S12. descriptive

S13. use of METAPHOR: evocation of rustic pastoral IMAGE, strong contrast of materialism vs. 'the earth'

S14. the LITERAL meaning of this phrase – i.e. property 'harvest' is not what is required. The words are used here in a whole new context + it relies on us to have a wide understanding of these words to understand the author's true subtle meaning.

S15. it is a METAPHORical term and explains how he is now able to reap his rewards

S16. stylistic. METAPHORically to harvest, growing of crops, etc.

S17. a METAPHOR. The seeds have been sown over the years – now it's time to reap the benefit

S18. use of METAPHOR

S19. METAPHOR: you cannot 'harvest' people

S20. METAPHOR, is a literary symbol, meaning that the property is 'there for the taking'

Table 3.5: Average proportion of previously underlined metaphors, grouped by degree of metaphoricity, identified explicitly by two groups of students (standard deviations in brackets)

	Degree of metaphoricity	
Literary socialization	*High*	*Low*
Beginners	0.65 (0.38)	0.25 (0.39)
Advanced	0.75 (0.23)	0.36 (0.35)

metaphoricity was not statistically significant. This indicates that there was no difference between the two groups of subjects with regard to their underlining of either high-metaphorical or low-metaphorical metaphors. But this finding is immaterial to our hypotheses.

3.2.4 Discussion

Let us first review the effect of literary socialization on the experience of metaphors as literary. H1 predicted that the advanced group would relate more metaphors to literary experiences than the beginners. In the first task, underlining for typical literariness, the comparison between the two groups of subjects yielded a significant main effect. This suggests that, during underlining, literary socialization does influence the attention paid to metaphors as literary. However, the means of proportional explicit identification were not affected by literary socialization. There is no good reason for this difference between subjects' performance during underlining and explanation. In all then, there is only partial evidence for an effect of literary socialization on readers' attention to metaphors.

Perhaps the operationalization of 'literary socialization' in terms of the presence or absence of explicit instruction in the language of literature was not felicitous. It might be argued that if one took groups of subjects with more widely diverging reading experiences, the difference in literary socialization would be based on rather more personally internalized conventions, which could make a difference. It is doubtful whether this would bring much relief, though, because there was a large age difference of more than six years between the two groups of subjects (section 3.2.2 above). This age difference has not made a difference in the present case either. Another point is the fact that only one text was used in the present experiment. This affects the representative value of the findings, for the present text may have contained too many conspicuous metaphors for the group with a lower degree of literary socialization to miss them. These issues will need to be determined by future research.

Next, there is the matter of the effect of 'degree of metaphoricity'. The lack of an effect of this factor on the underlining of stretches for literariness is also contrary to expectation — it constitutes an anomaly with respect to the theory. Fortunately, this problem is less big when we include the role of metaphoricity in the explanations of the underlinings. Explicit identification of metaphors is affected by degree of metaphoricity, in that readers explicitly identify highly metaphorical metaphors more frequently than low-metaphorical ones. This is in accordance with the prediction. Again, the findings of this study provide only mixed support for the hypothesis, that degree of metaphoricity affects the experience of metaphors as literary.

Perhaps the operationalization of degree of metaphoricity by means of ranking by two experts measured only one trait of metaphoricity, such as linguistic deviance. Thus metaphors having other potentially important attributes for literariness, like clarity or beauty, could have ended up in the low-metaphoricity category in the ranking. But they might still be underlined as typically literary by the subjects. In that way, any effect for metaphoricity would have been obliterated. The fact that this did not happen in the explanation task can be understood from the much closer relation between metaphor as linguistic deviance on the one hand and its noticeability as metaphor on the other: highly metaphorical metaphors in the sense of deviance will be identified explicitly more often than low-metaphorical ones.[5]

Let us now turn to the relation between underlining and identification. A good number of the underlined metaphors were also explicitly identified as such. However, this finding needs to be developed in follow-up studies which are able to compare explicit identification across conditions of literariness and non-literariness. But the initial evidence produced by this study is encouraging in this area at least. It suggests that readers consciously experience many metaphors as literary.

This leads me on to a further issue concerning the relation between the explanations and the underlinings. In Chapter 2 it was proposed that metaphors may also be related to literariness by their sheer quantitative presence. The fact that many more metaphors were underlined as typically literary than identified in retrospect as explicitly metaphorical may be interpreted as providing some support for this view. Readers may be more alert to language in literary texts than elsewhere without going to the extent of identifying figures of speech or providing labels for a particular style. A test with longer texts containing a representative number of metaphors for their respective discourse types could show whether this suggestion is valid: I would expect that the metaphors in the literary text(s) would be underlined more often as typically literary than the metaphors in the non-literary texts are underlined as typically journalistic, scientific, or whatever. This is what I begin to explore in the next study in section 3.3.

A point to be made about explicit identification is that it is clearly dependent on the availability of a metalanguage to the readers. Subjects indicated the presence of 'flowery language', language that went 'contrary to fact', and so on, but these sorts of phrases were not deemed to be fully adequate indicators of explicit metaphor identification. Examples from Table 3.4 include the following cases. Subject 2 talks about 'choice of words' and reference; although the analysis of the problem of metaphorical meaning is adequate, it is not identified as such by means of reference to the idea of non-literal comparison. Subject number 3 is much vaguer, using 'unnatural' and 'out of context'; only by presuming that the latter term carries a highly specific technical meaning could this explanation count as explicit metaphor identification. Subject 7 speaks of 'a type of saying', but cannot specify it clearly, apart from the idea that it is not 'factual language'; but many types of sayings are not 'factual language', so this was not counted as explicit identification of metaphor. Subject number 8 is the borderline case *par excellence*: the problem of reference is singled out, and the two domains of 'abstract' and 'concrete' are identified. However, the abstract can also be referred to by means of metonymy, synecdoche, symbolism, and allegory. So this still remains too unspecific an explanation for inclusion in the data. We are interested in explicit *metaphor* identification, not in general perception of non-literal reference. Subject 12 illustrates a tendency conspicuous throughout the sample of using the term 'description' and its variants in an apparently significant manner (compare subject 2 above), but this term is empty of content when it comes to explicit metaphor identification.

It is clear that subjects have often felt that *something* was there, but that their analytic abilities and metalanguage were insufficient for a specific recognition of the phenomenon. What may jump to the eye of the critic as a significant figure of speech of a particular kind, having a particular stylistic effect, is part of a much vaguer feeling for the ordinary reader about literary style.

3.3 Effects of discourse context

3.3.1 Introduction

Having investigated the influence of the two factors of reader knowledge and text structure on the experience of metaphors as literary, we can now turn to the other important factor discussed in the previous two chapters, literature as discourse context. The central assumption formulated in Chapter 2, that metaphors in literature afford readers an opportunity for having literary experiences, has received a beginning of empirical support in the previous study because many readers underlined many metaphors as typically literary and did so with some degree of consciousness. But we have not explored how metaphors function in non-literary discourse. Therefore, we cannot make any statements about the *discourse-typical* role of metaphor in understanding literature, because we lack a comparison. To make such a comparison between attention to metaphors in literary and non-literary discourse is the aim of the study we will now discuss.

I have argued in Chapter 2 that the discourse-typical function of metaphor in text processing is dependent on the nature of the discourse context in which metaphor processing takes place. Therefore the question arises how the effect of context on metaphor processing can be investigated empirically. A number of researchers in the empirical study of literature, for instance Schram (1985) and Meutsch (1987), have solved this kind of problem by manipulating the mode of presentation of the stimulus text. The general argument is that text processing becomes literary text processing when the reader has information that the text is to be regarded as literary. To the everyday reader, this information is basically contextual: it may involve the appearance of a text in a literary magazine, or its provenance from a particular section in the library or the bookshop. There may also be textual cues, such as the indication that a particular text is labelled as a novel, or the typical lay-out of a poem but to the reader, these usually are secondary features which follow from the primary, context-based classification of a text as literary. Readers read a literary text because they have selected it for that purpose, not because they have first investigated the features of that text as to their suitability for arousing literary experiences.

This argument facilitates an experimental design for empirical research in which the text, the words on the page, is separated from the context, the classification as literary. One group of subjects can be offered an originally literary and an originally journalistic text with the explicit contextual information that the texts are indeed literary and journalistic. Another group of subjects can be offered the same originally literary and journalistic texts, but this time with the opposite contextual information. In other words, the two texts are presented twice, once in their intended, authentic contexts for reading, and another time in a perverse, manipulated context for reading. For a graphic illustration of this design, see Figure 3.1. For both context conditions, it is expected that the text *which is presented as* literary induces the greater proportion of attention to metaphor. In other words, this design predicts that two groups of subjects, each linked to one of the contextual conditions, should perform in opposite ways. In the authentic context, it is the originally literary text which should trigger more attention to metaphors, because it is presented as literary: the means of cell 11 should be larger than those of cell 12. But in the perverse context condition, it is the journalistic text which should exhibit more attention to metaphors, because in that context condition, the journalistic text is presented as literary: the means of cell 22 should be larger than those of cell 21. In statistical terms, we are looking for an interaction effect (for an explanation of this term, see the analysis of the data of Table 3.3 in section 3.2.3).[6]

These predictions were tested by the same method as in the previous

Text		
Context	(Originally) literary	(Originally) non-literary
Authentic (1)	Literary (11)	Journalistic (12)
Perverse (2)	Journalistic (21)	Literary (22)

Fig. 3.1: Design

study. Subjects were first asked to underline those stretches of text which they deemed literary and journalistic, and then they had to explain their underlinings in writing. This provides us with a test of the following hypothesis:

H3 Context determines attention to metaphors (underlining task) and explicit identification of metaphors (explanation task).

Unlike the previous study, this experiment did not go into the effect of literary socialization and degree of metaphoricity on attention to metaphors. This was done for reasons of simplicity. The design of the present study is complicated enough as it stands. Another reason for leaving these issues aside is the fact that I was also interested in exploring an alternative method of underlining. In the previous study and in Steen (1990) I asked subjects to select ten stretches of maximally five words each. This method implies that subjects will begin by reading the text and then calculate the number of ten stretches and measure them out within the required five-word boundaries. In Steen (1990) I noted a refusal on the part of two subjects to underline more than six or seven stretches as journalistic because they could not find any more. These are important limitations on the validity of the data reported in those studies, because the procedure caused a degree of distance from ordinary reading. I was eager to see this distance reduced as much as possible.

Therefore this study experimented with a less controlled underlining task. If there are no restrictions on the number of stretches and their number of words, we should have a better indication of what is spontaneously experienced as typically literary and typically journalistic in these two texts. Moreover, if subjects are encouraged to underline stretches as they go along, then we are much closer to the undisturbed process of reading than before. However, this method does require careful attention to the comparability of the general underlining patterns before they can be used as data for the study of metaphor processing. I will devote sufficient discussion to this issue in the results section.

3.3.2 Method

SUBJECTS

University students of the Free University Amsterdam (N = 30) who had signed up for a course on literary text analysis took the test as part of their first hour of the course in the autumn of 1992. Their average age was 21 years.

MATERIALS

Fragments of a literary and a journalistic text were used. The literary text was narrative prose fiction, dealing with a confrontation between riot police and demonstraters on the day of the Coronation of Queen Beatrix in Amsterdam in 1980. It was an edited portion from the novel *De slag om de Blauwbrug* (The Battle of the Bluebridge) by the Dutch author A.F.Th. van der Heijden, being a slightly revised version of the text used in Steen (1990). The journalistic text was an impression of the first two days after the opening of the Berlin wall in November 1990, describing the events in the streets in narrative prose. It is an edited portion from a reportage by the Dutch journalist Cees Zoon for the Dutch 'labour' quality daily *De Volkskrant*. The main texts were roughly equal in length (379 and 397 words, respectively).

The texts contained a similar number of metaphors (twenty-seven and twenty-four, respectively). Analysis of the metaphors was carried out by myself, and discussed with a colleague. Metaphors ranged from novel compounds such as 'mist-curtain' for 'cloud of gas' to entire sentences such as 'Thousands of Alices entered their wonderland' for 'Thousands of East Berliners entered West Berlin'. They also ranged from highly original to quite conventional and dead metaphors, the latter including the designation of the battling arena in the literary text as a 'stage'. The nature of the metaphors will be discussed further in Chapter 9.

As indicated above, the texts were offered in two contexts: in the authentic context condition, they were offered in their genuine identities of literature and journalism, respectively. But in the perverse context condition, the literary text was offered as a piece of journalism and the journalistic text was offered as a fragment from the prepublication of a new novel. To enhance the effect of the instruction in the perverse context condition, that the originally literary text was a piece of journalism from *De Volkskrant*, I added a self-invented title − containing one metaphor −, the name of the author of the journalistic text, Cees Zoon, and the placename 'Amsterdam' at the top of the text. This part was discounted during analysis. To present the journalistic text as a piece of literature, the title originally appearing in the newspaper − containing two metaphors itself − was removed, and subjects were told that the text was a fragment from a prepublication of a new novel by the writer of the literary text, A.F.Th. van der Heijden. This part was also left out of consideration during analysis.

PROCEDURE

Subjects were randomly assigned to the authentic and perverse conditions of text presentation. In both conditions, the order of the texts was counterbalanced across subjects to prevent order effects: in the authentic context condition, eight subjects first received the literary text and then the journalistic text; and seven subjects first received the journalistic text and then the literary text. In the perverse context condition, seven subjects first received the (originally) literary text and then the (originally) journalistic text; and eight subjects first received the (originally) journalistic text and then the (originally) literary text.

Subjects received a written questionnaire with the information that they were to take part in a test designed to improve the course of literary text analysis they had enrolled for. They were told that I was interested in their personal opinion of what literature was. They were also told that in each pair of experimental texts only one was literary, so that the nature of literature could be determined better by means of comparison.

Subjects first had to read each of their two texts and underline stretches of text for their discourse-typical nature as they went along. The instruction made it clear which text was presented as literary and which was journalistic. Subjects were free to underline any stretch of text they found relevant. It was emphasized that it was first impressions that counted. They were told to wait until everyone had finished this stage of the test. It lasted for about twelve minutes.

Next, subjects were asked to continue with the second part of the test, and explain in a few words why they had underlined the stretches in the two texts as typically literary and journalistic. They had to number the previously underlined stretches in the margin, take over their first and last words on a separate sheet, and then add their explanations. Again, it was

Table 3.6: Mean percentage of metaphors underlined as typically literary and journalistic in two contexts of presentation (standard deviation in brackets)

	Text	
Context	*(Originally) literary*	*(Originally) non-literary*
Authentic	0.47 (0.21)	0.24 (0.11)
Perverse	0.10 (0.15)	0.27 (0.11)

emphasized that all reasons for underlining were relevant. I also stressed that all underlinings had to receive an explanation. Finally, subjects had to fill in a few questions about their sex, age, experience with literary text analysis, and interest in the course. This part of the test took about thirty minutes. After the test, subjects were debriefed about the rationale of the study.

3.3.3 Results

UNDERLINING DATA

Let us begin by taking a first look at the metaphor underlining data. For every subject, I counted the number of metaphors figuring in the stretches he or she had underlined as typically literary and typically journalistic. Then I calculated the mean number of metaphors per subject underlined in both texts by averaging across subjects. Finally I derived the average percentage of metaphors per subject underlined as typically literary and journalistic for each text by dividing by the total number of metaphors in each text, twenty-seven and twenty-four, respectively. Table 3.6 presents the mean percentages for the two texts divided over the two conditions of presentation.

In both context conditions, the mean percentage of metaphors underlined for literariness exceeds the mean proportion of metaphors underlined for their journalistic nature. When the texts were presented in their authentic identity, subjects underlined about half of the metaphors of the literary text as typically literary, but only one quarter of the metaphors of the journalistic text as typically journalistic. In the perverse context condition, the other group of subjects underlined about one quarter of the metaphors of the originally journalistic text as typically literary, but only one tenth of the metaphors of the originally literary text as typically journalistic. Both groups of subjects hence underlined twice as many metaphors during literary reading than during journalistic reading.

The data presented in Table 3.6 cannot be taken completely at face value. The method utilized in this study left subjects free to determine both the number of stretches of the text which they underlined, and the number of words which they included within each and every stretch. As a consequence, there may be important differences between the mean number of stretches or words underlined as being typically literary or journalistic, which in turn may have affected the percentages of metaphor underlinings. In other words, because the texts themselves may well be differentially typical or untypical of the respective discourse types, this may have raised or lowered the relative number of metaphor underlinings. Therefore we will have to take into account how many stretches and words were underlined in total in both texts as typically literary and typically journalistic.

This can be done by adding these variables (number of stretches and length of stretches) as *covariates* to the planned analysis of variance. The idea of such an analysis of covariance is to remove the effect of the covariates on the means of the groups before testing whether there are reliable differences between the remaining means. For instance, suppose that the literary text triggered 10 per cent more underlinings than the journalistic text in the authentic context condition. This would also raise the chance of underlining the metaphors in the literary text by 10 per cent. In such a case, the average number of underlined metaphors in the literary text would be 10 per cent too high for a fair comparison with the underlined metaphors in the journalistic text. The number of underlined metaphors would not be solely due to the experimental factors of text and context, but also partly to 'accidental' effects of the free method for underlining. Therefore, in such a case the means of metaphor underlinings in the literary text would have to be reduced by 10 per cent before the comparison with metaphor underlinings in the journalistic text could be made. This is what has been done in the analysis of covariance reported in note 7.[7]

It turned out that some of the difference between the proportion of metaphors underlined in the two texts (Table 3.6) was indeed related to differences among the texts in proportions of underlined words for typical discourse nature. In particular, there was a significant effect for the two covariates 'underlined proportion of words in the literary text' and 'underlined proportion of words in the journalistic text'. Interpretation of the test statistics suggests that (i) the literary text is more representative of literature than the journalistic text is of journalism (authentic context), and (ii) that the journalistic text is more representative of literature than the literary text is representative of journalism (perverse context). Indeed, the analysis showed that some 10 per cent of the metaphors underlined in the literary text as typically literary may be explicable by this excess in typicalness, and need not be due to the effect of the factors of literary versus journalistic reading themselves. The reverse argument holds for the perverse context condition: there, some 10 per cent of the difference between the percentage of underlined metaphors in the literary and the journalistic texts may be due to the higher potential for literariness of the journalistic text, in comparison with the potential for journalism of the literary text. These influences were removed by the analysis of covariance before the resulting means of underlinings were further analysed.

Now let us move on to the central results. As noted in the introduction (section 3.3.1), we are interested in the question whether there was a statistical interaction between the factors of context and text, because this would mean that there are differences between the two groups which can be related to the distinct contextual conditions. It turns out that the interaction effect was highly significant (after adjustment of the means for the covariates). When we look at the means of each group in Table 3.6, it is clear that this significant interaction effect can be interpreted as supporting the hypothesis that it is the literary reading task which promotes attention to metaphors. Even when the means of the two relevant cells (11 and 22) are reduced by 10 per cent on account of the effect of the covariates, there still remains a considerable, and statistically significant difference between the adjusted means and the means of the other text in the same group of subjects. The hypothesis that context determines attention to metaphors has been supported by these data.

The main effect of contextual condition of presentation was also significant. In other words, after adjustment for the covariates, the averaged means of the authentic context condition turned out to be significantly different from the averaged means of the perverse context condition. Looking at the means of Table 3.6, this shows that the authentic context condition received more underlinings for typical discourse nature than the perverse context condition. However, it can also be observed that this *overall* difference between the two context conditions is largely due to the different mean scores of the literary text alone, for the journalistic text has about an equal number of literary and journalistic underlinings. The finding of a significant main effect of context is therefore solely attributable to the dealings of readers with the literary text in the authentic and perverse conditions of presentation. It should be said that it is not uncommon for a significant main effect to be 'meaningless' when there is a significant interaction effect.

Finally we have to report that there was no significant main effect of the factor of text. In other words, there is no significant difference between the average means of the two columns in Table 3.6, after adjustment of the means by the covariates. But this part of the analysis was of no interest to our hypothesis either.

Table 3.7: Average proportion of previously underlined metaphors identified explicitly in two contexts of presentation (standard deviations added in brackets)

	Text	
Context	(*Originally*) *literary*	(*Originally*) *journalistic*
Authentic	0.49 (0.27)	0.00 (0.00)
Perverse	0.00 (0.00)	0.22 (0.25)

EXPLANATION DATA

How many of the stretches underlined for typical literariness and journalistic nature were motivated by the explicit identification of their containing metaphorical language? A summary of these data is given in Table 3.7, which contains the average number of stretches per subject featuring an explicit recognition of metaphorical language as contributing to the typical literary or journalistic nature of the passage in question. There were some missing values in the explanations, because not all subjects had kept to the instruction that all underlinings should receive a written explanation. However, this can be interpreted simultaneously as signalling a lack of explicit metaphor identification, so that these missing values are also null-results for the category under investigation. Therefore they are not disturbing.

Only two key terms kept recurring in these data, namely *metaphor* and *comparison*. A third term for metaphor identification, *image*, was used less frequently. These were the only explicit identifiers for metaphoricity. Despite the language difference of a change from English to Dutch, the data were just as clear as the ones of the previous study, so that additional checks on reliability of analysis were unnecessary.

It does not take a statistician to conclude that the data reported in Table 3.7 are quite special. There were no explicit metaphor identifications whatsoever in the explanation task for underlined journalistic passages in both conditions of text presentation. However, these data are also special from a statistical point of view. They cannot be usefully subjected to an analysis of variance because of the lack of variance in two of the four cells. This remarkable fact is indicative of the fundamental difference between the two tasks of explaining literary versus journalistic underlinings. When stretches were marked for literariness, about a quarter to half received an explanation by the subjects in terms of their metaphorical language. But subjects never did this for typically journalistic passages. This is good evidence for a relation between metaphor and literariness in terms of attention to metaphors.

3.3.4 Discussion

The hypothesis that attention to metaphors is determined by context is confirmed. The task of selecting typical text stretches for literature guided the attention of subjects towards metaphors, whereas the task of marking stretches as typically journalistic did not, or did so to a lesser extent. And the task of explaining why passages were chosen as typical of literary or journalistic discourse revealed that explicit metaphor identification played a prominent role in the experience of passages as typically literary, while it never induced subjects to mark a passage as typically journalistic.

This study was designed to provide further evidence for the finding of the previous study that there is a relation between metaphor and literariness. The addition of a non-literary reading task for comparison with the literary reading task is one novel feature. It led to a confirmation of the findings of Steen (1990), namely that a journalistic reading context directs the attention of readers away from metaphorical passages. The fact that we have been able to show that this is the case by employing two different texts, one of which was originally literary and the other journalistic, for the two distinct tasks of literary and journalistic reading adds to the validity of the conclusions. There is an important difference between attention to metaphors in genuinely literary and genuinely journalistic texts.

Another novel feature of this study is related to the previous issue. The extra context condition in which the texts were offered in perverse identities ensured that any differences between literary and journalistic reading were due to the context and not due to the text. In effect, this design was a strong test of the idea that it is context which determines the experience of metaphors as literary. Both conditions of text presentation, the authentic and the perverted one, led to a predominance of attention to metaphor in literary reading in comparison with journalistic reading. This was according to expectation.

Another important feature was the experimental use of a free method for underlining. There was no predetermined number of passages and words per passage as in the previous study and in Steen (1990). This method was chosen so that data could be collected about typically literary and journalistic passages in a way that was as close as possible to the original reading experience of the subjects. It turned out that subjects experienced a similar number of passages as typical throughout the four conditions of reading, because there was no significant effect of the covariates 'number of underlined passages' in the literary and journalistic text. This result enhances the validity of the findings, because subjects were not deflected from ordinary reading by the task of measuring out two times ten stretches of maximally five words each.

This was not the case when we looked at the proportionate number of words which were underlined in both tasks for both conditions of presentation. That covariate did show a significant difference between the two texts. The literary text was more typical of literature than the journalistic text of journalism. For the originally literary text, there was a larger number of words per typical passage in the authentic context condition than for the originally journalistic text. Similarly, there was a smaller number of words per untypical passage for the originally literary text in the perverse context condition. These general differences among the two texts also proved predictive of a certain percentage of the underlinings of metaphors, as was shown by the two significant effects of the covariates in the multiple analysis of covariance.

3.4 Conclusion

3.4.1 'Metaphors are literary'

The special relation between metaphor and literariness which can be observed in literary criticism has proven to extend beyond that domain and can also be observed in the behaviour of ordinary readers. The data collected and analysed in this chapter provide sufficient support for the idea that readers who are not literary critics pay special attention to metaphor in texts they believe to be literature in comparison to metaphor in texts they believe to be journalism. The two studies in which this idea was investigated involved three different texts in two languages, two groups of subjects who were of different nationalities, and two variants of the method of underlining. This facilitates generalization of the findings towards other comparable subjects, texts, and metaphors. Metaphors play a special role in the literary as opposed to journalistic reading of narratives by educated young adults: metaphors are seen as typically literary, but not as typically journalistic.

Many subjects motivated their underlinings of stretches as typically literary by means of explicit metaphor identification. What is more, some also added the comment that metaphor is a literary device. It is striking that this was never said about the journalistic metaphors, in spite of the fact that metaphor can just as legitimately be seen as an effective and traditional rhetorical device for journalism. The explication that metaphor is non-factual was often found in the explanations. Some kind of fact convention is apparently seen as opposed to the use of metaphoricity. As was argued in Chapter 2, metaphors are small (and impossible) fictions themselves. Fictionality as opposed to factuality being one of the hallmarks of literature as a distinct type of discourse, the relation between metaphor and literariness can be understood without difficulty.

Chapter 2 emphasized that metaphor can be seen as contributing to literary discourse in all four respects which I have identified as characteristic of literature: subjectivity, fictionality, polyvalence, and attention to form and style. The present chapter has shown that the aspects of fictionality and orientation to style are of fundamental importance when it comes to explaining the role of metaphor in literature. Metaphors are impossibly fictional, and they are identified explicitly as ingredients of a typically literary style.

Although this is a confirmation of a common view of metaphor in literature, it ignores the fact that there are many other types of discourse which contain metaphors. This can be taken as a suggestion that readers do indeed experience what is literary and what is not on the basis of a set of fairly specific, context-based discourse expectations, and that the function of metaphor in reception is accordingly affected. The second study of this chapter, separating text from context, has provided us with strong evidence for this suggestion. It seems that the common opinion that metaphor is literary was successfully infused into these students by a number of years of secondary-school training in the modern languages.

The point that the relation between metaphor and literariness is common doxa will now lead us on to make another comment about the validity of the findings of this chapter. The conclusion that readers intentionally select metaphors as typically literary is tentative in one important respect. As the writing task for explanations was not concurrent with but retrospective to the underlining task, the subjects may have actually mobilized their discourse knowledge about metaphor as literary only when they were asked to explicate their underlinings. Their application of the common doxa that metaphors are literary to their own behaviour during writing up their explanations does not mean that they had activated this knowledge while performing the underlining task. They could have picked the metaphors on much vaguer grounds, and might have marshalled their discourse knowledge for explanation only in retrospect. A method other than underlining and subsequent explication will have to alleviate this drawback.

This will be the task of the next part of this book. There, the method of thinking out loud while reading will be used to collect data about the reading process. It will also provide us with a means of investigating understanding processes of metaphor other than explicit metaphor identification. In particular, such criterial processes for subjectivity and polyvalence as appreciation and vehicle construction, respectively, will also be included in that undertaking. This may shed further light on the issue of degree of awareness of metaphors as typically literary during the on-line reading process as opposed to retrospective recognition.

Of course the idea that metaphors are related to literariness is not original. The point I am making in this chapter is not that they are related, but that they are related in *the behaviour of ordinary readers*. I have argued in the previous chapter that literary criticism is twice removed from ordinary reading, because it is focused on the text and because it is based on a cycle of readings rather than embodying one more or less continuous reading process. The fact that I have been able to show that there is a relation between metaphor and literariness in ordinary reading is a significant finding. We might have suspected that something like this is the case, but we did not know to what extent and in what areas it held true.

The value of this kind of experimental work, which is strange to most literary scholars, may become more evident from the areas in which it failed. Two other common ideas about metaphor and literariness were not as clearly supported by the evidence as was hoped beforehand, namely the expectation of an effect of degree of metaphoricity and of literary socialization. This 'failure' has the merit of making one aware of the imprecision of the common doxa and of the difficulties involved in making such general ideas precise enough for them to be tested by means of empirical research. This entails that it is unclear what we mean by degree of metaphoricity and literary socialization. Thus even the present failure has contributed to our knowledge about these notions: it has made us aware of what we do not know. It will be the task of the next parts of the book to address these issues in greater detail.

3.4.2 A brief note on the function of empirical and critical approaches to literature

I am spending some time on explicating these points because the use of an empirical method, and particularly of quantification, has been anathema in literary studies. However, if one takes seriously the idea that 'literature' is what people do with a particular kind of texts, and that it involves a kind of mental activity, then there is no alternative to going out to gather facts about people's behaviour (Schram and Steen 1992). In empirical research, the real reader is placed at the centre of investigation, and as many means as possible are employed to find out what goes on when people have literary experiences. The common method of self-analysis by the literary critic cannot hope to come even close to this ideal, for reasons which I have suggested.

An experiment with an underlining and a writing task may seem somewhat removed from ordinary reading. I claim, however, that it is far less removed from ordinary reading than literary criticism. Literary critics are in a kind of experimental situation, too: they are paid to lock themselves away in their rooms, and allow themselves the luxury of inordinate amounts of time and access to reference works to study texts. My subjects did not have any reference books, limited time resources, and received no money to motivate their reading. It seems to me that the latter version of the reading process is much closer to ordinary reading than the former. Other methods will have to indicate how much closer we can get. But the conclusions of the present studies constitute a much closer approximation to a clear view of the role of metaphor in literary reading than those deriving from literary critical writings. This is not to undermine the value of literary criticism, but to point out that literary criticism is aimed at a different kind of object and state of knowledge.

Literary critics often suggest that the functions of metaphor they have uncovered in a particular text will also be experienced by other people, and may extend to other metaphors in other texts. Even if this may be the case, it only holds within the language-game of literary criticism itself. As soon as the parameters are changed to include ordinary reading, literary critics stand with empty hands, because they have not dealt with ordinary reading. The empirical method I have employed in these studies includes the sampling of representative texts, metaphors, and subjects from larger populations. This entails that I cannot extend my conclusions to poetry, nor to other kinds of readers apart from highly educated young adults, nor to other kinds of texts containing far fewer metaphors or metaphors with a totally different psychological make-up. These are matters for further research. But I can generalize beyond my particular samples of texts, metaphors and readers to other, similar texts, metaphors, and readers, and this is more than most literary critics are able (or willing) to do.

The overall aim of this book is to show that empirical research on understanding metaphor in literature is possible, necessary, and valuable. Therefore, the next two parts will be a further in-depth exploration of the processes of understanding metaphor in literature, and of the psychological dimensions of literary metaphors.

Notes

1. This study was carried out before I had finalized my views on the definition of metaphor as presented in Chapter 1. Hence the native speakers did not pick all passages from the text which could qualify as metaphorical according to that definition, such as 'bring back that old-fashioned harmony'. I will briefly return to this point in the discussion of the results.
2. They achieved a correlation of $r = 0.66$, which brings the reliability of their combined score to a sufficient 0.80 (Spearman Brown formula).

Table IIIA: Effects of literary socialization and metaphoricity on underlining of metaphors

(i) Calculation of F1

	Source of variation	SS	d.f.	MS	F
Between subjects	LIT. SOCIALIZATION	0.06	1	0.06	4.54*
	WITHIN CELLS	0.36	26	0.01	
Within subjects	METAPHORICITY	0.07	1	0.07	2.37
	LITSOC BY MET	0.04	1	0.04	1.40
	WITHIN CELLS	0.72	26	0.03	

(ii) Calculation of F2

	Source of variation	SS	d.f.	MS	F
Between items	METAPHORICITY	8.65	1	8.65	0.23
	WITHIN CELLS	646.24	17	38.01	
Within items	LIT. SOCIALIZATION	8.25	1	8.25	2.71
	MET BY LITSOC	5.09	1	5.09	1.67
	WITHIN CELLS	51.80	17	3.05	

$^{*}p < 0.05$

3. The data reported in Table 3.3 were analysed by means of a 2 × 2 analysis of variance. Following Clark (1973), the analysis was performed twice: once treating subjects as a random factor while collapsing over materials (*F1*, Table IIIA, *i*), and once treating materials as a random factor while collapsing over subjects (*F2*, Table IIIA, *ii*). The calculation of *F1* allows generalization over subjects, but not materials, and the calculation of *F2* allows generalization over materials but not subjects. Literary socialization ('high' vs. 'low') served as a between factor in the subject analysis and as a within factor in the item analysis. Degree of metaphoricity ('high' vs. 'low') served as a within factor in the subject analysis and as a between factor in the item analysis. Note that the calculation of *F2* does not work with average proportions, but with average absolute numbers: the average number of times a particular metaphor is underlined for literariness is made up of 9 cases for the high-metaphorical group, and of ten cases for the low-metaphorical group.

4. The data reported in Table 3.5 were analysed by means of a 2 × 2 analysis of variance on the dependent variable of proportional explicit metaphor identification. The analysis was again performed twice: once treating subjects as a random factor while collapsing over materials (*F1*, Table, IIIB *i*), and once treating materials as a random factor while collapsing over subjects (*F2*, Table IIIB, *ii*). The calculation of *F1* allows generalization over subjects, but not materials, and the calculation of *F2* allows generalization over materials but not subjects. If both calculations yield significant effects, calculation of *minF'* becomes interesting,

Table IIIB: Effects of literary socialization and metaphoricity on proportionate identification

(i) Calculation of F1

	Source of variation	SS	d.f.	MS	F
Between subjects	LIT. SOCIALIZATION	0.19	1	0.19	1.69
	WITHIN CELLS	2.85	25	0.11	
Within subjects	METAPHORICITY	1.97	1	1.97	16.90**
	LITSOC BY MET	0.00	1	0.00	0.00
	WITHIN CELLS	2.91	25	0.12	

(ii) Calculation of F2

	Source of variation	SS	d.f.	MS	F
Between items	METAPHORICITY	0.83	1	0.83	5.65*
	WITHIN CELLS	2.50	17	0.15	
Within items	LIT. SOCIALIZATION	0.08	1	0.08	0.92
	MET BY LITSOC	0.01	1	0.01	0.12
	WITHIN CELLS	1.44	17	0.08	

(iii) Result calculation minF'

For metaphoricity, $minF'_{(1,10)} = 4.23$, $0.05 < p < 0.10$.

$**p < 0.01$; $*p < 0.05$

showing whether one is allowed to generalize over subjects and materials at the same time (Table IIIB *iii*). Literary socialization ('high' vs. 'low') served as a between factor in the subject analysis and as a within factor in the item analysis. Degree of metaphoricity ('high' vs. 'low') served as a within factor in the subject analysis and as a between factor in the item analysis.

5. A minor point in this connection goes back to what was said in endnote 1, where it was pointed out that some low-metaphorical passages were not identified as such by the expert native-speaker analysts on account of definitional divergencies. If more metaphors with a low degree of metaphoricity had been included in the test, then the difference between underlining high-metaphorical versus low-metaphorical items might have become more pronounced, showing an effect of degree of metaphoricity in the underlining data just as in the explication data. This problem was not redressed in retrospect, because more informative data about metaphor properties (Chapters 8 and 9) were already available by then.

6. It should be noted here that this is not the only possible use of this design. It may serve to do precisely the opposite. When two texts are selected which are highly recognizable as literary and non-literary, say a Shakespearean sonnet and a newspaper report on the Gulf War, then one would predict that it is the text factor which would override the context factor: readers would, at a certain point,

Table IIIC: Average numbers of underlined stretches (*i*) and relative number of words (*ii*) for discourse typicality in two texts, classified by context of presentation (standard deviation in brackets)

(*i*) *Average number of passages*

Context	Text	
	(Originally) literary	(Originally) journalistic
Authentic	5.53 (2.30)	4.13 (1.46)
Perverse	4.00 (2.56)	3.93 (1.94)

(*ii*) *Average proportion of words*

Context	Text	
	(Originally) literary	(Originally) journalistic
Authentic	0.38 (0.15)	0.23 (0.08)
Perverse	0.16 (0.15)	0.23 (0.13)

have to decide that the Shakespearean sonnet is not a newspaper report but a poem, and the other way around. But this is not the place to go into the methodological intricacies of such research.

7. A 2 × 2 multivariate analysis of covariance was performed on a percentage of underlined metaphors, with the within-subject factor of text (literary versus journalistic) and the between-subject factor of mode of presentation (authentic versus perverse), and four covariates of number of underlined stretches for (a) literary and (b) journalistic nature, and relative number of underlined words for (c) literary and (d) journalistic nature. Mean scores of the covariates are presented in Table IIIC (see overleaf, page 80). Covariates were entered into the analysis on a stepdown basis. The results of the analysis of covariance are shown in Table IIID. Calculation of *F2* and *minF'* were deemed unnecessary, because the design of the experiment already includes a replication with different materials: the materials of the texts offered in the perverse context.

Table IIID: Effects of text and context on metaphor underlining adjusted for covariation of four variables

(i) *Effects of text, context, and covariates*

	Source of variation	SS	d.f.	MS	F
Between subjects	REGRESSION	0.67	2	0.33	53.61**
	CONTEXT	0.08	1	0.08	12.93**
	WITHIN CELLS	0.16	26	0.01	
Within subjects	REGRESSION	0.29	2	0.14	26.74**
	TEXT	0.00	1	0.00	0.54
	CONTEXT BY TEXT	0.15	1	0.15	28.39**
	WITHIN CELLS	0.14	26	0.01	

(ii) *Parameter estimates for effects of text, context, and interaction, adjusted for covariates*

Parameter	Coeff.	Std. err.	t-Value
CONTEXT	0.06	0.02	3.60**
TEXT	0.01	0.04	0.25
CONTEXT BY TEXT	0.08	0.02	5.64**

(iii) *Regression analyses*

Entered in analysis	Covariate	B	Beta	Std. err.	t-Value
Between subjects	NO. LIT WORDS	1.10	0.91	0.13	8.79**
	NO. LIT PASS	− 0.00	− 0.03	0.01	− 0.27
Within subjects	NO. JOUR WORDS	0.90	0.87	0.17	5.47**
	NO. JOUR PASS	− 0.01	− 0.07	0.01	− 0.47

** $p < 0.01$

PART TWO

Processes

CHAPTER FOUR

Aspects of metaphor processing

This chapter is the first of a series of three which will be concerned with the details of the process of understanding metaphor. In the previous chapters I only dealt with parts of this phenomenon, concentrating on the effect of text, reader, and context variables on selected aspects of understanding metaphor. In this chapter I aim to develop an integral theoretical view of metaphor processing during reading, and to situate various aspects that are familiar by now, such as explicit metaphor identification, in this framework. The result of this endeavour will be a provisional picture of metaphor processing in and outside literary reception, which can then be further developed and investigated by means of empirical research in the next two chapters.

I will first have to lay out the groundwork for such an excercise and give a very brief sketch of general aspects of text processing (section 4.1). The process of understanding metaphor can then be discussed with reference to those general aspects of reading in section 4.2. The specific nature of the processes involved in understanding metaphor in literature will then be addressed in the third section of the chapter.

4.1 Aspects of text processing

4.1.1 Goals and contexts

It is striking that there have not been many attempts to relate metaphor processing to a general theory of reading. One reason may be the lack of a sufficiently developed encompassing framework for the study of reading. There are several well-known psychological approaches to text processing, such as Van Dijk and Kintsch (1983; Kintsch 1988) and Just and Carpenter

(1980; 1984; 1987), but important elements of the reading process are left out of consideration in these approaches. Some of these components are essential for an integral view of metaphor understanding during the reading process.

For one thing, the construction of presumed author intentions is not accorded much attention in the above-mentioned accounts. Of course, there are other psychologists who have looked at this issue, notably Flower (1987), who proposes an 'author's main points' reading strategy. Van Dijk and Kintsch (1983) themselves also envisage that readers generally construct a so-called communicative context model, in which author intentions can be accommodated, but this notion is not elaborated in any concrete theoretical or empirical detail. By comparison, the reader's construal of author intentions has been an important focus for the empirical research on literary reading carried out by Vipond and Hunt (1984; 1989). They argue that the attribution of intentions to a presumed author is crucial for a kind of reading which they believe is typical of literature, called 'point-driven reading'. In point-driven reading, readers frequently demand a justification for properties of the text; this is opposed to story-driven reading, in which readers concentrate on having experience by proxy. In story-driven reading, readers engage with the characters and events in the story, not with the way they are represented by their author, as happens in point-driven reading. The latter kind of reading is very similar to another reading strategy discriminated by Flower (1987), called 'rhetorical reading': 'In creating a rhetorical reading, the reader often constructs scenarios in which readers and writers interact, observe, and have designs on one another' (1987: 125). What is important for our purposes about point-driven reading is Vipond and Hunt's (1989) idea that attention to metaphor is an integral part of it. The evidence of the previous chapter may be taken as explicit support for this view. Therefore, despite the relative neglect of the ascription of intentions to presumed authors in prominent theories of reading, this aspect will have to be incorporated in a general reading approach to metaphor processing in literature.

Variations among social contexts of reading, such as literary versus journalistic reading, have also been largely ignored in mainstream psychology. However, as suggested in Chapter 2, reading for aesthetic pleasure, for up-to-date information on current affairs, and so on, are distinct goals for the act of reading that are at least partly the result of differences between social contexts. Van Dijk and Kintsch (1983) have abstracted from this variation. Other psychologists have usually limited themselves to an exploration of the question whether different goals for reading can be operationalized as different tasks by means of varying experimental instructions for reading (Bransford and Johnson 1972; Anderson and Pichert 1978). But if reading is intentional and goal-directed, the role of social contexts in the formation of goals for discourse processing has to be incorporated in a general discourse theory of reading. Otherwise, a gap is opened up between the overriding contextual approach to literature as a social domain of discourse and its implementation in psychological research. As noted before, the effect of social contexts on reading processes has been demonstrated in a number of empirical studies of literature (Meutsch 1987; Vipond and Hunt 1989; Zwaan 1993). Moreover, the study reported in section 3 of the previous chapter demonstrated that context is also relevant to metaphor processing. Therefore the factor of context cannot be ignored either.

4.1.2 Decoding, conceptualization, communication

Most surveys of the psychology of reading begin with an enumeration of the different kinds of processes involved. A representative example is provided by Groeben (1982: 51), who quotes an early publication by Kintsch (see Figure 4.1).

Many of the processes depicted in Figure 4.1 are reflections of distinct levels of the linguistic organization of the text. They involve the use of textual structures and related knowledge structures by the reader. For instance, the process of word identification is based on the specific domain of knowledge called the mental lexicon that the reader has to mobilize in order to accomplish the task of reading. Another example, related to a higher level of linguistic organization, is provided by sentence processing: a reader needs to know and access the grammar of the language. These parameters and processes are relatively easily identified, but their interaction during actual processing is not entirely understood (cf. Simpson 1991).

Paradoxically, it can be argued that this dependence on the structure of the text as a theoretical starting-point for modelling distinct aspects of text processing can also be a disadvantage. It is true that the various levels of textual structure have to be taken into account, because they probably relate to different kinds of psychological structures and abilities that readers will have to possess for successful text processing; but this does not mean that all of these knowledge structures and processing abilities are of the same magnitude in the total act of reading. It is specially important to keep in mind that the goals for engaging in literary (or non-literary) reading pursuits and the accompanying strategies for accomplishing them are affected by social conventions of discourse behaviour, such as Schmidt's (1980) aesthetic and polyvalence conventions for literature, and the fact of monovalence conventions for other kinds of discourse. I will now discuss some common insights about the psychology of reading in such a way that they provide room for the connection with socially affected goals and strategies of reading.

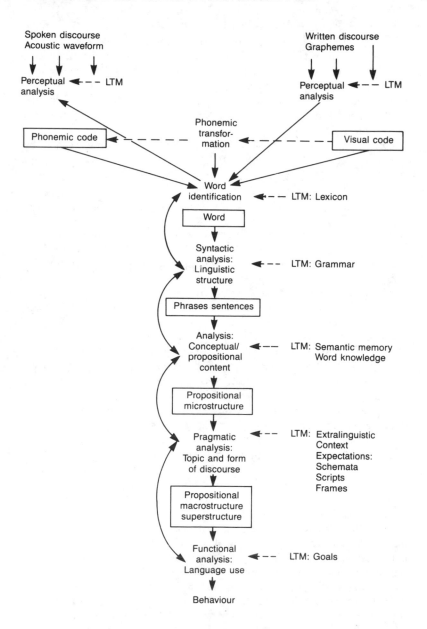

Fig. 4.1: Groeben's overview of the reading process

In the tradition of the empirical researchers of literature Schmidt (1980) and Groeben (1982; Groeben and Vorderer 1988), I assume that, at each moment in reading, there are three concretely identifiable factors involved: text, reader, and situation. We have discussed the text and the reader in some detail. Now I will clarify the notion of situation. Situations are the concrete, physical surroundings in which a reader processes a text. They include other objects, persons, and processes which are present during the act of reading. For instance, reading a cookery book typically involves another situation with a different *locale*, objects and actions than reading a novel.

Situations are crucially different from contexts in that they are independently observable. Contexts are a social categorization of the entire configuration of text, reader, and situation on the part of the reader himself or herself. Contexts are only accessible to researchers through reader knowledge and behaviour. We have to ask or determine by other means whether a reader thinks he or she is participating in literary reception. By contrast, situations can be observed independently: we do not have to ask whether a reader of literature is sitting in an easy chair.

For literary reading, situations are usually irrelevant. They predominantly offer 'noise' in the form of processes competing for the attention of the reader, such as a television programme or a record playing. Situations can hence interfere with the performance of the readers by distracting them from reading. Contexts are not irrelevant, because they define the reading process *as* literary. As a result, although I regard reading as involving an interaction between three material entities: text, reader, and situation, for literary reception, it is the context-affected interaction between text and reader which is fundamental.

At each moment of reading, readers are busy executing three analytically and empirically distinguishable types of psychological process, singly or in combination:

(1) They have to attend to the text as a semiotic, in particular *linguistic* object of signification.

(2) They have to build a *conceptual* representation of 'the world' it refers to in order to grasp it.

(3) They have to accept the text as the result of an *intentional*, meaningful action on the part of the writer.

These processes can be designated as *decoding, conceptualization*, and *communication*, respectively. Their products are partial mental models of the text. The distinction and interaction between these processes and their products is the subject of on-going research. For instance, here is Kintsch's (1988: 163) recent global division of the field of reading:

current theories use representations with several mutually constraining layers. Thus, there is typically a linguistic level of representation, conceptual levels to represent both the local and global meaning and structure of a text (e.g. the micro- and macrostructure, constituting the text base in Van Dijk and Kintsch, 1983), and a level at which the text itself has lost its individuality and its information content has become integrated into some larger structure (e.g. Van Dijk and Kintsch's situation model).

What I mean by *decoding* can be recognized in Kintsch's 'linguistic level of representation'. Van Dijk and Kintsch (1983) presupposed rather than examined decoding. The transition from decoding to conceptualization they handled as follows: 'We do not fully model the processes by which linguistic input is analysed and semantically interpreted; for the most part, we limit the model to the processing of semantic information' (Van Dijk and Kintsch 1983: 8). 'Semantic information' is the kind of decoded linguistic information that forms the basis for the conceptual propositions of the text base (Kintsch 1988: 166). In other words, when conceptualizing, readers 'process semantic information' in order to explicate linguistic meaning in terms of conceptual propositions. Just and Carpenter's model (1980; 1984; 1987) has much more to say about decoding than Van Dijk and Kintsch, but we do not have space to go into these details here.

As to *conceptualization*, in the above quotation Kintsch labels the construction of a text base as conceptual, but remains unclear about the nature of the 'larger structure' of the situation model. Van Dijk and Kintsch (1983: 11), however, suggested that the situation model 'is the cognitive representation of the events, actions, persons, and in general the situation, a text is about'. The situation model therefore contains more information than the text base:

> A situation model may incorporate previous experiences, and hence also previous textbases, regarding the same or similar situations. At the same time, the model may incorporate instantiations from more general knowledge from semantic memory about such situations. (Van Dijk and Kintsch 1983: 11–12).

As these knowledge structures are also based on conceptual representations, I regard the situation model as conceptual, too.

Finally, *communicative processing* is manifestly neglected in the passage from Kintsch (1988: 163) quoted above. Communication is the level of text processing concerned with 'functional analysis' and the application of goals in Groeber's quotation of Kintsch (Figure 4.1), but, as noted before, this aspect of Kintsch's theory has not been developed much. The difference between communication on the one hand and the territories of the linguistic and the conceptual on the other lies in the fact that communication has to do with the intentions readers impute to authors or texts, instead of the meanings or concepts and worlds that are expressed and evoked by their texts. Note that the construction of intentions does not mean that readers may not be wrong, nor that they need not think of real authors at all: what is meant here is that readers have to presuppose some sort of communicative intention on the part of the producer of the text they are actually processing.

The construction of a communicative mental representation for a text, which, with Van Dijk and Kintsch (1983), I will call a communicative context model may include several components, but three are fundamental: author, text, and reader. As Flower (1987) has shown, readers can construct intentional representations of texts by linking them to a presumed author, but they may also leave the author aside and concentrate on the main points of a text itself. Flower also indicates a third variation on this theme, when readers construct a communicative context model on the basis of the presumed effects of the text on the reader. If one of these situations obtains, I will say that the reader will have constructed a (partial) communicative context model.

The encompassing view of text processing I am proposing, which extends from decoding through conceptualization into communication, is indispensable if literary reading is the object of investigation. Readers' activation of literary reading strategies will have to be linked to the attribution (or at least presumption) of a literary intention to the author of the text, which is a matter of communicative processing. Contextual knowledge about the literary nature of the act of reading will hence, as a rule, be fed into the reading process through its effect on the construction of a communicative context model. However, it is not only the communicative level of processing that is influenced by the social context of reading: the conceptual and even the linguistic levels of processing are also involved. The effect of activating literary reading strategies on linguistic and conceptual aspects of the reading process was demonstrated empirically by Zwaan (1993). A theoretical framing of literary contextual effects on the reading process is offered by Schram and Steen (1992) and Steen and Schram (1993) in terms of subjectivity, fictionality, polyvalence, and form orientation.

The analysis of metaphor processing in reading is also bound to run into difficulty, as it has in the past, if all of the aspects of reading distinguished above are not taken into account. In the next section I will apply the above distinctions to a clarification of some central problems in metaphor research. They will prepare the ground for the last section of this chapter which will address aspects of metaphor processing in literature from the overall perspective of the reading process.

4.2 Metaphor in text processing

4.2.1 Are all metaphors understood in two stages?

The most famous controversy over metaphor processing has been concerned with the view that metaphor is understood in two stages. The standard philosophical and linguistic view is that the literal meaning of a sentence is computed first, but when that is matched with the context, it is rejected as inappropriate and replaced by a figurative meaning (Searle 1979). Seen against the distinctions introduced above, this looks like a view in which decoding is finished first, and is then followed by a round of conceptualization and communication, in which the results of decoding are evaluated as inappropriate. The basis of the two-stage model of metaphor processing lies in the componential, bottom-up, view of meaning which has informed linguistic research since the advent of Chomsky's generative grammar, and which has biased linguists to concentrating on abstract and formal sentence meanings (for a pertinent discussion, see Glucksberg 1986).[1]

In the past fifteen years, however, experimental evidence has suggested that people do not always have to compute the literal meaning of a metaphorical expression first before they arrive at a figurative meaning. For instance, provided they are given enough preceding context, people take no longer to understand some sentences in a figurative manner than if they understand them in a literal manner (Ortony et al. 1978; Inhoff et al. 1984). Thus, a sentence like (1):

(1) The hens clucked noisily

does not take longer to comprehend if it is preceded by a sufficiently long passage about a meeting of a women's club than when it is preceded by a text about a barn. This evidence goes against the two-stage model, because it would entail longer processing times for the non-literal reading condition (the women's club) than for the literal reading condition (the barn). The two-stage model in its boldest form is under heavy attack (for reviews and discussion, see Gibbs 1984 and Hoffman and Kemper 1987).

Interesting evidence that literal meaning sometimes does play a role has been provided by two studies. Gerrig and Healy (1983) manipulated sentences to the effect that one version offered a context before the metaphorical expression, but another version offered the metaphor first and then the context, as in (2):

(2) a. The night sky was filled with drops of molten silver. (context first)
    b. Drops of molten silver filled the night sky. (context second)

They argued that (2a) should facilitate metaphor comprehension because of the initial presence of the relevant context, but that (2b) would produce a garden path effect, requiring readers to construct a literal interpretation for *drops of molten silver* because of delay of the relevant context until after the metaphor, the garden path leading to longer sentence processing times. This prediction was confirmed. Thus there is some empirical support for the two-stage theory, but it is restricted to sentences which lack sufficient context. 'We propose that speakers and listeners skilfully use context with the result that the process of considering a metaphor's literal interpretation is rarely carried out in full' (Gerrig and Healy 1983: 673).

The second study demonstrating that literal meaning does play a role in the processing of metaphors is Janus and Bever (1985). They argued that the experimental paradigm based on sentence reading times used by Ortony et al. (1978) and Inhoff et al. (1984) may have been inappropriate for investigating the two-stage model:

> while differences between processing times of metaphoric sentences compared to literal ones may be attenuated at the termination of sentences because of 'contextual integrative processes' extraneous to the metaphor processed (Just and Carpenter 1980), or simply may have disappeared, this difference might have become more salient in a phrase-by-phrase measure. Therefore, Ortony et al. (1978) may have found no differences between literal and metaphor processing times, not because none exist, but because they did not observe reaction times at the point most likely to reveal these differences. (1985: 479)

In a small-scale replication, Janus and Bever corroborated the lack of any difference between literal and metaphoric processing times at the end of sentences, as reported by Ortony et al. (1978). In a second condition, however, Janus and Bever introduced a new phrase-by-phrase reading time measure, and this showed that metaphoric readings of phrases took longer than literal readings of the same phrases. For instance, they found a longer reading time for the phrase *the fabric* in (3), when it was read in a context requiring a metaphoric reading (4a) than in the one triggering a literal reading (4b):

(3) The fabric / had begun / to fray[2]

(4) a. *Metaphoric*
Lucy and Phil / needed a marriage counsellor. They had once / been very happy / but after several years / of marriage / they had become discontented / with one another. Little habits / which had at first been endearing / were now irritating / and caused many senseless and heated arguments. *The fabric* / had begun / to fray.

  b. *Literal*
The old couch / needed re-upholstering. After two generations / of wear / the edges of the couch / were tattered and soiled. Several buttons / were missing / and the material / around the seams / was beginning / to

unravel. The upholstery / had become very shabby. *The fabric* / had begun / to fray.

Janus and Bever interpreted this finding as support for 'the possibility of serial processing' (1985: 485), that is, for the two-stage theory, even for sentences in context.

What aspect of metaphor processing are we actually discussing here? Both Gerrig and Healy (1983) and Janus and Bever (1985) are concerned with a highly specific part of sentence comprehension, namely lexical access and integration. This process has been studied in great detail by Just and Carpenter, and they have come to an interesting conclusion which has a bearing on our present concerns. When accessing and integrating lexical items during reading, it is unlikely that readers build complete computations of *sentence meanings* before executing other kinds of processing, for example with reference to the situation model. In other words, readers cannot avoid starting conceptual processing while they are decoding. Just and Carpenter refer to this as 'the immediacy of processing':

> Immediacy of processing refers to the fact that a reader (or listener) tries to interpret each word of a text as he encounters it, rather than waiting to make an interpretation until a number of words have been encountered (Just and Carpenter 1980). 'Interpret' refers to several levels of cognitive processing, such as encoding the word, accessing its meaning, assigning it to its referent, and determining its semantic and syntactic status in the sentence and the discourse. . . . Interpretive processes of many levels occur as soon as they are enabled. Lower level processes are usually enabled as soon as the word is encoded. However, the point at which higher level integrative processes are enabled is unpredictable. But if the higher level processes are possible to execute immediately (i.e. without the benefit of information to follow), then they are executed immediately. (Just and Carpenter 1984: 166–8).

Decoding a sentence is not completed before conceptual and communicative processing are begun.

Immediacy of processing can explain the context effect on sentence reading times in the experiments by Ortony et al. (1978), Inhoff et al. (1984), and Gerrig and Healy (1983). When there is sufficient context, non-literal words can be integrated into the situation model just as fast as literal words, because available conceptual slots can be plausibly used for accommodation of the new words. When there is no context, the non-literal words are used in their default capacity of literal meaning to set up provisional contextual (conceptual) expectations about the situation model; these expectations have to be redressed later, when the full amount of semantic information is available (Gerrig and Healy's context second condition).

What remains to be explained is Janus and Bever's finding that metaphors do produce a delay during word-by-word intake, irrespective of the presence or absence of context. There is evidence concerning the processing of ambiguous and polysemous expressions that 'literal' word meaning is always activated momentarily before inappropriate meanings are suppressed (see Gibbs 1984: 292). Although the status of this evidence is unclear (Tabossi 1986; Glucksberg 1986; cf. Simpson 1991), the data of Janus and Bever seem to fall into this pattern. Janus and Bever's (1985: 485) conclusion that there is a 'possibility for serial processing' may therefore be limited to the process of word-by-word intake and retrieval from memory: 'literal' word-meaning is automatically accessed by the mind, but almost immediately afterwards inappropriate meanings (or aspects of meaning) are discarded, and the word is integrated into the context in a meaningful fashion (literally or metaphorically).

What is important to note here is that the original two-stage model, in which a full literal sentence meaning is computed before metaphorical interpretation is triggered, has now changed into a much weaker version, where we are dealing with 'the possibility of serial processing' of word and phrasal meaning. The initial, sentence-oriented view that metaphors are first processed semantically in their entirety and then matched against context has had to be abandoned. During language processing, semantic and pragmatic processing (decoding and conceptualization and perhaps even communication) do not take place cyclically at the end of clauses or sentences, but after almost every word. If this kind of serial processing, beginning with literal word meaning and then moving on to adapting literal word meaning to the situation model, is what the two-stage model amounts to, then metaphor is not treated specially at all, but follows the pattern of all language processing. Kintsch's (1988) new version of the earlier Van Dijk and Kintsch theory also departs from a 'dumb and seemingly wasteful process' of blind knowledge activation about meanings, which later has to be filtered with reference to context. Indeed, Van Dijk and Kintsch (1983: 313) wrote that 'What may be wrong about the classical conception may not be so much how metaphors are understood, but rather how literal expressions are understood. The knowledge check that occurs with literal expressions is not in itself sufficient, but must be followed up with further processing — very much as is the case with metaphors.'

Gibbs (1984; 1989) and Dascal (1987; 1989) have also examined research on language processing such as Just and Carpenter's and have drawn opposite conclusions as to its implications for metaphor processing. Gibbs (1984: 292) emphasizes that, even though there may be a momentary activation of literal meaning, 'The context-dependent interpretation of a sentence, however, may have little to do with its putative literal meaning'. Literal meaning and its role in processing are limited to the level of word recognition by Gibbs, his phrase 'interpretation' in this quotation probably referring to the sentence-representation as produced in the complex process of decoding and conceptualization and communication. On the other hand, Dascal (1989) uses processing research to posit a correspondence between word and sentence level processing:

> Just as a word is (tentatively) recognized and its lexical meanings are activated before its full sensory input is processed, so too a sentence is (tentatively) processed before its complete uptake. Such a processing includes, very early, contextual selection pressures. (1989: 254)

As I have suggested above, this seems to be an incorrect view of sentence processing as a whole. It is due to the traditional concentration in linguistics and semiotics on sentence meanings, and does not take the full complexity of the cognitive processing of language into account.

In sum, the issue is whether the activation of literal word meaning during word recognition is what was meant by the original proponents of the two-stage theory, when they claimed that literal meaning plays a role in processing metaphor. I believe that it is not, for in that formulation, a literal interpretation of the complete metaphoric sentence was supposed to be computed, and rejected, before a metaphoric, contextually appropriate reinterpretation of odd elements could be produced to repair the anomaly. For many metaphors, the evidence suggests that the role of literal meaning in metaphor processing is minimal, namely limited to its presence during automatic word meaning activation. Note that this probably does not hold for metaphors which are either very conventionalized (polysemy) or very difficult (problems with integration): in such cases, literal meaning is either not accessed at all (polysemy) or may be taken into account to solve the problem of lexical integration (Dascal 1987).

The answer to the question raised in the title to this section, whether metaphors are always processed in two stages, therefore has to be formulated with some care. There may be a question of serial processing, but not in the sense that full sentence meanings are computed and then rejected as inappropriate. Moreover, the roles of context and of individual differences regarding mental lexicons are essential in examining the incidence and depth of this kind of serial processing.

4.2.2 Are metaphors always recognized as such?

Another issue about metaphor which has preoccupied many linguists and psychologists is the matter of identification. It is crucial here to distinguish between metaphor identification as an activity in language analysis on the one hand, and metaphor identification in language comprehension on the other. For instance, Loewenberg (1975) and Kittay (1987) are concerned with metaphor identification as part of language analysis, in that it is their aim to define a class of expressions or utterances as metaphorical. By contrast, Grice (1975), Miller (1979), and Levinson (1983) all focus on the question whether there is a recognition stage which is presupposed for all adequate metaphor comprehension. In this section I am only dealing with the latter kind of identification. The former was dealt with in Chapter 1, section 5.

There is a clear link between metaphor identification by language users and the two-stage theory. Theorists have typically located metaphor recognition during language comprehension at the moment when listeners and readers recognize that 'literal meaning fails'. My previous discussion of the two-stage model therefore also has a bearing on the issue of metaphor identification. We can continue that line of investigation by inquiring whether the different delays in processing mentioned in section 4.2.1 all amount to metaphor identification. Let us consider a number of theoretical possibilities by means of Janus and Bever's (1985) example of *the fabric*, discussed in section 4.2.1 above. I will disregard the interpretation of the length of the delay they found in their processing data, and merely concentrate on kinds of representations that could be involved in producing some kind of delay.

Imagine a reader who has a twofold representation of the lexical item *fabric* in his mental lexicon: 'cloth' and 'structure'. When comprehending (4) above, both meanings of *the fabric* are automatically activated during the stage of lexical access. The 'cloth' meaning of *fabric* is suppressed and the 'structure' meaning is retained. This filtering process could cause a brief delay during processing. The delay can be explained by processes of decoding or conceptualization: disambiguation could be triggered by temporary semantic knowledge about the preceding text or by the more permanent conceptual knowledge regarding the current situation model. I will call this the polysemy scenario.

Does the hypothetical delay in the polysemy scenario indicate that there has been a stage of non-literal meaning recognition? The crucial point about the polysemy scenario is that there has been no moment when 'literal meaning failed', because there were two literal meanings ('cloth' and 'structure') available. Even though language processing might be slowed down for a moment because of the required filtering of unneeded information (*fabric* can mean 'cloth'), this does not mean that there have been two stages for the comprehension of *the fabric* as 'structure', one literal and one metaphoric. If there are two stages, they can be characterized, with Kintsch (1988), as construction (activation of two meanings) and integration (filtering of relevant meaning), which are general stages for all language comprehension. Note that I do not say that this is what happened in the

Janus and Bever (1985) experiment; I am only pointing out that such possibilities can be imagined, and that they are fruitful thought experiments for improving our view of varieties of metaphor identification. My conclusion about the polysemy scenario is that the presence of the linguistic metaphor in the stimuli and the delay in the reading times cannot prove beyond doubt that there has been a stage of metaphor identification. These data are compatible with a situation in which no literal meaning has failed. How to determine when we are actually dealing with such a polysemy scenario as opposed to other possible scenarios is another difficult matter, but it is irrelevant to our present purpose.

The above situation can be contrasted with a second scenario, in which a reader has only one meaning for *fabric* available to him, the 'cloth' meaning. Sentence comprehension then begins with accessing this meaning and proceeding with the attempt to integrate this meaning within the text base and situation model. In other words, the reader will construct a proposition to the effect that:

(5) EXIST (fabric)

and the situation model will be searched for a slot in which the fabric can be inserted in a meaningful fashion. At some point, the cognitive system will then have to conclude that there is no question of a literal 'cloth', and *the fabric* is reinterpreted metaphorically as 'structure'. Here literal meaning does fail, and some form of identification does take place.

Note, however, that this scenario departs from a theory of lexical access and integration in which one literal word meaning is recovered in full from the mental lexicon. Evidence that this presumption is incorrect is discussed by Tabossi (1986). Word meanings can be accessed and activated selectively depending on the preceding context, and there is no reason why *the fabric* could not be activated in such a way that the features exclusively belonging to 'the cloth' meaning are downgraded while the ones required for a 'structure' interpretation are upgraded. In such a case, *the fabric* could also be integrated into the situation model without an explicit moment when literal meaning failed. I am not taking a general position on these issues. I am only attempting to spell out the consequences of a number of scenarios for clarifying the idea of metaphor identification.

If a literal matching between word meaning and situation model fails and a metaphorical interpretation is attempted, then it is a matter of serial processing which extends into conceptualization. However, this is a kind of recognition stage (Miller 1979) which is not necessarily conscious. It belongs to automatic language processing which usually goes by unnoticed. Therefore, if we wish to include this phenomenon under metaphor identification, we will have to decide about its relation to the kind of explicit metaphor identification on the part of the language user which we encountered in Chapter 3. It seems to me that much of automatic metaphor processing only involves a kind of *implicit* metaphor identification: it hardly ever causes readers to become aware of a 'literal meaning problem' which their cognitive system has solved in a matter of microseconds. *Explicit* metaphor identification, by contrast, is a process which involves the awareness of the language user about the fact that there is a gap between literal language meaning and the way it is used in a certain context. Although there may be a relation between implicit and explicit identification, this is no foregone conclusion.

Gibbs (1989) has denied that explicit metaphor identification *follows from* some course of processing that begins with literal and ends with metaphorical meaning. He sees explicit metaphor identification as a post-hoc process, *constructing* the contrast between metaphorical and literal meaning in retrospect. The phrase 'post-hoc' refers to the moment after the completion of the process of decoding and/or conceptualization. The basis for such a construction of literal meaning is the *product* of metaphor understanding, not the *process* of metaphor understanding: it does not follow *from*, but *upon* metaphor processing at the levels of decoding and conceptualization.

This view is quite problematic for Dascal (1989). He claims that there is prominence of literal meaning after the act of metaphor understanding and takes it as a proof of its *reactivation* rather than construction. In his view, the activation of literal meaning during decoding naturally leads to a heightened awareness of the contrast between literal and metaphorical meaning after the process of understanding has been completed. This is a familiar view in formally oriented approaches to metaphor and is due to the starting-point of compositional semantics which leads to the bottom-up computation of literal sentence meaning before inserting it into context.

However, there are a number of arguments against Dascal's view. First, we have seen that the role of literal meaning during metaphor processing has to be constrained to such an extent that the notion of *reactivation* itself becomes questionable. The brief and partial activation of lexical meaning during word recognition often does not extend into having a function for the decoding of the sentence, as we have seen above. Activation of literal meaning during word recognition is of rather a different order from the subsequent use of literal word meaning during explicit metaphor identification, where literal word meaning is contrasted with the figurative usage constructed during metaphor processing. The latter might just as well be characterized as post-hoc functional activation.

Second, the arguments offered by Dascal for the 'uncontested rapidity' of what he calls recovery are at best impressionistic. I do not know of any pertinent data that bear on the hypothesis that people always and rapidly recover the contrast between literal and non-literal meaning. This also holds for the argument that 'People not only identify the content of a metaphorical remark, they identify it immediately qua metaphorical, that is, as contrasting with a possible (or impossible) literal reading' (1989: 256). There is no empirical evidence to support this view as it stands. Indeed, my data on explicit identification presented in the previous chapter suggest that there are different forms of identification, which might serve different functions and occur under different conditions. Moreover, many of the metaphors underlined as typically literary in those texts were not explicitly identified as such, even though the task should have promoted such a kind of performance if Dascal's claim is correct.

Third, Dascal does not only assume that the ambivalence between literal and metaphorical meaning is recognizable and recognized, but also that it is used for special efficacy by speakers:

> A theory that views this identification as a *post factum judgment*, and the alternative reading as a late *product* separated from the main understanding process, is both unparsimonious and unable to explain the special *communicative* efficacy of indirectness in general, which lies precisely in its recognizable ambivalence.

This claim about communicative efficacy presumes a great deal about human behaviour which is at best unproven. In my view, Dascal's starting-point in semiotics has biased his view of metaphor as a kind of non-literal meaning which is automatically identifiable, identified, and efficative. However, as we have noted before, the fact that a metaphor may be analysable as such does not necessarily correspond with its actual realization as a metaphor by language users. Whether it is explicitly identified after the act of processing, or whether it is implicitly and automatically identified as part of the process of decoding and conceptualization, are contingent possibilities which do not follow automatically from the metaphorical structure of the language that is processed by the reader. Any consequences about the efficacy of such a situation are also highly contingent. In short, metaphor identification is necessarily, but not sufficiently, dependent on the presence of metaphor in a text: the actions, attitudes, and knowledge of the reader also have to be taken into account.

4.2.3 Metaphor in decoding, conceptualization, and communication

We can now attempt to integrate these views by means of the distinct aspects of processing of decoding, conceptualization, and communication. When a reader encounters a linguistic metaphor, several things may happen:

1. A metaphor can be decoded in a process of automatic, unconscious meaning computation, and treated as a case of polysemy. Considerations of preceding text as well as situation may be instrumental in resolving the problem of polysemy. There is no stage where literal meaning fails.
2. A metaphor may also be decoded and conceptualized with reference to some part of the literal meaning of the vehicle. Depending on the nature of word access processes, this kind of metaphor processing can lead to a stage where literal meaning fails. Literal word meanings and the ideas they evoke then have to be adjusted in a metaphorical fashion. In this case, there is the possibility of a stage of implicit metaphor identification, in that literal meaning is evaluated as inappropriate with reference to context.
3. Metaphors may also be identified explicitly once the act of comprehension has finished. Then the metaphor is taken as a special verbal sign, intended to express a particular view or intention of the speaker. Explicit metaphor identification may hence be assigned to communicative processing, an aspect which has not featured very much in this section. It is not very likely that all explicit identification is a result of previous implicit identification. Indeed, some metaphors may not have required non-literal processing by the individual at all, and still be (analytically) recognized as metaphors after the act of processing.

4.3 Metaphor in literary text processing

4.3.1 Time-limited and leisurely metaphor processing

What is the relation between the aspects of metaphor processing discussed above and literary reception? In the previous chapters, I distinguished some parts of metaphor processing, and pointed out their relation to literature. In Chapter 1, I made a division between non-analogical and analogical processing. In Chapter 2, I divided analogical processing into one-way and two-way analogical processing, two-way analogical processing, in turn, leading to the discrimination between focus processing and vehicle construction. Chapter 3 gave a first view of the process called explicit metaphor identification. I also emphasized that there was a typical relation between two-way analogical processing and literature, and between explicit identification and literature. The former is based on the fact that two-way processing, also called metaphoric processing, causes polyvalent representations during reception, which is supposed to be characteristic of literary text processing. The relation between metaphor identification and literature resides in the attention to style traditionally associated with literary reception. It is now time to place these ideas in a more systematic framework by relating them to the above discussion of aspects of text processing. How can metaphor processing in literature be situated in the more encompassing view of reading as a psychological process? Can it be better understood by their insertion into such a framework? And are there other aspects of metaphor processing in literature which are suggested by a closer examination of the relation between metaphor and reading? These are the questions for the present section.

The crucial notion in this discussion will be *time*. It will have become clear from section 4.2 that time is of fundamental importance to a theory of metaphor processing. In this connection, Gibbs and Gerrig have introduced a 'total time constraint' (Gibbs and Gerrig 1989; see Gerrig 1989; Gibbs 1990):

> There is a unique total time associated with the recovery of a speaker's meaning when an utterance is performed in an appropriate context. . . . At issue is exactly what we mean when we say that a listener has understood a metaphor (see Gibbs, 1987, for a discussion). A computational theory should describe the representations of meaning that listeners arrive at when they experience metaphors in the theatre, in conversation, or other time-limited circumstances, as well as the representations that result when a particularly elegant metaphor can be enjoyed at leisure. The first type of understanding can be called *time-limited comprehension* and is governed by the total time constraint; the second type can be called *leisurely comprehension* and may well involve types of processing that are largely specialized for metaphor. (Gibbs and Gerrig 1989: 237–8)

Gerrig goes on to suggest that a theory for the understanding of metaphor in literature may have to straddle both domains, whereas most psycholinguistic theories of metaphor processing have remained limited to the first type of comprehension. Gibbs (1990) makes essentially the same point. I will now develop this approach in more detail with reference to the various distinguishable aspects of metaphor processing.

Gibbs has postulated a simple temporal series of metaphor processing aspects:

> The continuum of temporal moments is best reflected in different theorists' attempt [sic] to explain either metaphor comprehension, recognition, interpretation, or appreciation. Comprehension refers to the immediate moment-by-moment *process* of creating meaning for utterances. Recognition refers to the *products* of comprehension as types (i.e., determining whether the meaning of an utterance is literal, metaphorical, metonymic, and so on). Interpretation refers to the *products* of comprehension as tokens (i.e. determining the specific content of

the meaning type). Appreciation refers to some aesthetic judgment given to a *product* either as a type or a token. (Gibbs 1990: 75–6)

The general approach outlined here is fully compatible with my own (Steen 1989; 1991a). We now need to refine these ideas from the perspective of the general aspects of reading.

I first wish to address the question of how Gibbs's 'comprehension' relates to text processing. I presume that it is not limited to 'the process of creating meaning' in the narrow sense of decoding, as I have used it with reference to Van Dijk and Kintsch and Just and Carpenter. Given the discussion of the total time constraint by Gibbs and Gerrig (1989), the 'click of comprehension' probably only occurs after the reader's integration of the metaphor in the situation model. And if metaphors are used ironically, then their relation to the presumed purposes of the author will also have to be established, a process which takes place by building a link with the communicative context model. In other words, building linguistic, conceptual, and communicative representations may all be involved in the first 'moment' of metaphor processing, or Gibbs's comprehension. This is also true for the 'time-limited comprehension' Gerrig referred to above.

Thus the 'click of comprehension' involves a number of processing aspects that cannot simply be covered by appealing to the vague notion of 'meaning'. Meaning in the linguistic sense is crucially different from meaning in the referential and intentional senses. Non-literal processing which remains limited to decoding produces a different kind of meaning from non-literal processing which extends into conceptualization and communication. Moreover, as we have seen, these meanings may also be more or less explicitly identified as metaphorical. So, the notion of meaning will have to be used carefully.

Situating metaphor comprehension in a general model of reading can also account for the availability of the information required for the additional processes of explicit identification, interpretation, and appreciation. The possibility of seeing metaphor as an expression type, of elaborating its content, and of estimating its value is foreseen, as it were, by the initial, albeit partial, representation of metaphors (and indeed all language) within situation models and context models during time-limited comprehension.

The combination of the two kinds of comprehension called 'time-limited' and 'leisurely' which Gerrig (1989) deems necessary for the study of understanding metaphor in literature can thus be placed on one basis. There is a continuum between the two kinds of activities, which makes reference to aspects of comprehension which are not limited to literary understanding alone. This enhances the general plausibility of the approach.

4.3.2 Identification, understanding, and appreciation

Explicit metaphor identification or recognition is the classification of an expression as a particular kind of message on formal grounds. This may take place as a result of the striking nature of the expression in question, for instance when it is highly original, difficult, or moving. But it may also take place as a consequence of a particular interest in the text as linguistic form on the part of the reader, an interest which consequently increases the chance of metaphors being noted as one instance of special forms. Whichever of these two factors is operative, what we are dealing with here is the reader's reflection upon the linguistic expression as a type of message used by the author to convey a particular message to the reader. As suggested in section 4.2.2, this information can be represented in that part of communicative context model which pertains to the text as a message from the author to the reader.

Of course I do not believe that all metaphors are explicitly represented as such. My point is that when the process of explicit identification takes place, it is facilitated by the availability of at least partial models of author and text, which can be updated and elaborated by the reader's recognition that the author has used a 'special' kind of expression to make clear what he or she wants to say. This makes the explicit identification of metaphor intelligible as one viable option to readers who are involved in the 'leisurely comprehension' (Gerrig 1989: 238) of a text.

However, 'recognition' is not necessarily restricted to the product of the total comprehension process, as is suggested by Gibbs. In particular, metaphors requiring on-line analogical processing must involve some kind of 'recognition' of a non-literal analogical comparison which has to be processed. As a result, an implicit form of recognition can also take place once the grammatical meaning of the metaphorical expression has been constructed; it is the basis for a conceptual analogy which has to be understood as a kind of puzzle or problem. As argued in the previous section, this is a form of *implicit metaphor identification*, which is based on the detection of the non-literal meaning of a decoded expression. Like Gibbs's form of recognition, it also involves the processing of a product of comprehension, but not of the total time-limited comprehension process, as Gibbs argues. Instead it is dependent on one part of decoding, namely word access; but it does take place within the boundaries of the time-limited form of comprehension, and is automatic and unconscious. Therefore it is opposed to *explicit metaphor identification*, which is a process taking place with reference to a product of the total form of time-limited comprehension. That this is the kind of 'recognition' Gibbs has in mind can be seen from (Gibbs 1990: 68):

This position denies any fundamental difference in the psychological mechanisms used in understanding literal and figurative speech at least insofar as very *early* cognitive processes are concerned. Individuals may at a later point reflect on the *products* of these interpretations and make different judgments about these meanings – i.e., whether what has been understood is a literal or a metaphorical meaning. But such judgments reflect later stages in the time-course of interpretation and do not accurately reflect the earliest moments of comprehension.

Proceeding to what Gibbs calls *metaphor interpretation*, I believe that it is plausible to assume that *focus processing* is part of the initial comprehension process, precisely because it serves to integrate the current sentence into the overall concerns of text processing. Hence it would have to provide the basis for the further interpretation process. By contrast, *vehicle construction* would probably be an additional process, because it uses the analogy at first constructed for focus processing for a second time, for instance in order to develop the imagistic part of the metaphor. Vehicle construction could be part of interpretation, because it departs from information made available by the initial comprehension process based on focus processing.

But this is not the whole story. Focus processing itself may also go beyond the 'click of comprehension', if a more precise understanding of what the metaphor is about is needed. Literary critics are often concerned with this elaborate kind of understanding, and it may be just as typical of literary reading as vehicle construction is. Moreover, as pointed out in Chapter 2 (section 2.3), literary metaphors can have a typically complex nature, simply forcing readers to spend more time on their focus processing. Even though it is true that theatre-goers also have to understand an expression like 'Juliet is the sun' in the few seconds which the actor allows them for processing (Gerrig 1989), literary reading offers a different, more special experience, because it is self-paced. Evidence of longer processing times of texts when they were offered as literary as opposed to non-literary is presented in Zwaan (1993). One factor in such longer reading times might be the drawn-out nature of the focus processing of metaphors.

Note, however, that it is not clear at all that the only way to construct the vehicle for a metaphor is on the basis of *prior* focus processing. Activation of the vehicle domain may take place in parallel with the processing of the focus of the metaphor. Such questions are simply too difficult and too vague to handle at the present stage of knowledge. As a provisional formulation, I suggest that focus processing is a relatively initial, automatic and unconscious affair, which belongs to comprehension; while vehicle construction is an additional process (comparable in that respect to identification), which is part of interpretation. But as focus construction may itself extend into elaborate processing when the reader has the freedom to spend extra time on unusually interesting or difficult metaphors, it may also be part of interpretation.

Metaphor interpretation in literature may take yet another form. The function of a metaphor may be expanded beyond its original sentential context in order to achieve additional coherence with other aspects of the text as a whole, such as the portrayal of character or the evocation of mood. For instance, Freeman (1993) discusses the metaphors of *King Lear* in terms of a BALANCE and a LINK schema, governing the play's thematic concerns with financial accounting and filial bonds. And Black (1993) takes the metaphors of William Golding's *The Inheritors* as indicators of the way characters experience the world.

I have called the phenomenon whereby metaphors are given an additional (textual) function *metaphor functionalization* (Steen 1989). In particular, when metaphors are linked to suprasentential features like character or mood, they are given the extra function of literary (as opposed to linguistic) signification. Holyoak (1982) has also discussed this issue in terms of analogizing between linguistic and literary signs. It can now be pointed out that this process of functionalization is only possible when readers have a mental representation of the communicative context, for it appeals to the special nature of the text as literary, or the literary designs of the author with the text upon the reader (see the foregoing discussion of Flower 1987).

Metaphor functionalization is highly characteristic of literary interpretation, and it contributes to another layer of coherence regarding the total representation of the text. I do not know of any other kind of reading, for example journalistic or scientific reading, which would want to do the same. Functionalization is a form of additional processing in the same manner as explicit identification, and the question arises as to when these additional processes occur in the on-going activity of reception. The difference between identification and functionalization, however, should also be evident: functionalization is another form of meaning attribution to the text, whereas identification is not. From that angle, identification is a yes or no affair, whereas functionalization may be a laborious process, as a reader tries out various possibilities for connecting the metaphor as a literary sign to the literary text as a whole. These are relatively untrodden ways in metaphor processing research, which we will follow further in subsequent chapters.

As to *metaphor appreciation*, Gibbs (1990) and Gerrig (1989) argue that this process is more or less divorced from comprehension. Gibbs (1990: 69) writes that 'judgments of metaphor aptness entails [*sic*] a different kind of psychological act, one which demands more conscious reflection'. Evidence for this view was put forward by Gerrig and Healy (1983). They showed that good and bad versions of the same metaphor did not influence metaphor comprehension times, but that they did affect quality ratings. However, the question then arises as to how appreciation *is* related to comprehension.

Gerrig (1989: 240) has expressed what I feel about this issue: 'The exigencies of time-limited processing — in conversation or in the theater — may preclude the possibility of a strong relationship between comprehension and appreciation.' The tell-tale term is 'strong': it suggests that there may be a relationship, but that it is weak during ordinary comprehension, and has little effect on the subsequent elaboration of a value judgment during appreciation. I believe that it is part and parcel of metaphor processing (as it is of any other kind of language processing) to exhibit an affective response to the metaphor in question. This may be limited to having a vague feeling of a positive or negative attitude. However, it may also turn out to be the starting-point for a fully-fledged process of appreciation, a process which may be critical of the original response, or which may elaborate it to such an extent that the original response disappears from the final appreciation. Thus, although there need not be a particularly *strong* relation between comprehension and appreciation, there may be a *definite link* through the aspect of response. Initial affective response may hence be seen as a form of *implicit appreciation*. This provides the interested reader with a natural bridgehead for developing a more *explicitly* critical or appreciative mode of processing after the click of comprehension, a process which characterizes literary reception.

4.3.3 Conclusion

The attractiveness of Gibbs's (1990) proposition of a time series of metaphor processing aspects lies in the fact that it can serve to discriminate between essential and additional processes for metaphor understanding. We have seen that explicit identification, vehicle construction, functionalization, and explicit appreciation are probably all additional. It is not accidental that these operations also play a prominent role in literary criticism. They can be drawn out and monitored, and their product can be evaluated. They can be guided by the conventions for literary discourse: if readers adopt a literary reading attitude, they can focus on particular aspects of additional metaphor processing. It can add meaning (polyvalence) in the cases of vehicle construction and functionalization, or it can extend meaning into areas that are not needed for intersubjectively satisfactory communication (subjectivity) in the cases of vehicle construction and appreciation. Moreover, additional processing can boost the attention to literature as linguistic form and style (identification and functionalization). It might be supposed, then, that all of these processes are more frequent in literary as opposed to non-literary reading. At least one qualification should be added here: focus processing may also be frequent in literary reception, because of the allegedly complex nature of literary metaphors. These ideas will be explored in the following chapter.

Notes

1. Note that there is not one name for the issue: Janus and Bever (1985) refer to it as the 'three-stage model', while Hoffman and Kemper (1987) speak of the 'two-process theory'.
2. The slashes indicate the division of the stimulus materials into phrases as projected for reading time measurement onto the computer screen.

CHAPTER FIVE

Metaphor processing in thinking out loud

One excellent means to collect data on metaphor processing is the think aloud task: readers can be given texts for processing and asked to verbalize their thoughts out loud as they read. The verbal protocols thus obtained provide invaluable information about their mental activities during the reading process. It is remarkable that thinking out loud has not been used for the study of understanding metaphor in literature, for it has become a popular tool in the empirical study of literature and in problem solving. Many aspects of text processing can be seen as demanding some form of problem solving, and this certainly holds for understanding metaphor in literature, with its associated additional processes identification, vehicle construction, functionalization, and appreciation, and thinking out loud thus provides us with a good means to explore metaphor processing during the process of literary reception.

This chapter addresses two questions. First, can thinking out loud show that the processes described in the previous chapter are part of literary reading? Second, are there any other processes which will have to be incorporated into the general view of metaphor processing? Before we delve into these questions, however, I will first introduce the thinking out loud method in more detail.

5.1 Thinking out loud in the empirical study of literature

The thinking out loud method has enjoyed increasing popularity in recent years among empirical researchers of literature. Meutsch and Schmidt (1985) were among the first literary scholars to apply it in an empirical study of literary reading. At the First International Conference for the Empirical Study of Literature in 1987, there were quite a few more participants who reported research based on thinking out loud studies (de Beaugrande 1989). At the next two conferences, almost half of the researchers in the sections on reading processes employed think aloud tasks (see Ibsch et al. 1991; Kreuz and MacNealy 1993).

Olson et al. (1984: 255) point out that 'the TOL [thinking out loud] task is best used to study higher level processes in reading: the inferences, predictions, schema elaborations, and other complex cognitions that occur as part of skilled reading'. Thus described, thinking out loud is a methodological godsend to literary scholars inspired by reception theory and reader response criticism for they focus on precisely those aspects of cognition. Moreover, thinking out loud promises access to these aspects of the literary reading process through the basic and best-known unit of discourse, the sentence:

> The major focus of the TOL data will be on the processes responsible for integrating the semantic representation of an individual sentence into the various cognitive structures being constructed during comprehension. These data should reveal the kinds of strategies used by readers in accomplishing these tasks, the kinds of knowledge sources employed, and the kinds of representations constructed. (Olson et al. 1984: 257)

This makes the method highly suitable to the study of metaphor in literature, because explicit identification, vehicle processing, functionalization, and appreciation can all be approached as forms of 'integrating the semantic representation of an individual sentence into the various cognitive structures being constructed during comprehension'.

Initial enthusiasm for thinking out loud, however, may be dampened by other considerations. Verbal data in the form of introspective and retrospective reports constitute a controversial case as a form of scientifically acceptable evidence about psychological processes, as is noted in the introduction to a recent special issue of the journal *Text* devoted to 'verbal reports as data in text comprehension research' (László et al. 1988; compare Ericsson and Oliver 1988). Moreover, thinking out loud data may be rich, but they are not the most attractive data to work with from the point of view of reliable analysis. They are out of the control of the researcher, as it is the test subject who determines the length, aptness, clarity, and complexity of the goods delivered (Steen 1991b). For this reason de Beaugrande (1989: 22) says that 'new techniques may be called for, especially when research generates messy discursive data, such as when test subjects spontaneously report their responses to a literary discourse'. Another option, which I will follow here, is to use thinking out loud for a limited purpose of investigation; I will restrict my analysis of thinking out loud data only to those passages that are related to metaphor processing.

The turning-point for the reputation of thinking out loud data has been Ericsson and Simon (1984). The method has since been utilized as an efficient tool in a number of disciplines. The contribution by Ericsson (1988) to the aforementioned special issue of *Text* reviews the results to date in the field of text processing. The journal also presents a number of new studies which demonstrate that thinking out loud data are rich materials for text processing research which can be exploited in fruitful and innovative ways.

The fundamental idea of thinking out loud is that the information heeded by a subject carrying out a task may be verbalized concurrently or retrospectively and that such a report provides evidence of the information processing that is going on. The crucial issue is, of course, the relation between heeded and verbalized information: a one-to-one relationship between the two cannot be presumed on *a priori* grounds. Is the verbalized information complete, or even representative of the heeded information? Does the verbalization task disturb or influence the information processing? Ericsson and Simon (1984) discuss these problems at length, and evidence is put forward which suggests that the most urgent difficulties can be overcome by sensible research strategies. Ericsson and Oliver summarize the research as follows:

> Ericsson & Simon (1984) found that the verbal report instructions that change performance do not merely require that subjects verbalize their thoughts, but also require that subjects give reasons or motives for their thoughts and actions. It is not surprising that there are changes in thought processes as well as in performance when subjects must think of rationalizations, which they would not normally do when performing the task silently. (Ericsson and Oliver 1988: 405)

Similar methodological work was carried out by Deffner (1984). He also contributed a study to *Text* (Deffner 1988), extending his concerns with thinking out loud to text processing. Deffner (1988) agrees with Ericsson and Simon (1984) in concluding that thinking out loud does not interfere with the quality of task-relevant processes, although it may slow them down.

5.1.1 Task analysis of reading

Unwarranted hopes about the potential of thinking out loud may be allayed by realizing that it can tap only certain levels of mental activity, and that success or failure depends upon well-founded theoretical expectations. Ericsson and Oliver (1988) emphasize the use of a task analysis for the advance specification of those features of mental activity that are deemed to be of interest. This is where the analysis of reading presented in Chapter 4, and its relation to metaphor processing, will prove useful.

First, we should not expect to obtain insight into the ordinary grammatical rules applied during text processing. The reason for this is that the application of these rules is much too fast and automated to be heeded by the reader while reading a text. Even ordinary inferences and schema elaborations need not become explicit when a text is easy and well-written (Ericsson 1988). Many linguistic and conceptual representations are built without coming to the surface of the reader's attention. It might very well be that, as a rule, the processes falling within Gibbs and Gerrig's (1989) total time constraint for metaphor processing are inaccessible to the thinking out loud method of data collection.

However, such processes may impinge on the reader's consciousness as soon as 'semantic problems' need to be solved in order to achieve coherence. If the goal of reading is to construct a coherent representation of the text, any difficulties arising with the integration of new semantic material into the current text, situation, and context models may cause the reader to consider explicitly the structure of both the new information and the current state of his or her knowledge. In the context of metaphor, this can produce conscious attention to focus and vehicle processing. It may also induce reference to the presumed intentions of the author in conveying the information in a particular way. Again, in the context of metaphor, this can elicit explicit metaphor identification and appreciation. This is where it becomes clear that there is a grey area between comprehension and additional processing, as suggested at the end of the previous chapter. So, a task analysis has to refer to both textual and reader aspects in determining what counts as a 'semantic problem'. Metaphor is an obvious candidate for causing such reading difficulties, but it has not been singled out for special attention in thinking out loud research until now. There is sufficient evidence that this multi-dimensionality of reading is manifested in thinking out loud data triggered by text processing (Kintgen 1983; Meutsch and Schmidt 1985; Waern 1988; Andringa 1990; Graves and Frederiksen 1991).

5.1.2 Validity

One important problem concerning the application of the think aloud task is its validity in the context of literary reception. Larsen and Seilman (1988) doubt whether the concurrent thinking out loud procedure can be used for the study of literary reading because of its interruptive and disturbing character, especially when texts are presented sentence-by-sentence. They attack the familiar analogy between reading and problem solving as misleading, and claim that literary reading is 'automatic', subconscious, 'effortless', not 'reflective', 'a well-practiced skill', and without 'an extrinsic purpose'. 'One may come across a moot point that makes comprehension a problem, of course, but that is precisely an instance where the mode of reading appears to change' (1988: 415). All the same, I hope to show that these considerations need not dissuade us from the further exploration of metaphor processing through thinking out loud during literary reading.

First, it is a consequence of these remarks that thinking out loud is eminently suitable for tracking down such processing problems as may exist. It is an empirical question of some importance whether metaphor, or a specific class of metaphors, belongs to this kind of problems. Thinking out loud may clarify the strategies and knowledge sources employed by readers to arrive at a solution, and it may also shed some light upon the latter's representation.

Second, it is not at all clear that all or even most literary texts lend themselves to the kind of reading suggested by Larsen and Seilman (1988). Literary texts are famous for their complexity, richness, and sometimes difficulty. One could draw up a whole list of potential problems for examination. Metaphor certainly would have to feature on such a list.

Third, the applicability of thinking out loud also depends on the kind of reading one wishes to study. Someone reading for pleasure may be content with a superficial understanding of the text, skimming over many details. But careful reception may indeed be more 'similar to close study rather than to effortless enjoyment', to use a phrase from Larsen and Seilman (1988: 414). There is no principled reason to privilege either of these kinds of reading as the basic object of study, and it is not clear beforehand how different think aloud procedures relate to different kinds of reading anyway. True, it should also be stressed that the implications of research into these types of reading may differ widely. In particular, the former may be representative of literary reading as it occurs outside academia, whereas the latter may be representative of what may be called canonical or 'typical' literary reading, if such a thing exists. Whatever the case may be, the need for empirical study in this area is evident.

5.1.3 Optimal data

A demonstration of the suitability of thinking out loud as a method for the study of this kind of reading is provided by the only book-length study of literary reading making use of it, Kintgen (1983). Kintgen's express concern is with so-called pre-aesthetic reading, or 'the kind of reading academics undertake to discover information about a poem in preparation for presenting their knowledge to other academics' (1983: ix). Elsewhere Kintgen puts it like this: '. . . we are talking about a statistically abnormal kind of reading, the preaesthetic or professional reading one undertakes to prepare for formal discussion of a poem' (1983: 167). Granted the limited scope of pre-aesthetic reading, however, Kintgen justly makes a point of contrasting this object of research with the concerns of Culler (1981b) and Fish (1980): 'they tend not to deal with the process of reading, preferring instead to treat the complex ways in which knowledge resulting from that process is made public' (Kintgen 1983: x).

I wish to emphasize at this point that this 'statistically abnormal' kind of reading is of crucial importance in the empirical study of literature. It provides the bridge between the study of what Schmidt (1980) would call 'reception' and 'post-processing': on the one hand, it is the most complex and richest kind of reading that may still be considered and studied as one kind of reading process, and on the other hand, it is presupposed by all further critical activity normally called 'interpretation'. It thus provides an upper limit to what may be studied as 'reading', and a lower limit to what may be studied as 'interpretation'. I wish to refer to these data as 'optimal data', which may be used to explore 'less optimal (and less abnormal) kinds of reading' as subsets.

There is one restriction that should be put on this claim. Kintgen (1983) allowed his readers to *study* rather than read their texts – to read and reread parts in different sessions. This is interpretation rather than reception. If this procedure is replaced by one in which literary reading is requested of experts in one continuous session, then pre-aesthetic reading may be taken as canonical literary reading in the sense of reception as opposed to post-processing. It is the best possible kind of reading of a particular text by a particular reader in one spontaneous reception process. In such a set-up, thinking out loud provides the researcher with optimal data functioning as an upper limit to what is possible in ordinary literary reception. This may be applied to the specific aspects of metaphor processing put forward in Chapter 4 in order to refine our view of understanding metaphor in literature.

Kintgen's work was exploratory: he was one of the first literary researchers to study literary reading as a form of problem solving, and to apply the views of Ericsson and Simon. He does not aim for generalization on account of his small sample of readers (six) and texts (three). In his analysis, the categories are determined inductively, and a hedge is included in this connection which betrays a certain naïvety regarding empirical research: 'There is an obvious danger of circularity here, since one tends to find what he expects to find' (1983: *x*). This remark partly reveals a lack of theoretical foundation to the analyses. It also manifests a lack of experience concerning ways of validating one's analysis: there is an almost frivolous, certainly too liberal, generosity when it is asserted that 'since the protocols are included in the Appendix, the reader can test his own favorite schema on them' (1983: *x*). Reports of inter-coder reliability would have been the proper means to convince the reader of the strength of the analyses.

Despite these weak points, Kintgen has some interesting conclusions to offer on the validity of thinking out loud as a method for data collection concerning literary reading. Although it is granted that thinking out loud may increase consciousness during reading to some extent, Kintgen argues that this is not a hindrance but a benefit: in this way, one receives optimal and explicit data. The objection that thinking out loud may affect the quality of the reading process in that it may boost its level of analyticity is countered by a number of considerations. First, pre-aesthetic reading is of itself quite analytical, so that the extent of consciousness can only be a matter of degree. Second, none of Kintgen's readers was at a loss or surprised when they had to think aloud. This suggests that their verbalized behaviour was rooted in a fairly routine activity. Moreover, Kintgen found that particular strategies of reading such as biography-oriented or intertextuality-oriented operations were used often and consistently by all of the readers: it is implausible to assume that these were invented for the task. It is more likely that they reflect ordinary reading behaviour. In sum,

> The aim of protocol analysis is precisely to reveal these natural but unnoticed activities, to provide a record of the temporal flow of mental activity that would be impossible for the reader to construct for himself because the self-monitoring required would interfere drastically with that normal mental activity. Verbalization also interferes, but since so much of understanding a poem, especially for these readers, involves verbal manipulation, that interference is not likely to be great. (Kintgen 1983: 167)

It could be claimed that this also goes for pre-aesthetic reading in the more restricted form of one continuous session proposed above. Moreover, the analytical nature of pre-aesthetic reading may be decreased by the very limitation of only one session, and by using a sentence-by-sentence reading task, which may be expected to arouse curiosity in the further development of the text and maintain sufficient reading speed.

Kintgen argues that pre-aesthetic reading is characterized by a number of traits that can be called 'form-orientation', 'polyvalence', and 'subjectiv-

113

ity'. Subjectivity is explained in terms of idiosyncrasy as opposed to public acceptability of the response, and polyvalence refers to both alternative meanings at the same level and continued processing beyond the literal level. These features are seen as belonging to what Kintgen refers to as 'a script, a predetermined, stereotyped collection of actions' (1983: 168). They are encouraging for the further development of thinking out loud research regarding less 'abnormal' reading processes such as spontaneous and consecutive reception processes.

5.1.4 Outlook

Given its special status in linguistics, psychology, and literary theory, there is no reason to examine extensively why metaphor may constitute a semantic difficulty for text processing. Thinking out loud data ought to be a good means for revealing whether this is the case. They will be collected and analysed in order to investigate whether the proposals made in the previous chapter can be given an empirical foundation. In particular, do the verbal protocols exhibit focus processing and vehicle construction, explicit identification and functionalization, and explicit appreciation? Do the postulated underlying analogies also occur in the data? And are there any other processes which are triggered by the processing of metaphor as a semantic problem?

That some metaphors may be more problematic – or typically 'metaphorical' – in this regard than others is beyond doubt. This will be taken into account in Chapter 8, by collecting data on metaphor properties, and feeding them into an analysis of thinking out loud data during literary reading in Chapter 9. The other factor possibly influencing metaphor as a semantic problem is that of differences between readers regarding their degree of literary socialization. It is well known that experts in various fields behave differently from novices, and this has also been established for thinking out loud (Ericsson 1988). For literature, the case has been summarized by Vipond and Hunt (1989: 169): 'In brief, skilled readers talked more, talked about different things, and talked about them differently.' Meutsch (1989: 68) found that 'The realization of polyvalent reading experience is strictly bound to literary skills.' He calls this 'the dominance of the subject factor.' Therefore, if metaphor is understood in a special way in literary reading, then the best place to look for such a special treatment is in the reading of experts. Whether metaphor constitutes a semantic problem for other readers in the same way as it does for experts is another important question for research, and will be addressed in Chapters 6 and 9.

5.2 Pilot studies in thinking out loud

5.2.1 Introduction

In order to make optimal use of the thinking out loud method, a number of pilot studies were performed with two main aims. First, the appropriate instructions, procedure, texts, and subjects were determined for the experimental study to be presented in Chapter 6. Next, these data were used for the development of a method of data analysis regarding metaphor processing. How can criteria be formulated for encoding the relevant categories in the verbalizations? These are the concerns of the rest of this chapter.

First, there are such general issues as the selection of the experimental texts, the phrasing of the think aloud instruction, the necessity of a warming-up stage, the suitability of the sentence-by-sentence procedure, and the selection of the subjects. These are aspects of data collection rather than analysis. They will be examined in some detail in order to give a clear view of the decisions taken in setting up the think aloud study reported in the next chapter.

The selection of texts is determined by whether they contain metaphors to begin with. However, for the purposes of this chapter, it is also important to have various genres in order to have available a sufficient range of potentially different verbal reactions. Both literary and non-literary texts, as well as poetry and prose must be included. This also implies that some texts, poems, can be used in their entirety, while other texts have to be presented as fragments. Connected to this is the point that the length of a text is also a relevant aspect, for it is not precisely known how fast people read when they think aloud, nor how long they can keep this up without becoming tired. Finally, texts should not be too easy, because this may lead to underverbalization, but, on the other hand, they should also be immediately intelligible in order to prevent an overrepresentation of metacognitive processes needed to monitor problem solving.

Next there is the phrasing of the instructions for the think-aloud task. Ericsson and Simon (1984: 378) provide the following example of a 'general instruction':

> In this experiment we are interested in what you think about when you find answers to some questions that I am going to ask you to answer. In order to do this I am going to ask you to THINK ALOUD as you work on the problem given. What I mean by think aloud is that I want you to tell me EVERYTHING you are thinking from the time you first see the question until you give an answer. I would like you to talk out loud CONSTANTLY from the time I present each problem until you have given your final answer to the question. I don't want you to plan out what you say or try to explain to me what you are

saying. Just act as if you are alone in the room speaking to yourself. It is most important that you keep talking. If you are silent for any long period of time I will ask you to talk. Do you understand what I want you to do?

Is this enough information to make a reader think out loud about a literary text? Or does the change from the task of problem solving to the task of text processing require additional instructions? At the time of the pilot studies, there were no reports on this issue available.

To obtain optimal results, it is also desirable, in problem solving, that a subject should go through some 'practice problems'. There were no relevant publications on this issue in connection with reading. Should there be a practice text, and if so, how long should it be? Should it come from the same text or not? In the case of the presentation of an entire text, such as a poem, this is impossible: what other practice text is to be used? And is a short practice text sufficient to induce an appropriately 'literary' or even 'poetic' attitude of reading? The latter question is probably easier to pose than to answer, but it cannot remain unmentioned.

The format of the sentence-by-sentence presentation of the text seemed somewhat artificial. It could result in a series of sentence processing tasks rather than in text processing, let alone typically literary reading. However, the goal of collecting data on the level of sentence processing with an eye to processing metaphor and general literary reading processes was not to be abandoned, either. After all, this is the level of information processing at which metaphors get integrated into the larger mental structures which the reader has constructed for the text. Therefore, a way had to be found to reduce to a minimum the potential interference with the literary reading process from the sentence-by-sentence procedure.

Finally, another important aspect of the general issues pertaining to the method of thinking out loud about literary texts bears on its relation to the various kinds of test subjects. It is self-evident that one requires subjects with a high degree of literary socialization, as they will provide us with the desired optimal data. Arts students and lecturers are an obvious choice. Are there special problems with thinking out loud for readers with such a comparatively high degree of literary socialization? Are they over-articulate, or, on the contrary, do they experience the intricacies of a literary text to such an extent that they may become hampered in their expression? Again, no reports on this matter were available.

There have been many approaches to the analysis of verbal data; for a discussion of most of the crucial issues, see Schnotz et al. (1981); Brunner (1982); Fischer (1982); Huber and Mandl (1982); Ballstaedt and Mandl (1984); Ericsson and Simon (1984). In general, the selection of the method of segmentation and analysis depends upon the ultimate goal of the investigation. In the present case, the aim of segmentation is fairly clear:

units of segmentation have to allow for an analysis of metaphor processes in terms of focus processing and vehicle construction, identification and functionalization, and appreciation. Only those parts of the verbalizations that can be related with sufficient certainty to a particular metaphor are to be included in the data-pool for analysis. It is only these parts that have to be analysed in terms of distinct processes. The pilot studies will have to show how this kind of analysis can be developed in concrete terms.

5.2.2 Method

MATERIALS

Following a suggestion by Olson et al. (1984: 283), I set out with eight rather different texts. I will not go into any detail about the (Dutch) texts and their characteristics, because we are merely concerned with general methodological issues here. Suffice it to say that the texts were natural, that is not constructed by myself, and dealt with important themes and events. There were two poetic texts, one piece of non-literary prose, and five pieces of literary prose. The non-poetic texts had been edited to manipulate their length and appearance of unity, as all of these experimental texts were fragments. The length of the texts ranged from approximately 250 to 400 words. Suitable very short stories with a sufficient number of metaphors had not been found in the first search for materials.[1]

SUBJECTS

Seven students from the Department of General Literary Studies and nine lecturers from the Faculty of Arts of the Free University Amsterdam acted as expert readers. The students had completed approximately three years of study in a modern language and literature course, and were on the point of graduating. They were naïve about the purpose of the experiment regarding metaphor, and knew they were being used as guinea-pigs for methodological purposes. The lecturers were all experts on modern literature (English and Dutch) and (after reading) asserted that they had not been aware during thinking out loud of any special concern with metaphor on my part.

PROCEDURE

Thinking out loud data for these texts were collected in three runs between December 1987 and April 1989. Each subject was tested individually and offered one of the experimental texts. First, an instruction sheet was presented to the subject which he or she had to read. The instruction emphasized that subjects should read the text as if they were alone. It was also stressed that no attempt should be made to provide an interpretation or explanation of the text. This was to ensure that readers stayed as closely as possible to reception rather than post-processing. However, the subjects were also told to verbalize everything that crossed their minds. The tension between restraining interpretative tendencies on the one hand and encouraging exhaustive verbalization on the other was retained to see how subjects dealt with this potential conflict. An opportunity was then given to ask questions about the instructions. After the first subject had taken the test, instructions were added that every new sentence was to be read out loud and tackled in smaller chunks if necessary. This was to avoid long periods of silence and embarrassing complications during verbalization.

A warming-up period immediately preceded the actual test for each subject. For each type of text, a fragment was included from the same text or, if the text was presented in its entirety, from the same genre. This was done in order to make the subject adopt an appropriate attitude of reading – although no instructions to this effect were added. The tape-recorder was tested and switched on at this point to make subjects familiar with the situation. If there were any problems after the warming-up stage, these were discussed. If there were not, the subject was encouraged to continue reading.

Presentation of the texts was done on paper in a sentence-by-sentence fashion. Every new sentence was presented on a new page, but it was underlined and added to the text previously read by the subject. This technique allows subjects to take new sentences in as part of an existing context, and was intended to solve the problems involved in the serial presentation of sentences. At the same time it allows the analyst a view of what happens during sentence-processing itself. An instruction was added that subjects were to concentrate immediately on the new, underlined sentence every time they turned the page, and to refrain from re-reading the preceding text from the beginning. It was also indicated that back-reference was allowed whenever the subject felt necessary.

After the experiment, a brief interview followed to obtain information about the subject's experience of the test. Then the subject was debriefed.

5.2.3 Results and discussion

CONSIDERATIONS OF PROCEDURE

There were two significant additions to the original think aloud instruction of Ericsson and Simon (1984: 378) quoted in section 5.2.1 First, there was the request that subjects read out loud the sentence they were newly taking in. This had two motivations: first, it allowed the analyst to keep track of the current sentence being processed by the subject, and, second, it kept the subject in a talking mode. Only occasionally did subjects read their new sentence silently before reading it out loud. The second new instruction was the advice to treat longer sentences chunk by chunk. This means that much of the comprehension stage was already completed when subjects began to verbalize, and that the bulk of the thinking out loud data pertained to additional processing of the integrated sentence parts.

Adding every new sentence to the previously read text by presenting it on a new page with underlining was a procedure that worked well. In general the procedure makes subjects focus primarily on the novel informa- tion presented in the new sentence, while it also allows them to look back for problems of co-reference and the like.

On the whole, the warming-up period worked quite effectively. It got readers used to their situation and task in a very short time. Usually, one could hear that they were at ease with their situation after they had read two sentences or so. Whether they had also marshalled what may be called an appropriate attitude of reading is difficult to judge until we have more experience with the method.

CONSIDERATIONS OF MATERIALS

The next methodological issue is that of the texts selected as stimulus material. The two poetic texts were not deemed very difficult beforehand. However, they did present several reading problems to both the students and the lecturers. It is perhaps important to note that the poems were not narratives, but a combination of reflexive and lyrical statements. Moreover, they contained metaphorical connections at the macro-level of the text. It appeared that a first, more or less linear process of reading was only able to scratch the surface of what the subjects felt was suggested by the poem as a whole. These texts were clearly too complex for our purpose of studying the spontaneous incidence of special metaphor processing during ordinary literary reception.

The above differentiation between micro- and macro-metaphorical struc- ture is also crucial. It caused a problem not just for the analysis of the stimulus text, but even more so for the verbalizations. It was very difficult to keep track of what was part of the literal frame of reference and what was part of the metaphorical frame in the subjects' verbalizations when their reactions might have related to local and global metaphoricity. For the sake of clarity and simplicity, it was decided after the pilot test that texts with only small-scale metaphors would be included. Hence these two texts, and poetry in general, were not used in the main experiment. Perhaps such poetic texts can be used when they are shorter and when general reading difficulties can be resolved more easily and quickly at a global level of processing. This possibility was partly borne out by the readers' verbalizations about the quatrains which served as practice texts, and could be followed up in future research.

The only non-literary text was used for purposes of contrast. It, too, was quite a complex text. What is more, it was rather badly written according to the subjects who read it (a student and a lecturer), who criticized, indeed ridiculed, the overkill of metaphorical language.

Three fragments of literary prose from one particular author were used, because he seemed an excellent candidate for providing us with an experimental text on account of his sophisticated use of metaphor. But there always seemed to be something wrong: subjects underverbalized or oververbalized because of the involved metaphors, and one subject almost walked out because of his annoyance with the text. Therefore I had to turn to another author of literary narrative prose containing metaphoric language. These fragments turned out to be unproblematic for my purposes.

CONSIDERATIONS OF SUBJECTS

All students but one produced a verbal report of about four times the length of the original text. The exception was a student who used twice as many words as the other students. She was much more like the lecturers, who all produced much more protocol than the other students. If the ratio between stimulus text and response averages 1:4 for the bulk of the students, it exceeds 1:6 for the lecturers.

This difference requires careful attention, and can be explained with reference to two points. First, there is the matter of literary knowledge. What I mean by this is that one finds references to other texts, to biographical information and the like, which are clearly due to the fact that the lecturers are experts in this domain, while the students are not. Moreover, this also implies that the lecturers had developed decided preferences, and had at their disposal many standards of comparison which may all have been mobilized during reading to a greater extent than is the case for the students. Finally, another aspect of this same factor was the tendency to attempt to find justifications for elements of the text to a greater degree than the students (see Vipond and Hunt 1984 on point-driven reading). Such global features of expert literary reading are not only reflected in the kind of attention paid to metaphor, but also to other stylistic phenomena such as alliteration and rhyme, intertextual allusions, and potential symbolic, structural, and thematic significances beyond surface meaning. It should be noted that some of these features could also be found in the protocol of the older, more experienced student. This does suggest that the extent of literary knowledge is at least partly responsible for the large difference.

There is an important complicating factor, however, which disturbs this simple portrait – what I would like to call the social role of the expert as teacher. The usual daily practice of explicating texts to students in class may be pivotal in the performance of lecturers in think aloud tasks as well as their greater store of literary or textual knowledge. This feature can be deduced from the fact that most lecturers in the pilot study adopted a systematic search for meaningful elements in the text. This resulted in a relatively analytic mode of text processing that was not manifested by the students to the same extent.

The students predominantly reported moments of semantic synthesis at sentence level or engaged in problem solving when they met with particular textual problems. An exception was the mature student discussed above, who was also an experienced teacher and fifteen years older than the other student readers. Lecturers complemented their analytic move-ments at word and phrase level with synthetic ones at sentence level. On the whole, however, their attention to language features below the gram-matical level of the sentence considerably exceeded that of the students.

One might suppose that this particular feature of the protocols does detract from the validity of the data as bearing on literary reception proper. If it is true that we are encountering some influence from post-processing (the role of the teacher) here, then the experimental situation may have interfered with 'normal' literary reception. The only obvious way to circumvent this problem in the experiment reported in the next chapter, while not abandoning the university experts as an eligible group of subjects providing the optimal data we are after, was to use another group of university lecturers to represent a lesser degree of literary socialization.

DATA ANALYSIS: METAPHOR PROCESSING

The main aim of this section is to present an argument for the feasibility of both theory and method in terms of empirical findings. Therefore, no hard figures will be given concerning the incidence of the various processes. Rather, examples will be discussed in order to illustrate some main points. Moreover, these empirical data will be used to refine the model of metaphor processing in literature in the conclusion to this chapter. The incidence of various processes will then be investigated in Chapter 6. Some tendencies will be reported impressionistically in this section.

I will begin by reporting the results regarding *explicit metaphor identifica-tion*, which we examined by means of the retrospective explication task in

Chapter 3. Explicit metaphor identification was provisionally operational-ized as being signalled by a metalingual term labelling the linguistic structure as non-literal and/or comparative. *Metaphor, analogy, comparison, image,* and *figure of speech* are examples. All other criteria, such as hesitation, emphasis in speech at the location of the metaphor, or isolated mentioning of the metaphor itself (that is, without any addition by the subject) were taken as tendencies towards identification. In later research, such phenom-ena may have to be incorporated on a scale of identification markers, so that our grasp of this process can be refined.

Explicit identification of metaphors occurred frequently enough. Some readers identified about 30 per cent of the total number of metaphors present in a text, others zero. Lecturers identified many more metaphors than students. Terms used to identify metaphors with were *metaphor, metaphorical comparison, metaphorical interpretation of, comparison, imagery, image, 'image-language', figuratively, figure of speech.* The thinking out loud methodology thus provides rich data for the study of explicit metaphor identification.

An example of explicit identification can be found in the following translation of one subject's response to a passage about a police helicopter watching over a demonstration:

(1) <u>I walked to the place where</u> **the bird of prey hung ready over its quarry**
Oh my, now we get a very strong metaphor poured out over us. You first have to think what that may mean, for when you first see that bird of prey in the text you think: 'Bird of prey? What bird of prey, what are we talking about?' But it is clear that that is the helicopter and it is clear that it is seen as a very dangerous animal and moreover it is suggested that this bird of prey might come down any moment to eat the poor pedestrians walking below, for it says 'hung ready over its quarry'. With this sentence my worst suspicions are confirmed. I think it's a false sentence for there has never been a helicopter in The Netherlands which ever dived down upon the people to assault those people or to attack them.

This example requires a few remarks about method of presentation. I will adopt the graphic convention that parts underlined are stimulus material, and **bold** parts are metaphors. The verbalization constitutes one unit of analysis in that it relates in its entirety to the metaphor in the stimulus. In analysis, it receives scores for particular kinds of metaphor processing, where applicable. As will be clear, this particular verbalization is first coded as containing explicit metaphor identification on account of the occurrence of 'metaphor' in the first line.

However, it also receives another coding, for *explicit appreciation*: the qualification 'a very strong [metaphor]' clearly expresses a judgement by the reader on the nature of the metaphor. For explicit appreciation, any evaluative term expressing the opinion of the subject about the metaphor in question counts as good evidence. It is crucial here to distinguish between the affective purport of a metaphor realized as part of its meaning on the one hand and the attitude of the reader indicating his or her critical judgement of, for instance, the aptness of the metaphor on the other. Evaluative terms in the think aloud data ought therefore to be connectable to the opinion of the subject, not to the meaning or implication of the metaphor.

In general, for explicit appreciation, large group and individual differences were found. Four lecturers appreciated over 50 per cent of their metaphors explicitly, while four students produced no appreciations whatsoever. None of the students appreciated more than 15 per cent of their metaphors, while only one of the lecturers dropped below this level. Literary socialization seems a good candidate for explaining this group difference. It is also noteworthy that some lecturers often began by pronouncing their gut feeling about a metaphor. When they continued with other kinds of processing, they hardly ever changed their original judgement. However, other lecturers exhibited a much less evaluation-oriented approach, and only occasionally had explicitly appreciative comments to make. This difference between personal styles of critics is striking.

Examples of explicit appreciation range from statements about clarity, imageability, and difficulty, to beauty, emotionality, and scariness. Furthermore, many terms of appreciation manifest themselves as quasi-descriptive modifiers of the identification, as in 'a surrealist metaphor', or 'a traditional metaphor'. It is my opinion that most of these terms do not only classify or characterize, but also express a (covert) judgement. For the moment, we will take all of these as functioning at least partly as appreciative comments. They include categorization ('erotic', 'medical', 'biological', 'marxist'; 'neologism', 'lexical resemblance'), but also some kind of connection to author's intentions ('sarcastic', 'ironic', 'cynical', 'untrue').

Having illustrated identification and appreciation, let us now turn to other kinds of processing in (1) above. In general, their definition is determined by different kinds of frames of reference in the think aloud data. First of all, focus processing is signalled by a reaction to the metaphor in terms of language belonging to the topic domain of the metaphor. Next, a change in the frame of reference of the verbalizations from the topic domain to the vehicle domain will be regarded as signalling vehicle construction. Third, a change in the frame of reference from the topic or vehicle domain to an extrasentential or cotextual frame of reference, such as plot or theme or character, is the process of functionalization. Let us apply these criteria to (1).

First we encounter the basic metaphor process of *focus processing*: 'that is the helicopter'. This phrase shows that the reader draws the focus of the metaphor, 'bird of prey', into the domain of the literal topic of the metaphor, 'demonstration'. It involves the reader's use of the metaphor in terms of the current literal topic of the passage. In principle, metaphor processing could stop here.

However, in this case, focus processing is followed by another process, namely *vehicle construction*. The latter is signalled by 'this bird of prey might come down at any moment'. This part of the verbalization is a sign of interpreting the focus, 'bird of prey', not in terms of the demonstration, as before, but in terms of 'wildlife', its normal cognitive domain. It takes into account the literal meaning of the focus, 'bird of prey', and activates the associated vehicle domain of 'wildlife' at the temporary expense of the topic domain.

This process of vehicle construction in (1) is followed by yet another type of elaboration: 'to eat the poor pedestrians'. What happens here is that the metaphor is elaborated in terms of the relation between topic and vehicle domain. The language derives from the domains of 'street life/ traffic' ('poor pedestrians'; topic domain) and 'wildlife' ('to eat'; vehicle domain), respectively. As this elaboration depends upon the relation between topic and vehicle, this process may be called *metaphor construction*.

Metaphor construction is a new category emerging from the data which will have to be included when we later revise the model of metaphor processing. However, it is not an odd element to take on board; it follows automatically from our method of analysis in terms of frames of reference. Moreover, it can be accorded a position in the general theoretical framework by relating it to the procedure of Lakoff and Johnson (1980). They analyse conceptual metaphors in terms of analogical entailments that also use terms from both topic and vehicle domains. Metaphor construction is hence a natural addition to the categories of focus processing and vehicle construction. It suggests that the reader's view of the factual situation model is temporarily heavily affected by the figurative view promoted by the metaphor.

In general, focus processing was much more frequent than either of the other two processes for almost all of the subjects. This is what one might expect following Reinhart (1976). It goes against the idea that focus processing would not be accessible to the thinking out loud methodology, as speculated at the beginning of this chapter (section 5.1.1). It could be argued that thinking out loud produces focus processing as an additional process because readers have to talk about the text. But it might also be the case that focus processing lies in the grey area between the 'click of comprehension' and the specific realization of comprehension by further 'interpretation'. I will not pronounce upon these issues here, because other methods and kinds of data will have to put these findings into relief first. Conspicuous differences between the lecturers and the students did not manifest themselves for focus processing, but, again, this statement is only impressionistic because of the lack of comparable quantitative data. For the moment it may be safely concluded that vehicle and metaphor construction are two spontaneously occurring processes in thinking out loud.

Let us now turn to the presumed basis of focus processing and vehicle and metaphor construction, that is, *analogizing*. There was very little sign of subjects relating metaphor verbalizations to underlying analogies. Hardly anywhere was there an attempt to set up a structural relationship between the objects or relations involved in the metaphor and their respective cognitive domains. One example, translated again, out of a total of some ten instances, will suffice:

(2) In Brother's head there now **hung a loveless icon** of the boy
     This is quite a long jump to erm Brother, erm that boy. So that boy that's erm this friend, that friend of his, and he only has this recollection of him and the recollection isn't alive anymore – it is a kind of picture, the way an icon is a representation of something, too; does not resemble a human being, but is a kind of schematic representation of it, and that's the way he also has a schematic representation of this friend.

The analogy which is constructed in this verbalization may be summarized as:

(3) memory: reality :: icon: representant

The ground of this analogy is explicated by the reader too: both parts of the analogy are 'schematic'.

Only ten cases of analogizing out of a possible total of some four hundred is a very low proportion. The relative absence of analogical reasoning from the protocols may be explained by the observation that analogizing is quite a difficult and indeterminate (that is open) thing to do. Moreover, analogizing as a conscious reasoning process is apparently unnecessary for the adequate processing of metaphors. Perhaps the role of analogy in metaphor processing does not pertain to interpretative reasoning but to automatic comprehension; in other words, analogizing may take place largely unconsciously. This would also explain why thinking out loud does not exhibit many traces of analogies.

Note that the thinking aloud method does allow for the development of analogical reasoning. This is shown by Clement (1988) and Gick and Holyoak (1980). Indeed, explicit analogical reasoning (as opposed to automatic computation) may belong to the general domain of scientific analysis or education rather than to text processing in particular. If this is correct, then its absence from the present data suggests that the lecturers act more like readers than like teachers or academics in this respect, which is a comforting thought for the methodological validity of the task.

A matter related to analogizing is the multiple construction of metaphorical meaning on the basis of different realizations of the underlying or presumed analogy. This was referred to as one manner of polyvalent metaphor construction as described in Chapter 2. It will not come as a surprise after the previous remarks that this happened very seldom: only five polyvalent cases occurred over a total of more than 400 metaphors. An example is provided by the double affect of 'snout', realized as both positive ('funny') and negative ('scary'). Therefore, polyvalence in the form of constructing more than one basic meaning does not seem very prominent in thinking out loud about metaphors.

By contrast, the one remaining form of meaning attribution, contextual usages or *functionalizations* of metaphors, was clearly detectable in the data. They ranged from 0 to 25 per cent of the metaphors interpreted contextually per reader. There seemed to be a tendency for the lecturers to interpret metaphors contextually more often than the students. Poetic texts seemed to promote this kind of processing in the case of the students, too.

An example of functionalization is the interpretation of the phrase 'the experiment in the laboratory of solitude'. This phrase refers to a character's lonely survival as an unemployed person. It was accorded an extra, contextual meaning in terms of the 'intellectual development' of the character. This is a frame of reference that is not an immediate part of that needed to process the metaphor as such:

(4) this also brings it about that words like 'report', 'precision', 'experiment', 'laboratory', that they also are reminiscent of his intellectual development, which perhaps does not, which perhaps clashes with the state of loneliness in which he appears to be.

Such a contextual use provides an additional perspective upon both the topic and the vehicle of the metaphor. The metaphor does not strictly need such a new contextual perspective to function semantically: meaning is doubled here. Thinking out loud seems a suitable method to allow for the natural incidence of this kind of additional meaning construction.

Besides the processes discussed above, there were four other phenomena in the data that need to be incorporated in the model of metaphor processing. The first was foreshadowed in the methodological discussion at the beginning of this chapter, but its importance as a distinct aspect of metaphor processing only became clear through a study of the data. This is the experience of metaphor as a semantic problem, as in (5):

(5) because of **the rain which irrigates the centres** of the imperialist powers, **the** extensive suburbs of the system **get submerged**.

Well, what that may mean

The student 'solved' this metaphor in seventy-two words, but the lecturer used 449 words, because he found fault with the internal consistency of the metaphoric comparison. There were more readings that contained such moments of puzzlement. I will refer to this phenomenon as *problem identification*.

A second process which requires our attention is illustrated by the following excerpt:

(6) as a result of **the incorporation within** the universal **wheels of capitalism**
    Capitalism as a universal wheel, universal machine, which rolls on relentlessly

The interesting phrase is 'capitalism as a universal wheel'. It is partly identification and partly conceptual processing, for there is a degree of awareness of a non-literal linkage between two domains (identification) and a description of the terms belonging to the domains concerned (conceptual processing). Other examples are 'that has to be a description, that body, of death'; and: 'the last inhabitant, well, that has to be an evocation of a last consciousness concerning everything that has got lost'. Note that there is neither complete explicit identification nor fully-fledged conceptual processing. Rather, what is happening is that the metaphor is labelled: it receives a twofold name, almost in the way of the 'A IS B' formula of Lakoff and Johnson (1980). This analysis was suggested by the occurrence of the following verbalization:

(7) Everything, the ground, its fruits and **her intestines** which are rich in raw materials
    Mother Earth so to say as an image underneath in the deep

In this case, explicit identification does take place ('an image'), but a label of the metaphor is attached to it ('Mother Earth'), which sums up the point of the metaphor in more or less conventional, and certainly schematic terms. *Labelling* will be used as a new category, then, representing a hybrid between identification and conceptual processing.

It also happened that metaphors were taken up again at a later stage in the reading process. This is the other side of functionalization discussed above. Functionalization takes place at the moment of processing the metaphor itself. However, the reader may subsequently take up a particular metaphor to enrich the processing of a later passage in the text. Alternatively, metaphors may be reactivated to elaborate their previously developed representation with the help of the subsequent text. For instance, the metaphor of the icon discussed under (2) was reactivated later when the reader was considering the wrinkles in the face of the character:

(8) Those wrinkles had even completely disappeared; he had a smooth face and that probably also makes him think of an icon, which I think always has a smooth shape too.

This is an important additional source of potential meaning complexity and polyvalence related to metaphor processing. I will refer to it as *refunctionalization.*

Finally, as was foreseen by the model sketched out in the previous chapter, metaphors may be processed in the explicit terms of the communicative context model constructed by the reader. They are then seen as intentional uses of a particular kind of language by the author in order to convey a particular message or achieve a particular effect. One example of such a process is displayed in:

(9) [The helicopter] did not **travel over** the town but **persisted** in a circular movement.
Yes, what strikes me in this sentence, except for the picture that it suggests, is the verb 'to persist': that has, to my taste, a certain emotional charge, and the writer did not put that word there for nothing. To me that is the word that comes most to the fore. Apparently a kind of, the word has a particular, expresses a particular energy, which the writer wants to go against in some way or another, I think.

The first reference to 'the writer' embodies an invocation of the intentions of the author, and the second expresses the beginning of an interpretation of those presumed intentions. On the basis of the notion of a communicative context model, this process will be referred to as *context construction.*

5.3 Conclusion

The novel application of the think aloud task to the study of understanding metaphor has proved to be useful. There are some restrictions on its initial success when we look at the role of different texts and different readers, but these difficulties can be overcome in subsequent research. On the whole, the method gives access to the on-going process of the actualization and integration of metaphors in the developing representation of the text at various levels.

From this finding, a number of things may be concluded. First, *pace* the query about the validity of the method by Larsen and Seilman (1988), one may believe that at least some metaphors are sufficiently problematic to receive explicit attention during thinking out loud. Another view of the method is that thinking out loud reflects the kinds of processing occurring after the 'click of comprehension' mentioned by Gibbs (1987) and Gerrig (1989) and Gibbs and Gerrig (1989). In that case, it is eminently suitable to track additional processes like extended interpretation and so on. This would mean that other methods are needed for the on-line study of metaphor comprehension, an observation which is in line with the stand-point of Larsen and Seilman. A third position in this respect would constitute a compromise. Against Larsen and Seilman it can be argued that not all texts afford such smooth reading as they suggest, and against Gibbs and Gerrig one can say that some metaphors may not trigger a well-defined moment, or a 'click', of comprehension. This could also explain the frequent presence of focus processing in the data. However, as we noted above, focus processing may also be partly explained as resulting from the method itself, in that readers cannot but talk about the topic of the text. This caveat is not very detrimental, however, for readers also have to think about the topic of a text when they process it. Therefore, if metaphors receive attention at times in the form of focus processing, this is a reflection of the need to keep the construction of a coherent text representation on course.

But perhaps the most interesting result of the pilot studies is the view they offer of the process of understanding metaphor in literature as a whole. The theoretically distinguishable categories of identification, various kinds of meaning attribution, and appreciation have done their job as a preliminary model, but the richness of the thinking out loud data has provided us with the outlines of a clearer picture. I will therefore review all of the processes once again with the help of one *constructed example*. This will lead us on to an integrated description of metaphor processing.

Suppose we had collected the following idealized data:

(10) But then the Dutch **blasted** the German defence
    what does this sentence mean?
    it seems a metaphor to me
    football as war or something
    the Dutch find a possibility to score a goal, I think
  5 they blow up the resistance
    and they use the gap to score
    the room to score is like a hole in a war line
    it is an opening or something
    this is rather different from the chess-football mentioned earlier
 10 the reporter is not very consistent in his views
    but it is rather a cliché too

Line 1 of this constructed verbalization is an example of what I wish to call *problem identification*, in that a semantic problem is recognized but not understood. Line 2 is an illustration of *explicit identification*: the metaphor is labelled explicitly as a figure of speech of that kind. In line 3 we find the newly distinguished process of *labelling*, a combination of partial identification and conceptual processing.

Focus processing is exhibited by line 4: it involves the conceptual integration of the figurative term, or the focus, within the cognitive domain of the literal topic. In the next line, however, our hypothetical and perfect reader focuses attention on the vehicle domain by itself, which therefore is to be classified as *vehicle construction*. A combination of both focus processing and vehicle construction is contained by line 6, involving implications of the metaphor as a whole; this is the newly introduced process of *metaphor construction*.

A specific case of conceptual metaphor processing is the discovery of the analogical structure of the metaphor, as can be seen in line 7. Given the difficulty and low incidence of this phenomenon, it is not unfitting to call this process *metaphor analysis*. When it is a matter of the analogical comparison having been constructed, it may be further explicated in terms of its ground, as happens in line 8. This process may hence be referred to as *metaphor explication*.

In line 9 we observe the by now better-known phenomenon of the relation of a metaphor to extra sentential meaning or knowledge in terms of the preceding context. It is a case of *metaphor functionalization*. The next statement constructs a communicative context model by referring to the author of the metaphor: this is what I called *metaphor context construction*. Finally, line 11 is a clear example of *explicit appreciation*.

The only process not exemplified by (10) is the reader's return to a metaphor at a later stage in the reading process to resume its processing in connection with a later passage. It cannot be illustrated because of the constructed nature of the example. I called this process *refunctionalization*.

One advantage of this description is that it is based on a logical task analysis related to empirically founded criteria. This model assigns a different position to those processes called analysis and explication. As we have seen, such processes do not seem to occur very often. They may be the prerogative of only certain readers in certain contexts, and are probably much more tied to educational or scientific analysis and study than to other kinds of text processing. The other processes are likely to be more frequent in thinking out loud while reading.

Notes

1. In retrospect, it may be advisable to return to somewhat longer experimental texts such as very short stories: they have the advantage of being complete and uncut, as long as their length does not become too excessive.

CHAPTER SIX

Metaphor processing in literature and journalism

6.1 Introduction

The last chapter developed a classification of different aspects of metaphor processing on the basis of an analysis of thinking out loud protocols. This classification system being available, we can now proceed to a more precise investigation of the incidence of these processes in literary reception. We are interested in the relative frequencies with which these processes can be observed within and outside literary reading. Given the results presented in Chapter 3, the general expectation is that metaphors are accorded more attention in literary reading than in other kinds of reading, such as journalism. The more interesting question is, of course, which processes are involved in this larger degree of attention?

Chapter 3 showed that metaphors figured prominently in the underlinings of passages as typically literary, but we cannot be sure of the nature of readers' processing of these metaphors. For instance, how often are the vehicles of these metaphors constructed? How often are they related to their extrasentential contexts? And so on. The think aloud task can provide further insight into these matters by showing how often readers talk about these specific aspects of the metaphors while they are processing the experimental text. It is particularly interesting to examine how often readers identify metaphors explicitly as metaphors. Chapter 3 showed that readers explicitly identified 25 to 50 per cent of the metaphors which they had previously underlined as typically literary. However, as was noted there, these explanation data do not provide evidence about the on-going act of reading itself, as they were collected after the reading process had finished. Therefore the question arises how often readers identify metaphors as metaphors during the process of reception itself.

We have seen that some of these aspects of metaphor processing are probably more important for literary reception than others. Identification itself is expected to be one of these typically literary manifestations of dealing with metaphors, on account of its relation to the typical attention readers of literature pay to form and fictionality. But the same holds for vehicle construction and functionalization on account of the role of polyvalence and for appreciation on account of the role of subjectivity, to mention only the most prominent categories which we have discussed in the previous chapters. However, because the present study constitutes a first exploration of the incidence of the various metaphor processing categories, I included all of them without further distinction. Metaphor analysis and explication were left aside for the present purposes, though, because of their low incidence, observed in the previous chapter. More sophisticated predictions regarding separate aspects of metaphor processing in literature can then be based on the findings of this first investigation.

I investigated the idea that metaphors are accorded more attention during literary reading than non-literary reading by creating an opposition between literature and journalism. I did this by collecting and examining thinking out loud data about the literary and the journalistic text used in Chapter 3, section 3. After an analysis of the verbal data, it was possible to determine whether metaphors received proportionately more attention in literary reading than in non-literary reading and which processes were predominantly responsible for this predicted additional attention.

It should be observed that, in this design, any differences in metaphor processing between the two reading conditions may be due to two factors which are confounded in the opposition between the two reading conditions of literary and journalistic reading. First, there is the factor of context: as we have seen in Chapter 3, the instruction that a text is literary or journalistic can induce the application of different strategies of reading. Second, there is the unique nature of each text: even if readers set out to read a text *as* literature or *as* journalism, the text in question may stimulate or obviate the typical type of text-processing in question. Therefore it is impossible to say which of these two factors is responsible for any differences found between the literary and journalistic reading conditions used here. However, the finding of such differences is an interesting result by itself, which may be explained by conducting further research on the relative weight of the factors of 'context' and 'text'. Given that my primary interest did not lie in the separate contribution of 'context' and 'text', but in the observability of their joint effect upon metaphor processing, there was little harm in following the present route. To obtain some more control over the potential role of the texts apart from context, I carried out an additional check on the general comparability of the two texts for their use in thinking out loud (see section 6.5).

Using two different texts also implies that the metaphors to which the test subjects are responding when they are thinking out loud are not the same. Technically speaking, I am using different test items (metaphors) between the two reading conditions in order to measure the relative incidence of metaphor processing. This problem will be handled further in Part Three. There I will present a framework for a theory of metaphor properties in Chapter 7, and, related to that, data on the properties of literary and journalistic metaphors in Chapter 8. In Chapter 9, I will then be able to examine the differences between the literary and the non-literary metaphors present in the two experimental texts used here; and subsequently to determine the effect of these properties upon reader performance in thinking out loud.

Reader performance was also seen to be dependent on differences between readers: Chapter 5 reported that there was a considerable difference between arts students and faculty members in this connection. Two factors were deemed criterial: degree of literary socialization and professional experience with text explication. It was suggested that the latter factor had to be held constant in order to obtain a better view of the role of literary socialization. If one wants to examine as high a level of literary expertise as is practically possible, arts students are judged to be less appropriate as test subjects than faculty members. Therefore the preferred solution to the problem of professional experience with text explication was to recruit another group of academics who had similar experience with explicating texts while having a lesser degree of literary socialization than members of the arts faculty. This operationalization of literary socialization was achieved by using groups of 'experts' and 'controls' from literature and anthropology departments, respectively.

The expert group of readers, with a high degree of literary socialization, were predicted to perform in greater accordance with our expectation than the readers with no professional experience in literary reading. When the same literary text is presented to two groups of readers who are comparable in all important respects except for their degree of literary socialization, any differences in reading results may be attributed to the greater or lesser degree of literary socialization. Moreover, literary socialization should not make a difference in journalistic reception because it is irrelevant to that type of reading. Hence in non-literary reading, the two groups should perform equally regarding the incidence of metaphor processing. In short, literary socialization determines attention to metaphors in literature, but not in journalism. Statistically speaking, we are looking for an interaction effect.

6.2 Method

SUBJECTS

Academic researchers and teachers in two disciplines, literary studies (N = 19) and anthropology (N = 18), served as subjects. Originally there was one more subject, but his data could not be used because of equipment failure. Moreover, three subjects from the literary group had to be removed because they provided interpretations and analyses rather than receptions of the texts. My initial impression of this problem was confirmed by a statistical examination of the data in terms of the number of words each subject used for thinking out loud.[1] From now on I will refer to the two groups as the 'experts' (N = 16) and the 'controls' (N = 18).

The experts were selected at random from the German and Dutch Departments of the University of Amsterdam and the University of Utrecht. The controls came from the department of anthropology at the Free University of Amsterdam. Subjects were approached by letter and sometimes suggested other test subjects who had not been on the list. All participants received a book token for their effort.

MATERIALS

The experimental texts were identical to the ones used in the Dutch underlining study presented in Chapter 3 (section 3.3). To repeat briefly, the literary text was narrative prose fiction, dealing with a confrontation between riot police and demonstrators on the day of the Coronation of Queen Beatrix in Amsterdam in 1980. The journalistic text was a narrative impression of the first two days after the opening of the Berlin Wall in November 1990, describing the events in the streets. The texts were roughly equal in length (approximately 400 words each), and contained a similar number of metaphors (twenty-seven and twenty-six, respectively). For more detailed information, see section 3.3.2.

PROCEDURE

The experimental texts were offered in counter-balanced order: half of the subjects in either group received the literary text first and the other half received the journalistic text first. Collection of thinking out loud data took place individually. The experts, for the most part, were interviewed in their offices. The controls, coming from my own university, usually had their sessions in my office. All sessions were recorded by a walkman tape-recorder.

Subjects received oral instructions about their task, the instructions being given according to a check-list. They were told that they were going to read two texts, with a small break for interview purposes in between. They were also told that the texts were literary and journalistic, and that the purpose of the investigation was to examine reading processes. It was explained that, to this end, the texts were being offered sentence-by-sentence, every new sentence of the text being added to the previous text so that subjects could refer back easily. Subjects were requested to verbalize everything that occurred to them. However, it was also added that they were not to explain to me what they said, but that they were to proceed as if they were alone in the room.

Before the beginning of the actual experiment, a number of trial sentences were offered from another portion of the experimental text that was used first in that session, in order to familiarize the subject with the situation and the procedure. In all cases except one, this warming-up part was successful. In this one case, the session was not pursued and the subject was removed from the pool.

At the beginning of the actual thinking out loud about each text, the author of the source was disclosed to the subject, and a short statement of the theme of the text was provided in the form used above in the materials section. In between the two texts, subjects were asked a number of questions concerning their background and literary reading habits to distract their minds from the previous text. After having read the second text, subjects were asked about their opinion of the representativeness of the think aloud data in comparison with silent reading, the general difference between literary and non-literary reading, and their estimation of the extent to which that difference had been reflected in this particular thinking out loud session. Then debriefing followed about the real purpose of the experiment.

6.3 Results

6.3.1 Metaphor processing analysis

All statements in the thinking out loud protocols that could be related with sufficient certainty to the metaphors in the stimulus sentences were analysed according to the classification system discussed in Chapter 5. For each test subject, every metaphor was scored for a particular process if the subject's think aloud verbalizations manifested the pertinent features. The scoring criteria for distinct categories of metaphor processing were as follows:

1. When readers express their difficulty or doubt with processing a metaphorical expression, this is *problem identification*.
2. When readers express their metalingual awareness regarding a metaphor as being non-literal, comparative, or an image, this is explicit *metaphor identification*.
3. When readers connect the topic and vehicle domains of the metaphor with an overt comparative linker such as *is* or *is like*, this is *labelling*.
4. When readers process a metaphor in terms of language belonging exclusively to the topic domain, this is *focus processing*.
5. When readers process a metaphor in terms of language belonging exclusively to the vehicle domain, this is *vehicle construction*.
6. When readers interpret a metaphor in terms of language belonging to both the topic and the vehicle domain, this is *metaphor construction*.
7. When readers connect the metaphor to other portions of the text or their interpretations thereof, this is *metaphor functionalization*.
8. When readers connect the metaphor to the intentions of the author, this is *metaphor context construction*.
9. When readers return to metaphors interpreted before the current sentence, this is *metaphor refunctionalization*.
10. When readers express their judgement concerning the class or the quality of the metaphor, then this is *metaphor appreciation*.

A first round of eighteen protocols (nine subjects) was scored by myself and a second rater who had been trained with the data reported in Chapter 5. However, this did not produce enough satisfactory reliability co-efficients. After discussion of these data and sophistication of the criteria for scoring, yielding the format reported above, we scored a second sample of sixteen protocols (eight subjects). This showed improvement: inter-coder agreement was estimated for each of the ten basic categories of metaphor processing with reference to the sixteen protocols analysed by myself and the second analyst, and statistical analysis demonstrated that reliability was sufficient for six of the ten categories.[2] I decided to investigate the incidence of only the following processes: focus processing, context construction and explicit identification, explicit appreciation, and refunctionalization. I analysed the remainder of the protocols in this fashion. The other processes will have to await further study until the difficulties with reliable analysis are solved. I also dropped problem identification although it was in fact eligible, because there were only four instances in the sixteen protocols successfully analysed for inter-rater agreement.

Table 6.1: Average proportionate incidence of metaphor processing in two reading conditions by two groups of academics (standard deviations in brackets)

		Reading condition	
Processing category	*Literary socialization*	*Literary*	*Journalistic*
Focus processing	Experts	0.20 (0.18)	0.13 (0.14)
	Controls	0.15 (0.10)	0.08 (0.08)
Context construction	Experts	0.16 (0.13)	0.09 (0.11)
	Controls	0.11 (0.08)	0.04 (0.05)
Explicit identification	Experts	0.17 (0.12)	0.08 (0.10)
	Controls	0.10 (0.11)	0.01 (0.03)
Explicit appreciation	Experts	0.18 (0.12)	0.12 (0.10)
	Controls	0.19 (0.12)	0.09 (0.11)
Refunctionalization	Experts	0.10 (0.06)	0.08 (0.06)
	Controls	0.08 (0.10)	0.03 (0.05)

6.3.2 Incidence of metaphor processes

For every subject I counted the number of metaphors realized in one of the five manners of focus processing, context construction and explicit identification, explicit appreciation, and refunctionalization. Then I divided these totals by the total number of metaphors in the literary and the journalistic text, respectively, in order to be able to compare the *relative* incidence of metaphor processing, and' averaged these proportions across subjects. Table 6.1 displays the resulting mean proportion of occurrences of every process, classified by group of readers, in the literary and the journalistic reading conditions. All mean scores of the literary reading condition are higher than the means of the journalistic reading condition. Also, almost all means of the experts are higher than the means of the controls. Can statistical analysis of these data show that these differences are significant? (I once more refer to section 3.2.3 for further information about any unfamiliar terms.)

An analysis of variance was planned with all five dependent variables of focus processing, context construction, explicit identification, explicit appreciation, and refunctionalization included in the same analysis. However, this analysis was prevented by the detection of singularity, which constitutes a mathematical problem in analysis of variance. In conceptual terms, singularity indicates that some of the variables whose means are compared are very highly correlated, and that one of the variables may indeed be a combination of the others (Tabachnik and Fidell 1989: 87). In such a case, the envisaged simultaneous analysis of all five distinct variables could amount to testing the same difference more than once, one time at a specific level and another time at a combinatory level. This is not the correct way to go about such a test.

In order to investigate the nature of the relations between the variables, compare the correlation matrix of the five metaphor processing categories; I give the averages of the two groups of subjects in order to maintain a relatively simple picture (Table 6.2). Inspection reveals that the incidence of the three communicative metaphor processing categories of context construction, identification, and appreciation was related to each other in both conditions of reading (with the exception of the pair 'context construction' − 'appreciation' in literary reading). Moreover, refunctionalization was also related to focus processing and context construction in the two conditions of reading.

I did not want to interpret these data one way or the other by deleting one or two further variables from the analysis on the assumption that they were combinations of the others. I did not feel I had solid grounds to make the appropriate selections. Moreover, the relations between the variables made sense on the grounds of the theoretical distinction between conceptual and communicative processes, the process of refunctionalization being indiscriminate in this regard. An alternative strategy to circumvent the problem of singularity was available. Instead of combining the five dependent variables of metaphor processing within one overall analysis, it was also possible to perform a series of five separate analyses of variance, one analysis for each metaphor processing category in turn. In other words, each of the metaphor processing categories was taken as a separate case of metaphor processing for which the predictions could be tested. To exclude the chance of obtaining fortuitously significant findings because of the repeated series of tests on data which are closely related to each other, the level of significance of each test was adjusted accordingly.[3] The results of these five analyses of variance can be grouped together and discussed by factor, reading condition and literary socialization, respectively.[4] I will first deal with the analyses treating the subjects as the random factor.

The most important result was the unanimous significant *main effect of 'reading condition'* on the average proportionate incidence of metaphor processing. This factor exhibited a statistically significant effect for all of the dependent variables of focus processing, context construction, identification, appreciation, and refunctionalization. Looking at the averages displayed by Table 6.1, this outcome suggests that all five metaphor processing categories exhibited a higher incidence in the literary reading condition than in the journalistic reading condition. There is a higher attention to metaphors in literary reading than in journalistic reading which is based on all five metaphor processing categories. The relevant

Table 6.2: Correlations between different metaphor processes in two conditions of reading, averaged across two groups of academics

(a) Literary reading

	Focus	Context	Identi-fication	Appreciation	Refunction-alization
Focus processing	1.00				
Context construction	0.30	1.00			
Identification	0.14	0.59**	1.00		
Appreciation	− 0.22	0.33	0.55**	1.00	
Refunctionalization	0.52**	0.41*	0.29	0.19	1.00

(b) Journalistic reading

	Focus	Context	Identi-fication	Appreciation	Refunction-alization
Focus processing	1.00				
Context construction	0.04	1.00			
Identification	0.14	0.79**	1.00		
Appreciation	− 0.01	0.68**	0.58**	1.00	
Refunctionalization	0.47**	0.39*	0.57**	0.25	1.00

Two-tailed significance: ** $p < 0.01$; * $p < 0.05$

test statistics were large: even if they are added together across the five separate tests, the result is still clearly statistically significant. Thus, the prediction was supported by the evidence.

The second *main effect* of these analyses was that of *literary socialization*, the between-subject factor. The results demonstrated that there was no significant difference between the average incidence of metaphor processing for the two levels of literary socialization operationalized by means of the groups of readers. The different means of the five dependent variables for the two groups were due to the effect of chance upon sampling. The present data do not support the hypothesis that literary socialization affects the incidence of various kinds of metaphor processing. However, some of the test statistics were fairly large, indicating that this factor did account for some proportion of the variance in the data. Specially noteworthy is explicit identification, suggesting that there was a tendency for the experts to explicitly identify more metaphors than the controls. We will come back to this finding in section 6.4. For the moment, however, we can conclude that the different averages of the metaphor processing categories manifested by the literary experts and the controls were caused by chance.

More pertinent to our present concerns, however, is the result regarding the *interaction between literary socialization and reading condition*. We expected that literary socialization would have a clear effect on the incidence of the metaphor processing categories in the literary reading condition alone. The results indicate, however, that there was no observable effect of literary socialization in this quarter. The test statistics were very small, indicating that the literary experts did not perform differently in the literary reading condition from the anthropologists for any of the metaphor processing categories. Hence our prediction was not confirmed by the evidence.

However, the above analyses only show that we can generalize beyond our present sample of subjects to other, similar literary experts and anthropologists. These analyses have treated the subjects as a random factor, but the materials as a fixed factor. If we wish to test whether we may also generalize the above findings beyond our specific materials, we have to turn to a second series of analyses, which treats the materials (metaphors) as the random factor (see Table VIB in note 4). An inspection of the test statistics of these analyses shows that all significant effects of the factor of *reading condition* recur here, except for the process of context construction. However, because of the large number of tests, these results have to be interpreted as tendencies. Moreover, *simultaneous* generalization over *both* subjects and materials yields fewer significant results: calculation of the relevant test statistic produces only two tendencies, for focus processing and explicit identification (see Table VIC in note 4). The previous conclusions about a clear effect of reading conditions on metaphor processing are limited: replication with other subjects and materials is needed before we can say that the prediction has been fully substantiated by the evidence.

We get quite a different picture when we turn to the other main effect, *literary socialization*, in the second series of analyses. The previous analyses, treating the test subjects as the random factor, did not show any effect of literary socialization, except for one tendency regarding identification. But this situation is completely reversed when we treat the materials as the random factor: all processes except explicit appreciation exhibited a reliable or tendentially significant group effect, indicating that the literary experts did accord more attention to the metaphors than the anthropologists. This indicates that, if these particular thirty-four subjects were to think out loud about another series of metaphors in a literary and a journalistic text, then the literary experts would again pay more attention to the metaphors than the anthropologists. But these results cannot be generalized towards other subjects, let alone to other subjects *and* materials at the same time, because there was no significant effect of literary socialization in the first series of analyses, treating subjects as the random factor.

Finally, there is no sign of an *interaction between literary socialization and reading condition* in the second series of analyses. The metaphors in the literary reading condition are not accorded more attention than the metaphors in the journalistic reading condition by either of the two groups. This would be the same if these subjects received a different set of metaphors. The interaction between literary socialization and reading condition has not yielded one significant effect in either series of analyses, with subjects or materials treated as the random factor.

6.4 Discussion

The idea that readers accord more attention to metaphors in literary than in journalistic reading was confirmed by the data collected and analysed in this think aloud experiment. It turned out that all five processes included in the analysis played a role in the greater attention readers pay to metaphors in literary reading:

1. Readers processed the focus of metaphors more often in the thinking out loud verbalizations about the literary text than in the journalistic reading condition.
2. They built contexts in terms of author intentions more often than in journalistic reading.
3. They identified metaphors explicitly more frequently in literary than journalistic reading.
4. They expressed their judgement about literary metaphors more repeatedly than when they thought out loud about journalistic metaphors.
5 They refunctionalized metaphors at later stages of the reading process more frequently while reading the literary text.

Although not all of these results can be generalized simultaneously beyond both subjects and materials used in the present experiment, the results obtained are in accordance with the expectations formulated in the previous chapters. Replication will have to confirm that context construction, appreciation and refunctionalization are involved in general patterns of literary metaphor processing just as focus processing and explicit identification.

One explanation for the attention paid to metaphors in literary reading lies in the context-affected factor of the reader, who activates specifically literary reading strategies. As argued before, there are several sides to literary reading which make it likely that metaphors receive more attention in literary reception than in other types of reading. If we assume that the general nature of literary reading can be described as subjective, fictional, polyvalent, and form-oriented, metaphors qualify as good opportunities to exhibit this kind of reading. As was shown in Chapter 2, metaphors require subject-dependent searches for meaning and reference across conceptual domains, and their indeterminacy often allows for the consideration of more than one alternative in this respect. This type of reading should be contrasted with the non-literary reading attitude in which metaphors are approached from a general need for factuality and monovalence. The evidence shows that, in the overall comparison between literary and journalistic reading, much less attention was paid to the metaphors in the journalistic reading condition than in the literary condition.

We have not been able to address the question whether metaphors were indeed frequently realized in a subjective and polyvalent fashion. This question requires a content analysis of the processes of focus processing, vehicle construction, metaphor construction, and functionalization. However, as they did not exihibit sufficient reliability co-efficients, it was impossible to pursue this goal, which will have to be the subject of future research.

The high incidence of explicit identification and of explicit appreciation can be taken as concrete evidence for the argument that literary text processing favours subjectivity, awareness of fictionality, and orientation to form. Explicit identification is concerned with metaphor as a figure of speech and related to the recognition of metaphor as an impossible fiction. Explicit appreciation of metaphors involves the reader's expression of a subjective judgement about the nature or the quality of the metaphor; the relevance of expressing such a subjective opinion is thought by subjects to be higher for literary than for other kinds of reading. The higher incidence of identification and appreciation in the literary reading condition hence provides good evidence for the general idea that literature stimulates subjective, fictional, and form-oriented reading processes.

The other context-affected factor that may have influenced metaphor processing in literary and journalistic reading is the text. When texts are produced with an eye towards literary versus journalistic reception, this may affect the structure of the metaphors they contain as well. If the average nature of the metaphors in these texts is indeed different, then this fact can also account for the different incidence of the various metaphor processing categories between the two reading conditions. Literary metaphors can stimulate literary processing. This is an alternative, equally plausible explanation of the present findings in comparison with the explanation in terms of reading attitude.

An interesting complication in this connection is formed by the varying discourse-typical nature of the two experimental texts. The analyses in Chapter 3 showed that the literary text is more representative of its type of discourse than the journalistic text. The journalistic text has a relatively high potential for literary text processing. This imbalance probably results from the fact that I was looking for a journalistic text with a sufficient number of interesting metaphors located in a comparable story and theme to balance with the literary text. Consequently, the distance between literary and journalistic reading performance was decreased in this particular think-aloud task. As a result, the average attention to metaphors may have been unusually raised in the journalistic reading condition. Nevertheless, the results of the experiment show that the attention paid to the metaphors in the literary reading condition differs significantly from the attention paid to the metaphors in the journalistic reading condition. The conclusion must be that the experiment has provided a strong confirmation of the prediction that metaphors in literature are accorded more attention than metaphors in journalism. If anything, the ordinary attention to metaphors in journalism may well be lower than what we have found here.

The other hypothesis that was tested in this study – whether expert readers pay more attention to metaphors in literary reception than less expert readers – did not receive support from the evidence. It turned out that all of the test statistics for the interaction effect were extremely small, not providing even a hint of a tendency in the right direction. Indeed, inspection of the statistics showed that, if there was a difference between the two groups, it was not limited to literary reading alone. Tendencies for differences between the two groups of readers were found for the main effects of literary socialization rather than for the interaction between literary socialization and reading conditions. The analyses treating the subjects as the random factor showed at least one clear tendency in this connection, namely the incidence of explicit metaphor identification. Even stronger evidence in this direction was found in the analyses treating the materials as the random factor: there, no fewer than four of the five processes manifested a significant difference between the two groups of readers. This provides some encouragement for future work in this area.

An explanation for these findings can be offered in the following form: the habitual attention of the literary experts to language as form, and to metaphor in particular, has probably become an ingrained habit of reading which is not restricted to literary reception. It thus seems that we have come across another manifestation of the 'dominance of the subject-factor' previously noted by Meutsch (1989: 68); see Chapter 5 section 5.1.4. It is natural that explicit identification is the process which exhibits this tendency most clearly: it is the key process for the reading strategy which highlights linguistic form. On the whole, however, the reception of literary metaphors was not as greatly affected by the degree of literary socialization of the subjects as expected. If literary reception is seen as a subject-dependent act, in that the attitude and abilities of the reader determine the degree to which reception becomes literary, then this idea does not extend as far as differentiating the processing of metaphors in the literary reading condition from their processing in the journalistic reading condition. In the thinking out loud study there was no appreciable difference between the group of literary experts and the anthropologists regarding the number of metaphors processed in various ways.

Before more general conclusions are based on this observation, however, there are various issues which have to be resolved. For instance, there is the matter of the choice of texts which may have diminished the influence of literary socialization. Too many conspicuous metaphors in too short a text may have boosted the performance of the group with a lower literary socialization. Second, the distance between the levels of literary socialization may have been too small for any effects to become clearly visible. And third, the operationalization of literary socialization by means of comparing two groups of academics (anthropologists) may have been too gross a means to capture differences between more skilled and less skilled literary readers. Finally, there is the issue of statistical power when using relatively small groups, as we did here.

The statistical tendencies discussed above did not attain significance because of the increasing of the level of significance for each separate test on account of the relation between the processes indicated by the detection of singularity. This is not *just* a mathematical problem, of course. It also has a bearing on the actual relation between the manners of metaphor processing themselves. The reliability co-efficients for each of the metaphor processing categories indicate that the distinction between them is solid, but the correlation matrix shown in Table 6.2 illustrates that their overall incidence is highly related in some quarters. In other words, the processes are not identical, but at the same time they are still variations on one theme: attention to metaphor. What is especially interesting is that the three communicative processes of context construction, identification, and appreciation can be observed to belong together. This is encouraging support for the overall theoretical approach adumbrated in this part of the book. More importantly, however, it raises the question whether there is a causal basis to these correlations. For instance, does attention to a metaphor in terms of author intentions also increase the possibility of attending to the metaphor in terms of its formal properties (identification)? Does identification also stimulate appreciation? And does the reader's appreciation of a metaphor involve some kind of check with the presumed intentions of the author? This kind of coherence in metaphor processing seems quite plausible and deserves further investigation. Such research would have to go into the relation between metaphor processing strategies *per metaphor*, going beyond the crude correlational measure employed here, which has only dealt with totals.

6.5 Additional analyses: textual interest and reader performance in thinking out loud

6.5.1 Introduction

Thinking out loud performance is partly determined by the text. The use of two different texts in the main experiment raises the question whether they are comparable as to their respective degrees of interest for processing and hence verbalization. Irrespective of the texts' contextual function as literature or journalism, one could merely turn out to be more interesting than the other. This might have affected thinking out loud performance in a fashion that has nothing to do with the difference between literary and non-literary reception. A higher textual interest could have stimulated thinking-out-loud performance which in turn could have had repercussions on the incidence of metaphor processes. It was therefore necessary to perform an independent assessment of the degree of interest of the two experimental texts and to relate this to the subjects' verbalizations about the texts during thinking out loud. This affords some helpful insight into the role of the text apart from its function in context.

As I used a sentence-by-sentence reading task in the main experiment, what we are talking about is the degree of interest of every individual stimulus sentence with a view to its potential effect upon thinking out loud. The interest of sentences can be estimated by independent judges. Sentences with an estimated high degree of interest could be expected to receive a more elaborate reaction from subjects who are thinking out loud than sentences with an estimated low degree of interest. This degree of local textual interest can be directly related to thinking out loud performance by the subjects in terms of the number of words they used: there should be a positive relation between estimated level of interest in the stimulus materials and number of words in the think-aloud responses. This comparison provides us with a measure of the relation between the *local* effect a text is *expected* to exert on readers on the one hand and the local reactions to that text *produced* by readers during thinking out loud on the other. The two reading conditions can be usefully compared on this score in order to determine the validity of the think aloud data about metaphor processing.

The estimates of local interest may also be summed and averaged to provide us with an indication of the *average* comparability of the two texts regarding interest. These data can then be related to the averaged number of words which subjects spent on the sentences of the two texts for the same purpose. The reason for this additional examination is the fact that a similar *correlation* between *local* interest and thinking-out-loud performance in literary and journalistic reading does not guarantee that the *absolute* magnitude of the relation is the same for both reading conditions. Readers may spend more or less words on more or less interesting sentences in both reading conditions, thus producing comparable correlations between interest and think aloud performance for the two texts, but the absolute number of words per verbalization could still on average be higher in one reading condition than in the other. Therefore both the local relation between sentences and responses as well as the overall means of these data will have to be compared in order to determine whether textual interest and thinking out loud performance correspond in the same manner in the literary and journalistic reading conditions.

The questions to be answered in the present section are therefore:

1. Is there a difference between the two experimental texts regarding estimated degree of interest?
2. Is there a relation between the estimated degree of interest of the two experimental texts on the one hand, and the observed degree of interest exhibited by the think aloud test subjects on the other?

6.5.2 Method

Subjects, procedure, and *materials* of the thinking-out-loud study are as in section 6.2 above. What remains to be reported here is the independent assessment of textual interest of the experimental texts.

The textual interest of the two texts was estimated in a small rating task. Interest was measured in terms of (i) the degree of attention demanded by a particular sentence and (ii) its arousal potential for continuation of the reading process. 'Attention' (i) is taken to reflect interest in a general manner at the level of sentence-processing itself: sentence length, sentence complexity, and sentence meaning can be seen as contributing to the operationalization of interest by means of attention. 'Continuation' (ii) is an operationalization focusing on the integration of a current sentence into the overall text representation. Attention and continuation are intended to be two relatively unrelated measures of degree of interest: one may need a high degree of attention for a sentence in a text independent of one's motivation to continue or stop reading.

This independence can be usefully checked by means of a crude analytic measure of degree of interest of the stimuli in terms of number of words in every sentence. I expected a positive relation between the assessed degree of attention demanded by every sentence on the one hand and the number of words in the sentences on the other, for attention is partly determined by the sheer amount of information expressed by a sentence. By contrast, the measure of 'continuation' did not have to be related to the number of words in the stimulus sentence at all: the motivation to read on does not depend on the amount of information but on the content of the sentence in question and on its function in the text.

The method of data collection for the interest measures of 'attention' and 'continuation' involved the application of sentence-by-sentence rating scales. The two experimental texts were offered as two series of separate sentences, each new sentence appearing in isolation on a separate page. Judges had to answer two questions about every sentence by filling in the two seven-point scales: (i) How much attention does the sentence demand of the reader? (ii) How insistently does the current sentence invite the reader to continue reading? The test was offered as two separate parts, one for each text, in counterbalanced order. Raters were informed that the aim of data collection was an assessment of the variation in the stimulus materials regarding estimated degree of 'attention' and 'continuation' for every sentence. They were also informed of the purpose of the stimulus materials, that they were to be used in a think aloud reading experiment. Rating took place individually. Academic staff of the Department of Psychology at the Free University Amsterdam (N = 6) acted as raters. Reliability of the mean scores 'attention' and 'continuation' was satisfactory.[5]

For each text, the resulting mean scores of every sentence on the two rating scales of 'attention' and 'continuation' were related to the analytic data of 'number of words per sentence', and are shown in Table 6.3. It can be observed that there is no difference between the two texts regarding the overall patterns of the correlations. As expected, rated degree of attention demanded by every sentence is closely associated with its respective number of words. Moreover, it is also true that the measure of 'continuation' is not related to either number of words or to 'attention'. Thus, 'attention' and 'continuation' provide us with two independent measures of the expected performance during thinking out loud.

Next, mean scores of the two scales were calculated for the two texts in order to compare their averaged degrees of interest. This was done by averaging the mean rating scores across sentences for each text. The mean overall interest scores of 'attention' and 'continuation' for the literary and journalistic text are presented in Table 6.4. Statistical analysis of these means showed that these differences were not significant: the two texts are entirely comparable as to their degree of demanded overall attention and their role in urging the reader to continue reading.[6]

6.5.3 Results

We now have to address the question whether each of the text's *estimated* degree of necessary attention and urge to read on, as measured in the

Table 6.3: Relation between sentence length and estimations of required attention and urge for continuation in sentences of two texts

(a) Literary text

	Number of words	Attention	Continuation
Number of words	1.00		
Attention	0.92**	1.00	
Continuation	− 0.12	− 0.04	1.00

(b) Journalistic text

	Number of words	Attention	Continuation
Number of words	1.00		
Attention	0.68**	1.00	
Continuation	0.21	0.23	1.00

One-tailed significance: ** p < 0.01

Table 6.4: Mean scores for rating scales 'attention' and 'continuation' for two texts (standard deviations in brackets)

Rating scale	Text	
	Literary	Journalistic
Attention	3.33 (1.12)	3.41 (0.68)
Continuation	4.44 (0.78)	4.71 (0.83)

'attention' and 'continuation' scales discussed above, was reflected in the *observed* sentence-by-sentence thinking out loud data. The prediction was that the average number of words per stimulus sentence in the think aloud protocols was positively related to the analytic measure of 'number of words per stimulus sentence' and to the rating scale of 'attention', but not related to the scale of 'continuation'. To test this prediction, the number of words in the think aloud verbalizations about each sentence were averaged across subjects in both groups. Correlational analysis of these data for both groups of readers and both texts shows that the expectations were confirmed (Table 6.5).

We can conclude that the expected degree of attention as established by the rating test relates closely to the actual degree of attention measured in number of words produced by readers during text processing while thinking out loud. By contrast, the expected urge to read on as established by the rating test was not related to the number of words produced by the test subjects. More important, however, is the observation that there was no difference between the two reading conditions in this regard, indicating

Table 6.5: Sentence-by-sentence correlations between estimates of interest and number of words in thinking out loud verbalizations of two groups of academics, divided by text

(a) Literary text

	Estimates of interest		
Number of words in thinking out loud verbalizations	Number of words	Attention	Continuation
Experts	0.75**	0.80**	− 0.20
Controls	0.82**	0.85**	− 0.09

(b) Journalistic text

	Estimates of interest		
Number of words in thinking out loud verbalizations	Number of words	Attention	Continuation
Experts	0.60**	0.67**	− 0.16
Controls	0.50**	0.41*	− 0.23

One-tailed significance: ** $p < 0.01$; * $p < 0.05$

Table 6.6: Mean response-stimulus ratios in thinking out loud by two groups of academics, divided by text (with standard deviations in brackets)

	Text	
Literary socialization	Literary	Journalistic
Experts	2.54 (1.77)	1.84 (1.19)
Controls	2.01 (1.09)	1.69 (0.89)

that general sentence-by-sentence performance in the think aloud task has not differentially affected the processes of understanding metaphor in the literary and the journalistic text. (The mean verbalization scores per sentence of both groups of readers were also related to each other in both conditions of reading.)[7]

I then calculated the average thinking out loud reaction score, relative to the total number of words in both texts: it consisted of the ratio between the total number of words in the thinking out loud reaction and the total number of words in each text. This is an index of the total interest invested by the subjects in the texts. Table 6.6 shows the average ratios between the number of words in response and stimulus, cross-classified by text and by group. The mean stimulus response ratios exhibit some conspicuous differences between the conditions: the literary condition manifests a higher average than the journalistic one, but within the literary condition, there is a considerable difference between the verbalizations of the experts and the controls. The significance of these differences was tested again by means of an analysis of variance.[8]

The results indicated that there was a significant main effect for the factor of reading condition. So the literary and the journalistic reading conditions did indeed appear to display different degrees of expressed interest, as operationalized by the ratio between number of words in the thinking-out-loud verbalizations and in the original textual stimulus. In thinking out loud about these two texts, the test subjects produced more response in the literary than in the non-literary textual condition.

There was no effect of the other main factor, literary socialization. The differences between the averaged ratios of the literary and the journalistic reading conditions were fortuitous. They do not indicate that literary socialization had an effect on the larger ratio observable for the group of experts. The experts and the controls can be regarded as fully comparable regarding their thinking out loud performance in terms of number of words.

There was no interaction effect either. The fairly large difference between the experts and the controls in the literary reading condition alone was not due to the effect of the factors of literary socialization or reading condition. The difference is explained by the effect of chance variation on sampling.

6.5.4 Discussion

From the significant sentence-by-sentence correlation it can be concluded that degree of local textual interest does exert an effect upon thinking out loud performance. For both groups of readers there is a positive relation between the number of words they spend on a particular sentence on the one hand, and the textual features of sentence length and rated degree of required attention on the other. Sentences with a high degree of estimated interest also receive comparatively extended verbal responses during thinking out loud. In this respect there is no difference between thinking out loud about the literary and the journalistic text.

In this light, the fact that the identical, average rated degree of interest of the two texts does go together with a difference in overall thinking-out-loud performance requires an explanation. Although comparative degree of interest itself is not irrelevant, as is shown by the local-level analysis, it is apparently still overruled by another factor which has produced the absolute difference between the literary and the journalistic texts in overall thinking out loud verbalizations. There are two possibilities, one of which is both more likely and more attractive. The first is the theoretical expectation that literary reading is more elaborative in that it triggers additional processing than non-literary reading. However, the alternative explanation is potentially damaging: the difference between the two reading conditions may have been caused by a variant of social desirability. When readers know that the researcher is from a department of literature, and that they are going to read a literary and a journalistic text, they may be more attentive and eager when thinking aloud about the literary text than when dealing with the non-literary text. Although this is not as likely an explanation as the first, it cannot be ruled out on *a priori* grounds.

However, the following considerations militate against this explanation. First, it would mean that an involving task such as thinking out loud is systematically affected by such a largely unconscious attitude as that of pleasing the researcher. On the presumption that most subjects would be willing to adopt such an attitude, they would be aiming at upgrading the literary part of the task at the expense of the journalistic part. With thirty-four adult academics who are used to explicating, reading, discussing, and evaluating different kinds of texts on the basis of well-developed personal critical standards, this does seem somewhat far-fetched. Moreover, I know of no such reports concerning researcher orientation by subjects in the literature on thinking out loud.

Second, it would also mean that those readers who had received the literary text second would have intentionally held back somewhat during the first part of their session and could have controlled the number of words spent on the second text sufficiently to produce this significant difference. This, too, is implausible, because it requires the subject to control the production of, on average, 1,300 as opposed to 1,100 words when thinking out loud about the literary and the journalistic text. With a highly involving task such as thinking out loud, this would mean presuming an intentional and successful control strategy on the part of the subjects regarding their quantity of expression.

Moreover, there is an important positive point which tilts the balance in favour of the literary elaboration explanation. In quite a few post-process interviews, subjects stated that the difference between literary and journalistic reading was precisely one of attention for language. Indeed, forcing people to read a text sentence-by-sentence was unproblematic in the literary reading condition, whereas in the journalistic reading condition some subjects commented upon the unnatural feeling they had during their thinking out loud. From that angle, the lack of a relation between textual interest and reading behaviour may be an understandable result, because it is overruled by the factor of adopting different attitudes of reading. Thus, even if the sentences of the journalistic text may on average be just as interesting as those of the literary text when judgements are requested by raters concerning the amount of attention it demands and the degree to which it invites the reader to continue, readers in thinking out loud still expect to deal with journalism somewhat more superficially than with literature. What is more, this expectation was observed to be uttered occasionally by the subjects during thinking out loud itself as well as afterwards in the post-process interview. Hence the validity of the difference between the two reading conditions does not seem in danger.

6.6 Conclusion

Let us briefly review the issues raised in this chapter. First, it was found that metaphors are indeed accorded more attention in literary reading than in journalistic reading. This is a confirmation of our hypothesis. The role of all five processes of focus processing, context construction, explicit identification, explicit appreciation, and refunctionalization was evident. This finding is probably related to a more general result concerning literary text processing, for it turned out that the overall degree of interest invested in the literary text was greater than the degree of interest manifested for the journalistic text. This more elaborate processing of the literary text took place in spite of the fact that the literary text was not deemed more interesting by a group of independent raters. The higher incidence of metaphor processing in the literary condition thus corresponded with a larger amount of verbalization in the literary reading condition in general.

The relation between these two findings can be interpreted in three ways. First, the greater attention to metaphors in literary reading may also have boosted the overall number of words spent on the literary text as a whole. Second, an overall increased attention to the literary text may also have raised the number of metaphors processed in more elaborate ways. And third, there may simply be a correlational relation between the two findings, both relating to a generally elaborative nature of the literary reception process. All of these possibilities are plausible.

The results may be interpreted with reference to a greater degree of elaboration in literary reading, but this raises more questions than it answers. The most pressing points are: How does such presumed greater elaboration relate to differences between the texts? Would it be caused by deeper processing of the same number of textual aspects, or would it be based on a consideration of a greater number of aspects of the text than in non-literary reading? Can it be explained as the addition of extra processing to ordinary, non-literary reading processes? These issues need to be investigated in future research.

By contrast, there was no relation between literary metaphor processing and the difference between the two groups of readers. The expectation that the literary experts would use metaphor processing strategies in literature more often than the anthropologists serving as controls was not confirmed. There is another aspect which indicates the lack of any overall large difference between the groups of readers used in this study. This is the fact that in the thinking out loud experiment there was no difference between the literary experts and the anthropologists regarding their quantity of verbalization. Both groups used a roughly equal total number of words in the two reading conditions, and both groups verbalized more extensively in the literary than in the journalistic reading condition. The explanation for this unexpected finding may lie in the length and nature of the materials, the operationalization of literary socialization, or the size of the groups. The alternative explanation is that the hypothesis was wrong.

If these are the most important empirical findings of the present study, it is now time to add one more prospect for the future. For it is to be hoped that the above effects will be confirmed when other metaphor processing categories are included which have had to be provisionally left out of consideration in this study. The processes of vehicle construction, metaphor construction, and functionalization each provide further opportunity for the reader to display subjective and polyvalent processing in literary reception. They are expected to occur more frequently in literary than in non-literary reading. Improvement of encoding instructions and achievement of satisfactory interrater agreement in this area is one of the first priorities for further research. They are a precondition for a further analysis of these processes in terms of subjectivity and polyvalence.

Notes

1. I examined the distribution of the ratio between average number of words per thinking out loud verbalization and average number of words of sentences in the stimulus texts and found three bivariate outliers among the literary experts. These subjects verbalized much more extensively than the other subjects, tending more towards analysis than towards reading in comparison with the other readers. This went against the instructions, and so their data were excluded from further examination. This is discussed further in section 6.5.
2. Both samples for second coding were selected evenly from the two groups of readers, and were distributed throughout the range of length of verbalizations. I used a relatively strict measure of reliability, which takes into account the role of chance in obtaining fortuitously identical results between two analysts, Cohen's Kappa. Its reliability coefficient was sufficient for six of the ten categories:

problem identification (0.80), focus processing (0.52), context construction (0.50), explicit identification (0.71), explicit appreciation (0.69), and refunctionalization (0.55). Note that these are not correlation co-efficients.

3. Adjustment of α to 0.01 was undertaken for each of the five tests in order to retain an experimentwise α of 0.05.

4. Screening for within-cell univariate and multivariate outliers revealed one univariate outlier for the variable of focus construction in the journalistic condition. Following the advice of Tabachnik and Fidell (1989: 70), the influence of this case was reduced by changing its z-score from 3.71 to 3.05. There were no multivariate outliers at $\alpha = 0.001$.

Each of the dependent variables of focus processing, context construction, identification, appreciation, and refunctionalization was tested in a separate analysis of variance. Each of the analyses was performed twice: once treating subjects as a random factor while collapsing over materials (F1, see Table VIA), and once treating materials as a random factor while collapsing over subjects (F2, see Table VIB). Independent variables were literary socialization (experts vs. controls), serving as a between factor in the subject or F1 analyses and as a within factor in the item or F2 analyses; and reading condition (literary vs. journalistic) serving as a within factor in the subject or F1 analyses and as a between factor in the item or F2 analyses. The combined treatment of subjects and materials as random factors yields minF', and is reported in Table VIC.

5. Crohnbach's α was 0.98 for attention and 0.91 for continuation (the judges were used as items).

6. The difference between the degrees of interest of the two texts was investigated by means of a profile analysis with the between-factor 'text' with the levels 'literary' and 'non-literary' as the independent variable and the within-factor 'scale' with the levels 'attention' and 'continuation' as the dependent variable. Using the criterion of Wilks, there was no effect for text (approximate $F_{[2,52]} = 0.75$, $p > 0.05$): the literary and the journalistic texts display an identical degree of interest as operationalized by the two scales. There was no difference between the application of the two scales to the two texts either ('difference' $F_{[1,53]} = 0.31$, $p > 0.05$; 'average' $F_{[1,53]} = 1.01$, $p > 0.05$). This suggests that neither of the two scales was specially geared to measuring one text or the other.

7. For the literary text, $r = 0.84$, $p < 0.001$; for the journalistic text, $r = 0.73$, $p < 0.001$.

8. Prior to analysis, the ratio between average number of words per thinking-out-loud verbalization and average number of words of sentences in the stimulus text was examined for the suitability of multivariate analysis. Three bivariate outliers were found among the literary experts, which were excluded from further examination (see section 6.3 above). There was one remaining univariate outlier, representing an expert subject who talked relatively much in the journalistic reading condition. Because of the validity of her literary data, and because the excess in the journalistic condition did not seem highly disturbing, I adopted the following strategy: I performed the ensuing analysis both with and without the data of this subject, and found that there was no difference between the results of the two tests. Therefore I retained the subject in the group of experts, and will

Table VIA: Effects of reading condition and literary socialization on metaphor processing, with subjects as a random effect

(i) Focus processing

	Source of variation	SS	d.f.	MS	F
Between subjects	LIT. SOCIALIZATION	0.05	1	0.05	1.80
	WITHIN CELLS	0.85	32	0.03	
Within subjects	READING CONDITION	0.09	1	0.09	13.44*
	LITSOC BY READING	0.00	1	0.00	0.01
	WITHIN CELLS	0.22	32	0.01	

(ii) Context construction

	Source of variation	SS	d.f.	MS	F
Between subjects	LIT. SOCIALIZATION	0.05	1	0.05	3.74
	WITHIN CELLS	0.42	32	0.01	
Within subjects	READING CONDITION	0.07	1	0.07	13.63*
	LITSOC BY READING	0.00	1	0.00	0.00
	WITHIN CELLS	0.17	32	0.01	

(iii) Explicit identification

	Source of variation	SS	d.f.	MS	F
Between subjects	LIT. SOCIALIZATION	0.07	1	0.07	5.38!
	WITHIN CELLS	0.44	32	0.01	
Within subjects	READING CONDITION	0.14	1	0.14	34.28*
	LITSOC BY READING	0.00	1	0.00	0.00
	WITHIN CELLS	0.13	32	0.00	

(iv) Explicit appreciation

	Source of variation	SS	d.f.	MS	F
Between subjects	LIT. SOCIALIZATION	0.00	1	0.00	0.29
	WITHIN CELLS	0.43	32	0.01	
Within subjects	READING CONDITION	0.11	1	0.11	9.52*
	LITSOC BY READING	0.01	1	0.01	0.54
	WITHIN CELLS	0.39	32	0.01	

(v) Refunctionalization

	Source of variation	SS	d.f.	MS	F
Between subjects	LIT. SOCIALIZATION	0.02	1	0.02	2.85
	WITHIN CELLS	0.20	32	0.01	
Within subjects	READING CONDITION	0.03	1	0.03	9.29*
	LITSOC BY READING	0.00	1	0.00	0.81
	WITHIN CELLS	0.10	32	0.00	

$\alpha = 0.01$; $^*p < 0.01$; $!p < 0.05$

Table VIB: Effects of reading conditions and literary socialization on metaphor processing, with metaphors as a random effect

(i) Focus processing

	Source of variation	SS	d.f.	MS	F
Between items	READING CONDITION	0.21	1	0.21	11.18!
	WITHIN CELLS	0.98	51	0.02	
Within items	LIT. SOCIALIZATION	0.12	1	0.12	22.94*
	READING BY LITSOC	0.00	1	0.00	0.00
	WITHIN CELLS	0.26	51	0.01	

(ii) Context construction

	Source of variation	SS	d.f.	MS	F
Between items	READING CONDITION	0.05	1	0.05	1.96
	WITHIN CELLS	1.22	51	0.02	
Within items	LIT. SOCIALIZATION	0.03	1	0.03	6.42!
	READING BY LITSOC	0.00	1	0.00	0.95
	WITHIN CELLS	0.22	51	0.00	

(iii) Explicit identification

	Source of variation	SS	d.f.	MS	F
Between items	READING CONDITION	0.11	1	0.11	6.32!
	WITHIN CELLS	0.91	51	0.02	
Within items	LIT. SOCIALIZATION	0.08	1	0.08	17.95*
	READING BY LITSOC	0.00	1	0.00	0.00
	WITHIN CELLS	0.22	51	0.00	

(iv) Explicit appreciation

	Source of variation	SS	d.f.	MS	F
Between items	READING CONDITION	0.18	1	0.18	4.67!
	WITHIN CELLS	1.95	51	0.04	
Within items	LIT. SOCIALIZATION	0.01	1	0.01	0.90
	READING BY LITSOC	0.01	1	0.01	1.50
	WITHIN CELLS	0.34	51	0.01	

(v) Refunctionalization

	Source of variation	SS	d.f.	MS	F
Between items	READING CONDITION	0.13	1	0.13	4.77!
	WITHIN CELLS	1.38	51	0.03	
Within items	LIT. SOCIALIZATION	0.09	1	0.09	12.56!
	READING BY LITSOC	0.00	1	0.00	0.12
	WITHIN CELLS	0.35	51	0.01	

$\alpha = 0.01$; $*p < 0.01$; $!p < 0.05$

Table VIC: Effect of reading conditions and literary socialization on metaphor processing, with subjects and metaphors as random effects

	Effect			
Process	Reading condition		Literary socialization	
	minF'	d.f.	minF'	d.f.
Focus processing	6.10*	1/81	1.67	1/37
Context construction	1.71	1/65	2.36	1/66
Explicit identification	5.34*	1/68	4.14	1/51
Explicit appreciation	3.13	1/82	—	—
Refunctionalization	3.15	1/82	2.32	1/47

$\alpha = 0.01$; *$p < 0.05$

Table VID: Effect of literary socialization and reading conditions on relative number of words used during thinking out loud

	Source of variation	SS	d.f.	MS	F
Between subjects	LIT. SOCIALIZATION	1.93	1	1.93	0.67
	WITHIN CELLS	92.53	32	2.89	
Within subjects	READING CONDITION	4.45	1	4.45	15.94**
	LITSOC BY READING	0.64	1	0.65	2.30
	WITHIN CELLS	8.93	32	0.28	

**$p < 0.01$

report the analysis including the data of this subject.

I investigated whether the two reading conditions differed regarding relative number of words in the thinking-out-loud verbalizations by performing a 2 × 2 analysis of variance with the within-factor reading condition with the levels 'literary' and 'journalistic' and the between-factor group with the levels 'experts' and 'controls' as the independent variables (Table VI D).

PART THREE
Properties

CHAPTER SEVEN

Dimensions of metaphor

In the previous chapters I discussed understanding metaphor in literature in terms of the on-going mental activities of the reader. I have shown how the specifically literary aspect of processing metaphor during literary reception can be explained by a discourse context which affects the social status of text and reader. Discourse contexts are an abstraction of social regularities demarcating one domain of discourse from another. They are operative in reading when text, reader, or situation are marked for their literary, journalistic, or whatever nature, triggering a mental representation of a discourse-typical context on the part of the reader. When a reader does perceive the discourse context as literary, then the various and partial mental representations of the text arising during reading are systematically influenced by this initial representation of the context as literary. This approach is supported by the evidence on general literary reception and on the understanding of metaphors in literature.

An explanation of the literary nature of the results of the reception process is usually given in terms of the reader and his or her activation of particular reading strategies, and I have developed this approach in some detail in Part Two. However, this is only half the story. Not all metaphors are equal, and it may be expected that differences between metaphors themselves have an observable effect on the reading process. For instance, some metaphors are more difficult than others and may be expected to promote more extensive focus processing. Others may be more imageable than others and perhaps stimulate vehicle construction. Still other metaphors are so worn-out that they may not trigger special attention at all. All of these differences between metaphors will have to be included in our general view of understanding metaphor in literature.

Moreover, metaphors in literature may be different from metaphors in other types of discourse. This is a common assumption among literary critics. If such a difference is corroborated by empirical research, it can be explained by the effect of context on the factor of the text during its production. Authors design their texts to achieve literary discourse, and metaphors may be an important means by which they are successful. However, at this time it still is an open question to what extent the common view that literary metaphors differ from non-literary metaphors can be sustained by empirical observation. What evidence there is available from empirical studies in psychology is conflicting. There is a study by Gentner (1982) which suggests that literary metaphors do differ from scientific metaphors, but there is another series of studies that concludes that there is no difference between constructed and poetic metaphors (Marschark et al. 1983; Katz et al. 1985; Katz et al. 1988).

This chapter is the first of a triad exploring metaphor as a textual entity. It will address the nature of metaphor in literature from the point of view of the cognitive discourse approach developed in the previous two parts of the book. Chapter 8 will then continue with an empirical investigation of literary metaphor. Two studies will be presented which were designed to test implications of the views of metaphor in literature developed in the present chapter. Finally, Chapter 9 will loop back to the processing data collected in the first two parts of this book, and investigate whether they can also be explained by analysing the effect of various dimensions of metaphors revealed in Chapter 8. Different kinds and incidences of metaphor processing in literary reception such as those found in the previous chapter need not only be due to different discourse-related strategies of reading. They may also be explicable with reference to any typical differences that may be found between literary and non-literary metaphors. Chapter 9 will hence bring back together again the factors of metaphor as a textual entity and the reader as a text processing agent.

7.1 Metaphors and types of discourse

The common parlance of 'literary metaphor' and 'poetic metaphor' suggests that there is a particular kind of metaphor which may be identified as literary or poetic. The phrases often involve an attitude about metaphor which attributes a set of properties to a particular class of metaphors leading to the identification of this class as literary in a unique fashion. For want of a better term, I will call this the essentialist view of literary metaphor.

I do not use the phrase 'literary metaphor' in this way. When I speak of 'literary metaphor', it is a shorthand alternative expression for the neutral and contingent 'metaphor in literature'. The advantage of 'metaphor in literature' is that it is clear in scope. It refers to metaphors in literary texts, but not to metaphors in other kinds of texts. By contrast, the essentialist use of 'literary metaphor' can also apply to metaphors outside the domain of literary discourse (for examples, see Fernandez 1991b; Friedrich 1991). However, if one sees literature as a social construct, as I do, then it is inconsistent to use 'literary' as a predicate for phenomena, like metaphors, outside the social domain of literary discourse. Those metaphors may resemble the metaphors often found in literature, but that does not make them literary. They may trigger typically literary processing operations such as vehicle construction, but that does not make them literary either. They are just non-literary metaphors manifesting interesting properties and triggering unusual processes. The interest of these properties and processes can be described by relating them to the domain of literary discourse, and readers may even experience these features in this manner, but this still can be accounted for in terms of resemblance, and does not require the postulation of a set of literary metaphors occurring outside literature.

There are many ideas about the characteristic features of metaphors in literature, leading to the postulation of a category of 'literary metaphor', but they have never been subjected to systematic empirical testing. Therefore, the definition of literary metaphor as a particular kind of metaphor would be a premature exercise. Instead of setting out from such an *a priori* definition of the nature of literary metaphor, it has to be the target for research. Only when the typical properties of metaphors in literature have been determined by comparing them with metaphors in other types of discourse, can we summarize these findings by setting up one (or more) stereotypical models for metaphors in literature. These may be designated as 'literary metaphors', but that does not change the fact that we are talking about an average based on the properties of metaphors occurring in literary texts. Only then will it be possible, should one wish to do so, to use another shorthand form of speaking by identifying a metaphor outside literature as 'literary', meaning that it displays the properties that are typically manifested by metaphors in literature. But I prefer the more precise manner of speaking which simply lists the relevant metaphor properties in themselves, while noting that they are more typical of metaphors in literature than of metaphors in other kinds of discourse.

The presumption that metaphors in literature differ from metaphors in other kinds of discourse can be motivated in a cognitive discourse theory of metaphor in literature by having recourse to the process of production. Producers of literary texts design their texts in such a way that they facilitate literary experiences. As suggested in Chapter 2, literary texts highlight the experience of subjectivity, and manifest a prominent construction of fictions, polyvalent meanings, and attention to form and style. By contrast, the design of non-literary texts is assumed to be directed at intersubjectivity, stimulating the construction of connections with the factual world, monovalence, and attention to content. As I have argued before, authors' uses of metaphors may vary according to these general designs. Some metaphors may be excellent means for the triggering of literary experiences as defined above, while other metaphors can stimulate non-literary reading experiences. This motivates the expectation that there are diverging typical properties for literary and non-literary metaphors.

However, it is improbable that all metaphors are used by their authors with this contextual design in mind. As pointed out in Chapter 1, many metaphors are part of our common language and conceptual apparatus, and these metaphors can be used in literary and non-literary text production alike. Moreover, not every aspect of text production is directed at the triggering of typically literary or non-literary reading experiences. Although readers may realize many parts of a text as typically literary, we have no certainty that they were designed as such. In other words, there will be many a passage in literary and non-literary texts which does not have to be in line with the tendencies typically expected of such texts on the basis of the discourse context.

It is not clear how these more or less neutral passages and metaphors affect the overall difference between the average nature of literary and non-literary metaphors. Perhaps the average differences do not lie very far apart, and only a handful of metaphors may be responsible for the attribution of a typically literary nature to 'the' metaphors of a text. These aspects have to be disentangled carefully in order to develop a detailed and sophisticated view of the role of differences between metaphors in the process of understanding metaphor in literature.

7.2 The role of the text

The recent concentration in literary studies on understanding processes has been the cause of some confusion when it comes to incorporating the role of the text in the empirical study of literary reading. Indeed, one of the main advocates of an empirical study of literature, Siegfried Schmidt, has called the text 'a pragmatic fiction' (Schmidt 1985: 14), because the text does not exist apart from its concrete realization by a particular individual, be this individual a reader or a writer. And the proponent of another contextualist approach, Roger Sell, has called the study of the text 'introspective' as opposed to empirical in a critical passage on my own proposal for empirical research on metaphor processing in literature:

Turning things round the other way for a moment, even an out-and-out empiricist must presumably devote introspective study to his chosen texts. How else can he set up his hypothesis for empirical investigation or locate those features whose reception he wishes to test – metaphors, in Steen's case? (Sell 1991: *xvii*)

Schmidt and Sell are two examples of a more general attitude in literary studies, in which the text has become such a flexible object that it cannot be approached as standing on its own, but needs the intermediary of a text processing subject. As a result, the study of the text is judged to be subject-bound or introspective. On this view, then, the text only exists as realized text, and only the realization of a text by a reader, critic, or analyst is accorded a reality of its own.

It should be noted that there are two highly damaging implications of this position, and they are equally characteristic of some modern attitudes in literary studies. First, the text itself cannot act as a corrective when diverging realizations are compared, for no representation of 'the text itself' is accepted as such. There are only more or less authoritative 'readings'. But according to the logic of the text as realized text, the ground for deciding which of these readings is more authoritative than another also has to lie in people rather than texts, for instance in the interpretative community (Fish 1980). I do not accept this extremely reader-oriented view of reading.

Another consequence is that the meta-texts which text processing subjects such as readers, critics, and analysts produce about an original text are in the same plight as their stimulus texts. For meta-texts are themselves texts. So they cannot be taken on their own accord either. They will also have to be processed by other readers, critics, or analysts. This leads to an infinite regress. Note that this latter line of reasoning also constitutes an argument often used in anti-empirical circles to prove that literary studies cannot be empirical but is necessarily hermeneutic or interpretative.

This devaluation of the text as an autonomous phenomenon is a mistake in my view. The fact that critics disagree about aspects of interpretation does not mean that texts cannot be analysed or described by themselves. Texts are objective phenomena displaying particular linguistic and textual structures, and they can be dealt with scientifically just as well or badly as other structured objects in the world. The fact that one has access to texts only by means of human processing does not make text analysis any different from the analysis of other phenomena which we perceive through the senses. This is an epistemological situation which holds for many if not most objects of scientific research. The structures scientists attribute to their objects of investigation are always partly dependent on their own sensory apparatus. True, some of the lack of consensus on the nature of particular structures may be due to this partial subject-dependence, but in good science this will be recognized as such, and attempts will be made to remove as efficiently as possible the disturbing influence of the human observer upon the structures observed. In the social sciences, when the object of investigation is a text this is done by means of so-called content analysis (Van Assche 1991).

Critical disagreement in literary studies is not explained by the fact that one has to process the language of a text in order to have a representation of it. There are many statements one can make about the structures of a text which are perfectly acceptable to every text analyst endorsing whichever creed. Instead, critical disagreement is due to the different uses made of these available structures by various critics. Critics attempt to impose additional and more comprehensive and interesting structure by offering interpretations on the basis of the intersubjectively describable structure of the text. Their debates cannot be regarded as evidence for the idea that texts cannot be investigated as things by themselves. On the contrary, they show that partial reference is inevitably made to some norm for arbitration, namely (aspects of) the text. The best illustration of this state of affairs is the critical debate engendered by Roman Jakobson and Claude Lévi-Strauss's analysis of Baudelaire's 'Les chats' (see Fokkema and Kunne-Ibsch 1977: 71–80).

Literary criticism is a meeting place of textual structures and reader expectations and operations. The critic and the text are 'set' towards literary experiences, both of these factors contributing to text processing with much greater weight in literary criticism than in 'normal' literary reading (see Chapters 2 and 3). But this assessment also suggests that the structures of the text can, and indeed must, be accounted for in an empirical manner. From a methodological standpoint, when an object consists of several factors (in the present case a text and a reader in a particular context) then it is imperative that we acquire independent descriptions of each of the factors in order to determine how they interact when making up the phenomenon under study, literary reading. An empirical study of the text and its metaphors are essential ingredients to any study of metaphor processing during reading.

The point about literary criticism is that it does not aim at such a methodologically valid description of the object of the text (compare Verdaasdonk and Van Rees 1992). It is a cultural practice which presupposes the text as text, and continues from there by making it more interesting, tangible, teachable, and so on in contemporary culture. There is nothing wrong with this practice; on the contrary, it is highly valuable. However, it is not an attempt at a scientific description of the text, nor an attempt at a scientific explication of the role of the text in the process of reading. The often observed failure of critics to reach agreement about properties of the text therefore has no bearing on the possibility of empirical text study, which has different aims. Its goal is intersubjective testability regarding the nature of aspects of the structure of the text.

Scientific text study can proceed in two ways. First, it can apply the analytic instruments of a particular discipline to unravel the text. Linguistics, text-linguistics, rhetoric, stylistics, and discourse analysis are the disciplines most often used in this connection. To ensure the reliability of such analyses, the ideal procedure would be to have two analysts investigating the same text and compare their results. As this procedure is not common practice in linguistics and literary studies, analysis often seems less trustworthy than it could be.

The second procedure is to collect judgements from independent subjects on particular aspects of a text. These data do not constitute an analysis of the text, but instead provide an empirically founded view of particular text properties. I will examine differences between metaphors in literary and non-literary texts in this way in the next chapter. Once one has collected such reliable data about metaphors as textual entities, the effect of metaphors upon text processing can also be determined without difficulty. Even if metaphor processing is influenced by different strategies of reading the activation of which is dependent upon the reader and his or her view of the context, metaphor processing may be affected simultaneously by differences between metaphors of various kinds. The interaction between these two factors of reader activity and text properties constitutes the most complex and interesting aspect of research in literary reception.

7 . 3   Dimensions of metaphor

I will now extend my general cognitive discourse approach to literary reading to include the factor of the text. In Chapter 4, I proposed a distinction between various aspects of text processing which was based on a global task analysis of reading. I divided the reading process into three basic aspects, namely decoding, conceptualization, and communication. Each of these aspects is related to the construction of a different mental representation of the text: linguistic, conceptual, and intentional models. I also accounted for the encompassing factor of context, which does not give rise to a mental model of its own: context systematically influences the nature of the other mental models constructed during reception. For literary reception, I claimed that the most important context-induced differences will reside in the relatively frequent construction of subjective, fictional, polyvalent, and form-oriented representations of the text. All of this turned out to be applicable to the micro-level of metaphor processing as well as to the global level of literary text processing.

How can this general approach be applied to the empirical study of the other important factor, the text? The fact that the reader's mental activities give rise to three distinguishable kinds of mental models may be taken as the starting point for the suggestion that texts can also be studied in relation to these three aspects of processing. After all, texts themselves are the product of another kind of mental activity, their production by the writer. It is consistent to assume that the writer was busy encoding, conceptualizing, and communicating during production just as much as the reader during reception. Just as these reception processes are reflected in think aloud protocols, so these production processes can be reflected in the structure of the text. Therefore I propose to regard the empirical study of texts as the search for the linguistic, conceptual, and communicative properties of the text. They are due to its underlying linguistic, conceptual, and communicative structure. Textual properties can hence be revealed by a description of the meaning of the text, the situation it refers to, and the signification of both meaning and reference.

This is not the place to develop this proposal into a full-blown discussion of the possibilities and problems for text study of this kind. Nor will I compare these ideas to other, similar divisions in linguistics and discourse analysis. Such a discussion would distract us from the main topic of interest, metaphors in literary texts. I will only say here that the proof of the pudding is in the eating, and that the application of this approach to such a salient aspect of texts as metaphors will have to show that it is a feasible method which deserves further development.

The rationale behind my approach to a study of properties of metaphors as textual entities is the same as that outlined above. When readers process metaphors, they are able to construct at least three different kinds of mental representations: a linguistic representation of the meaning of the metaphor, a conceptual representation of its referential content, and a communicative representation of the message it is attempting to convey. I believe that each of these aspects of metaphor processing is affected by the particular structure of the metaphor as a textual entity. This entails that I will have to assume that metaphors differ according to their linguistic, conceptual, and communicative properties, and gives rise to the questions: How can these properties be identified? How do they relate to each other? How can they affect processing? These questions will concern us for most of this chapter.

A further issue is the role of context. We have seen that metaphor processing takes place in specific discourse contexts such as literature or journalism, which influence the construction of the varying mental representations of the metaphor's linguistic meaning, conceptual content, and communicative purport. We have also noted that metaphors in a text are the result of a production stage in which authors may have constructed them in varying manners in order to achieve literary or non-literary effects in discourse. Therefore the various metaphor properties which are related to linguistic meaning, conceptual content, and communicative purport may display a specific distribution when it comes to comparing literary metaphors with non-literary metaphors. Although the dimensions of comparison are identical for all metaphors, their average value may exhibit different 'typical' characteristics for various types of discourse. For instance, literary metaphors may be more novel than journalistic metaphors. The question whether novelty relates to the dimension of linguistic form and meaning, the dimension of conceptual and referential content or both is an interesting one which will have to be addressed in empirical work (see section 2.3 in Chapter 2).

This approach also entails that I will not identify a distinct 'aesthetic' or 'literary' property of metaphors. My general discourse approach to literature and metaphor forbids such a solution, for I hold that the characteristics of 'aesthetic' and 'literary' are social composites. The basis of the aesthetic and the literary lies in distinctions between *social* domains of discourse, not in a separate *psychological* dimension for all discourse which would be comparable to linguistic form, conceptual content, and communicative function. Literary discourse is just one specific manifestation of all discourse, characterized by a specific combination of generally available discourse features. By implication, some metaphors are literary because they occur in literature, and they can be designated as typically literary when they exhibit a particular combination of discourse features, which can generally occur throughout all types of discourse. In other words, I am talking about literature and 'literary' metaphors in terms of a typical distribution of specific features of discourse; that is, we are dealing with relative frequencies.

The specific discourse features I am thinking of are of course the ones proposed in Chapter 2 as characteristic of literature: subjectivity, fictionality, polyvalence, and attention to form. Literary metaphors may be more emphatically fictional than non-literary metaphors, they may be subjective and polyvalent more often than other metaphors, and they may require more attention to their form than metaphors outside literature. Each of these features may contribute to the general difference between literary and non-literary metaphors, and a special literary or aesthetic dimension is not required.

There is one respect in which this issue will lead to a further elaboration of my general approach. The aspect of the 'literary' or the 'aesthetic' is sometimes regarded as a specific manifestation of a general, emotive, dimension of all discourse. We have hardly dealt with this dimension of discourse in previous chapters, but this does not mean it is not important. The emotive side of reading was at least partly included in the processing chapters by allowing for its appearance in explicit appreciation. But now we have to spend some time on its relation to metaphor. I do not wish to restrict the use of 'aesthetic' and 'literary' to an emotive phenomenon alone, because these terms serve much wider functions in terms of my general discourse theory of literature: 'literary' and 'aesthetic' discourse include both emotive and cognitive aspects of reading. This ordering implies that my basically cognitive model of text processing proposed in Chapter 4 has to be supplemented by an emotive side. For the moment I will therefore say that the construction of the various cognitive mental representations which constitutes the overall process of reading is accompanied by various emotive experiences, which may also exhibit typical properties between different domains of discourse.

The experience of beauty is probably one typical emotion in literary reception. However, its content and relation to other features of literary reception and literary texts is too complex to specify at present. Suffice it to say that metaphors may exhibit a particular emotive dimension, too, which can accommodate the typically literary experience of beauty.

There is a comparable way in which my general discourse approach will have to be extended. Our concentration on cognitive issues did not just leave the emotive side of metaphors relatively underdeveloped, but their moral purport as well. Schmidt's (1980) view of discourse as having a cognitive, emotive, and moral dimension provides a systematic basis for this extension (Schram and Steen 1992). Some metaphors can be judged as immoral, particularly when unfavourable comparisons are made about groups of people which can be taken as discriminatory. John Lennon's critical song title 'Woman is the nigger of the world' may serve as an example. I will not go into this issue any further here either, but simply wish to note that the moral properties of metaphors in texts also require a place in the system.[1]

I have discussed how empirical text study can aim for the description of the textual manifestation of metaphor in terms of its properties that are relevant for processing. I have distinguished between three cognitive properties, namely linguistic form and meaning, conceptual content, and communicative function and have added one emotive property, pertaining to the affect of textual entities, and one moral property, pertaining to their ethics. Each of these properties can be expected to vary systematically as a result of the influence of discourse context. For instance, literary texts and their components, including metaphors, are predicted to manifest more original linguistic and conceptual properties, and more beautiful emotive properties, than non-literary ones. I will now continue my exposition by discussing two psychological studies on differences between metaphors in order to show how they can be used for a further elaboration of the approach.

7.4 Metaphors in science and literature

In psychology, there are some studies on differences between metaphors which have a bearing on our subject. In a few cases, metaphor quality as such is equated with literary quality. Sternberg et al. (1979), for instance, speak of the 'aesthetic quality' of metaphors when they discuss the contribution of within-domain and between-domain distance to the aptness of metaphors (see also Tourangeau and Sternberg 1981; 1982). 'The participants, on the whole, preferred metaphors whose two subjects were drawn from distant domains and metaphors which confirmed their picture of the principal subject' (Tourangeau 1982). Gerrig and Healy (1983) distinguish between two kinds of metaphor goodness. The first has to do with ordinary communication: 'For on-line communication, a good metaphor is one that can be understood.' However, the second is connected with aesthetics: 'To appreciate a metaphor, in the literary sense, is to consider how elegantly the image evoked by the metaphor is coordinated with the segment of the real world it picks out.' In other cases, literary metaphors are part of the linguistic stimuli which have been used in experimental research. An example is McCabe (1984). She had metaphors, including literary ones, rated in and out of context for the degree of similarity between tenor and vehicle and overall quality. It turned out that the similarity between tenor and vehicle does not relate to rated metaphor quality in extended contexts, whereas it does in isolated sentences. McCabe concludes that metaphor research will have to take into account ratings of metaphors in context. Also important is the work by Katz et al. (see Marschark et al. 1983; Katz et al. 1985; Marschark and Hunt 1986; Katz et al. 1988). They present a series of no less than ten scales upon which literary and non-literary metaphors were rated to reveal their differences. At one place they suggest that these scales may go back to two underlying factors, one formal and one aesthetic (Katz et al. 1985). But in Katz et al. (1988), they seem to retreat from this position; I will return to their studies in the next section.

However, these studies do not present a theory of the specific, and perhaps special, nature of metaphor in literature. An important exception is formed by the structure-mapping approach of Gentner (1982; 1983). She presents a systematic, cognitive framework accounting for conceptual differences between literary and non-literary metaphors. In particular, Gentner has found that good literary metaphors seem to be typically richer than good scientific metaphors, which, by contrast, are typically clearer. She claims that the former are therefore usually understood as having an expressive function, whereas the latter will predominantly have an explanatory function. As these are matters of degree, this is a fruitful starting point for a further investigation of the conceptual structure and communicative function of metaphor in literature and in other types of discourse.

What is so attractive about Gentner's proposal is that it deals with almost all of the dimensions distinguished above. She does not quite label them in the way I have done, but most of the discourse dimensions I have distinguished in the previous pages recur in her discussion of differences between metaphors in science and literature. It is very encouraging to see the issues coming from the angle of a theory of reading also arising in Gentner's theory of knowledge representation and problem solving. The following discussion is not intended as a critique, but as a reformulation for my own purposes of Gentner's highly original contribution to the theory of metaphor.

The above-mentioned features of richness and clarity are two corner-stones of Gentner's conceptual theory of metaphor as analogical mapping. The knowledge domains involved in analogical mapping can be analysed as propositional networks, consisting of entities and relations holding between those entities.[2] Metaphor is characterized as a conceptual mapping which carries over only the relations holding between the entities, ignoring the inherent attributes pertaining to the entities. In Gentner's example, the hydrogen atom is like the solar system because the relations 'X attracts Y' and 'Y revolves around X' are mapped from the domain of solar systems to the domain of atoms, but the attributes of X, for instance that it is yellow and hot, are irrelevant. Metaphor and analogy are hence defined as a kind of conceptual structure mapping, because it is the relations holding between entities that count, not their inherent substances.

Given this structure mapping approach to metaphor, there are several properties of non-literal analogies which can be discerned. The ones most pertinent to our present concerns are clarity and richness. Gentner's own definition of clarity is very clear:

> The clarity of an analogy refers to the precision with which the object mappings are defined, that is, exactly how the base nodes are mapped on to the target nodes and which set of predicates gets carried across. Any case in which it is unclear which base nodes map on to which target nodes violates clarity. (1982: 114)

Given a structural analysis of a metaphor in terms of a conceptual mapping from one propositional network to another, this definition provides an approach to assessing the relative clarity of a metaphor by determining the number of one-to-one mappings. The precision of predicate carry-over is a structural criterion for the identification of the conceptual metaphor property of relative clarity.

The other characteristic of analogies, richness, has to do with the number of predicates that are imported from one domain to the other.

> More precisely, the richness of an analogy is its predicate density: for a given set of nodes, the average number of predicates per node that can be plausibly mapped from base to target. (1982 :114)

This constitutes another measure for a conceptual comparison between one metaphor and another, provided one has got a description of the propositional networks involved in the mapping. Richness is a second conceptual property of metaphors which can be derived from an analysis of conceptual structure.

What is most important in the present context is Gentner's view of the relation between richness and clarity: 'Richness is defined independently of clarity; a set of predicates can all contribute to richness even if they involve contradictory mapping assumptions' (1982: 114). This is the basis for her idea that scientific metaphors may be relatively clear whereas literary metaphors may be relatively rich. Good scientific metaphors can be teased out and made into explicit models which do not contain inconsistencies, for their mappings are one-to-one. This is not a requirement for good literary metaphors. Empirical evidence collected by Gentner turned out to support her approach:

> I asked people to rate scientific and literary metaphors for richness and for clarity. As predicted, scientific and literary analogies show an almost opposite relationship to richness and clarity. Good science analogies are rated high in clarity and low in richness; bad science analogies, low in clarity and high in richness. In contrast, good literary metaphors are rated high in richness and poor literary metaphors, low in richness. Clarity is about equal for good literary comparisons as for poor ones. This pattern fits with the prediction: clarity *must* be high in good explanatory analogy, and *may* be high in good expressive analogy. Richness is high in good expressive analogy, but not in good explanatory analogy. Correlations between the subjects' own ratings of scientific explanatory value and literary expressiveness and their ratings of richness and clarity show the same pattern. (1982 : 124–5)

This theory fully accords with the ideas in the empirical study of literature as derived from Schmidt (1980). Clarity is one manifestation of monovalence – consider the criterion of a one-to-one mapping – as opposed to polyvalence, and it serves to give metaphors a factual as opposed to an aesthetic function: clear metaphors can be developed into scientific models which can explain and predict the facts. By contrast, low clarity and high richness may contribute to polyvalence, because they raise the number of connections to be made between two domains of knowledge; this lowers their use for explanatory purposes, but increases their expressive potential, which is related to the aesthetic domain.

How can the above proposals be incorporated into my discourse theory of understanding metaphor in literature? I will make a couple of suggestions in the following pages by introducing a number of terminological and conceptual alterations to Gentner's theory. Note also that my discussion is concerned only with metaphor properties as textual entities. The relation between metaphor properties and their function in processing will be dealt with in Chapter 9. Let me begin by addressing the odd issue in Gentner (1982) of the relation between metaphor and analogy. Gentner (1982: 107) puts metaphor and analogy on a par, and relates them to what she believes are their natural discourse habitats, science and literature respectively. In other words, metaphors are literary, and analogies are scientific. Hence the title of her chapter: 'Are scientific analogies metaphors?' However, in my opinion this is a misleading and problematic division of the concepts 'metaphor' and 'analogy'. I have argued in Chapter 1 that all metaphors involve non-literal analogies. This view is also suggested in Gentner (1983: 162), where she says that 'Many (perhaps most) metaphors are predominantly relational comparisons, and are thus essentially analogies.' The use of 'essentially' suggests that analogies are in some sense more important than metaphors. This can be understood from the above observation that all metaphors involve non-literal analogies. However the title of Gentner (1982), 'Are scientific analogies metaphors?', shows that this was not her point. 'Essentially' also suggests that metaphors are superficially different from analogies, a view which, unfortunately, is not further elaborated. Both aspects can be approached from a discourse angle, clarifying the relationship between metaphor and analogy in one stroke.

My cognitive discourse approach agrees with structure-mapping theory that both metaphors and analogies involve non-literal comparisons, which in turn have to be distinguished from literal comparisons and abstractions (Gentner 1983: 159–62; Gentner 1989). Indeed, it is one of the outstanding merits of the structure-mapping theory that it has shown the continuum existing between these three kinds of domain comparison, which were informally related by Lakoff and Johnson (1980). The difference between the structure-mapping theory and my approach to metaphor, however, is that I wish to retain a distinction between talk about the formal properties of non-literal comparisons in the text on the one hand and their cognitive properties on the other. In other words, metaphors may relate to conceptual non-literal comparisons, or analogies, as we have seen in Chapter 1, but it is incorrect to say that all metaphors in texts are non-literal comparisons (or analogies). From a formal point of view, they are metaphors. Their formal structure as metaphors may be related to different properties for linguistic processing than the formal structure of analogies, for instance with respect to density and comprehensibility. Turning the perspective round for a moment, an expression like 'The hydrogen atom is like the solar system' can indeed be based on conceptual analogy, but in formal terms it still remains a metaphor, or, more correctly, a simile, rather than an analogy. Hence the distinction between metaphors, similes, analogies and so on on a formal level, and between literal comparison, non-literal comparison, and abstraction at a conceptual level.

At this point it has become clear that metaphors as textual entities reveal at least two distinct dimensions determining their properties. First, formally speaking, they are metaphors, and not similes, 'simple analogies' (Gentner 1982: 108), extended comparisons, and so on. Second, they express non-literal comparisons with a particular conceptual structure. These two dimensions of linguistic meaning and form on the one hand and conceptual content on the other can be subjected to structural analysis. Analysis of the conceptual structure of metaphors can yield the identification of properties such as richness and clarity. By the same token, analysis of the linguistic structure of metaphors can yield the identification of linguistic properties, such as density and comprehensibility. Density and comprehensibility may be determined by the rhetorical status of the non-literal comparison as a metaphor, a simile, or an analogy. By the same token, when the ground for comparison is verbally explicit, this may add to comprehensibility, while comprehensibility may be decreased when the ground is left implicit. Compare 'He was a bullet' with 'He was as hard as a bullet'. Other parameters of the linguistic dimension may be readily imagined, such as the grammatical scope of the metaphor (e.g. Dirven 1985; Graesser et al. 1989). The range of linguistic properties of metaphors need not be limited to comprehensibility either: from Lakoff and Johnson's work, we can see that conventionality may be an excellent candidate for another linguistic property of metaphors. I will not pursue this theoretical exercise any further at this place, however, because I first wish to develop the overall discourse view of metaphor properties by looking at other dimensions.

Genther's identification of analogy with science and metaphor with literature can now be dissolved by noting that the linguistic form of analogy can also be found in literature, and that the linguistic form of metaphor is also found in science. Metaphor and analogy are formal features of particular expressions whose definition is based on their being non-literal comparisons. In turn, the conceptual structure of both metaphors and analogies may vary in both literature and science according to their relative degrees of richness and clarity. The distinction Gentner wants to capture with the systematic opposition between literary metaphor and scientific analogy (Gentner 1982) will therefore have to be explained in another way.

The alternation in Gentner (1982) between the pairs 'literary metaphor' and 'science analogy' on the one hand and 'expressive' and 'explanatory metaphor' on the other is quite suggestive. This alternation implies another conflation of two aspects of reading I have distinguished. On the one hand, there is the type of discourse in which metaphor is located, that is, scientific or literary discourse. On the other hand, there is the presumable communicative function that may be attributed to metaphors in a particular type of discourse, that is, explanation or charged expression, respectively. (I will refer to 'charged expression' as 'evocation' from now on, in order to distinguish between this communicative function of metaphor and the general function of all language as expressive.) It will be clear that the communicative function of non-literal comparison may vary with its conceptual structure: explanation will go together with clarity, and evocation with richness. An analysis of the communicative structure of metaphors as explanations or evocations will therefore probably yield such communicative metaphor properties as 'enlightening' and 'suggestive', respectively. Speech act theory might offer the tools for such a communicative analysis of the structure of metaphors, through the concept of illocutionary force: metaphors can be used to express such illocution types as those mentioned above. In principle, Gentner's theory about the relation between conceptual structure and communicative function therefore seems unproblematic.

However, when we turn to her correlation between the conceptual and communicative dimensions of metaphor on the one hand and the types of discourse they occur in on the other, problems arise. There is no reason to believe that the combination of clarity and explanation is restricted to science. Clear and explanatory non-literal comparisons may occur in literature just as easily as in science, and rich and evocative non-literal comparisons can be found in science as in literature. This is also pointed out by Gentner herself. Similarly, the linguistic features of these types of non-literal comparisons can also vary between metaphor, simile, analogy, and extended comparison, whether we are concerned with literature or science. Therefore, the differences Gentner is trying to capture here need to be formulated in other terms.

In my opinion, it is misleading to call the scientific phenomenon 'analogy', and the literary one 'metaphor'. Instead, when metaphors and analogies are considered as textual entities in different types of discourse, the following aspects will have to be analysed.

1. There is the linguistic structure of non-literal comparisons, for which it is relevant to determine for instance whether the linguistic structures involved are metaphors or analogies. A metaphor property that is probably related to this aspect of linguistic structure can be designated as 'density' (metaphor) versus 'explicitness' (analogy) for the moment.

2. Conceptual analysis, by comparison, is concerned with distinct parameters of non-literal domain comparison for the case of metaphor and analogy alike. The identification of properties like metaphorical or

Table 7.1: Discourse dimensions of metaphor

Dimensions	Structure	Example	Property
linguistic	rhetorical status	metaphor analogy	density explicitness
conceptual	number of predicates precision of mapping	image model	richness clarity
communicative	illocutionary force	explanation evocation	enlightening suggestive

analogical clarity and richness may be the outcome of this conceptual analysis.

3. And finally, the communicative properties of metaphors will have to be attended to as well. They can be derived from an analysis in terms of such presumed intentions or illocutionary forces as explanation or evocation. Their labels may be provisionally determined as 'enlightening' and 'suggestive'.

Each of these three dimensions and their related properties can be found in metaphors both in literature and outside it. It is an empirical question, to be approached in terms of relative frequencies, which properties are typical of which types of discourse.

In sum, we have distinguished between the following dimensions and properties of metaphor in literature and other types of discourse, which are laid out in Table 7.1. There may be further parameters to be added to the dimensions. As mentioned before, two other parameters affecting the *linguistic* nature of a metaphor besides the one pertaining to the classification of figures of speech are grammatical scope of the metaphor and degree of deviance from conventionalized language use. Another *conceptual* property of metaphors for instance is imageability. It will be due to another parameter of the conceptual structure of non-literal comparisons, namely the relative concreteness or abstractness of the domains involved. The cognitive discourse approach to metaphor dimensions and properties has thus provided us with a workable manner of ordering important aspects of the field of research.

The questions raised earlier in this chapter about the identification of diverging metaphor properties and their relation to each other have now been dealt with. Their theoretical development will be undertaken later on, after further empirical study in the next chapter. An example of how such an empirical study can be conducted will now be discussed in order to assess the possibilities and problems for research in greater detail.

7.5 Poetic and constructed metaphors

Apart from Gentner (1982), the most provocative psychological study of differences between literary and non-literary metaphors is the one by Katz et al. (1985). In their large-scale investigations of psychological dimensions of metaphor, they found that there was no difference between a large pool (N = 260) of constructed metaphors on the one hand and a pool of a similar quantity (N = 204) of poetic metaphors on the other. Both groups of metaphors were presented in the formulaic form of *An A is a B* or *As are Bs*, such as 'An airplane is a migrating bird'. Subjects had to rate the metaphors on ten scales measuring what the researchers called metaphoricity and goodness. The qualities investigated with the aid of these ten scales were: overall imageability, subject imagery, predicate imagery, ease of interpretation, degree of metaphoricity, felt familiarity, semantic relatedness, metaphor goodness, number of alternative interpretations, and comprehensibility. These data were factor-analysed in order to determine the number of underlying dimensions which could account for the scores in the rating scales. In both the rating studies, and in an additional smaller replication study, one 'monster factor' (Marschark et al. 1983: 38) was found which accounted for some 75 per cent of the total variance and all scales were highly related to this single factor. It was labelled as 'metaphor interpretability'. The conclusion of the authors was that these scales apparently capture 'the nature of the beast', and that metaphoricity and goodness go back to the single origin of interpretability (1983: 38). The researchers also observed that the patterns of the relations between the scales and the factor (which are called factor loadings) were highly similar for the literary and the non-literary metaphors, although it was acknowledged that a direct comparison between the two pools of metaphors could not be made because of design problems (Katz et al. 1985).

However, there is a complication of this relatively simple picture:

> Metaphors rated as relatively good are easy to interpret, have only a few interpretations that are particularly salient, are easy to image, and have subjects and topics that are highly related. In short, it appears that better metaphors are those that can be labeled as being more readily interpretable. (1985: 377–8)

After this interpretation of the data, the researchers point out that this does not match other findings. With references to an unpublished manuscript by Gentner and to Tourangeau and Sternberg (1981), the authors note that 'goodness ratings may be multiply determined' (Katz et al. 1985: 378). They continue:

> Recent metaphor models . . . suggest that at least two factors are involved in

the making of goodness or aptness rating. One is characterized by such variables as clarity of expression, well-formedness of the utterance, similarity of topic and vehicle, and specificity of the interpretation. As such, this factor appears to emphasize nonaesthetic aspects of the sentence meaning. The other factor is described by trait terms such as *aesthetically powerful, insightful,* and *emotionally rich.* (Katz et al. 1985: 378)

Special reference is made to an unpublished study by Dawson (1982). Apparently 'interpretability' cannot be the only factor accounting for metaphor quality, for Dawson (1982) revealed a second factor 'with high loadings of scales such as aptness, beauty, and likeability'. This factor differs from the first factor revealed by Dawson (1982), which is reported to reflect 'the degree to which a metaphoric comparison was a well-formed sentence that one could easily understand (with high loadings on such scales as comprehensibility and the similarity of the constituent comparison nouns)' (Katz et al. 1985: 378). Dawson's first factor hence seems to be identical to the 'monster' factor captured in the three studies of Katz, Marschark, and Paivio. These authors therefore interpret Dawson's second factor as reflecting 'aesthetic properties'. They conclude that 'Further research is clearly needed to determine the multiple dimensionality of metaphor goodness' (Katz et al. 1985: 378).

It is interesting to observe that, at this point, the authors implicitly retreat from their earlier position that they have revealed 'the nature of the beast' (Marschark et al. 1983: 38). This impression is confirmed by a consideration of Katz et al. (1988), where the issue of multi-dimensionality is left aside. In sum, the question now remains unanswered whether metaphoricity and metaphor quality do derive from one common source or not, and whether literary and non-literary metaphors relate to this matter in the same way.

I believe that there are a number of theoretical aspects which have to be disentangled here. They have to do with modelling the relations between the cognitive and aesthetic features of metaphors as discussed by Katz and his colleagues in a systematic way, and their subsequent operationalization in a wide variety of measures. From the point of view of the present discourse theory, their scales and materials are hardly appropriate to measure either the nature of metaphor ('metaphoricity') or metaphor quality in the encompassing sense elaborated in the first half of this chapter: they are too clearly restricted to the domain of conceptual properties of metaphor. The inclusion of other dimensions such as linguistic form and communicative function and the metaphor properties related to them is essential for a full view of metaphor quality and its relation to different domains of discourse. Moreover, a control for linguistic form is desirable if the aim is to measure the conceptual properties of metaphors. When the target of research concerns the full range of metaphor properties in texts, then variation in linguistic form is an essential parameter for investigation, because the partly linguistic property of 'interpretability' is clearly dependent on formal variation between metaphors.

Apart from linguistic variation, there is also the methodological issue of sampling. Marschark et al. (1983: 28) admitted that there is question of a 'non-systematic manner of metaphor construction'. In Katz, Paivio, and Marschark (1985: 368), the sampling of the poetic metaphor pool is said to have been done by a professional writer of fiction, who conducted a systematic search of a number of anthologies and collections of poetry for figurative expression. However, the method of this 'systematic search' is not discussed. I cannot escape the impression that in both cases there may have been more bias in constructing or selecting a particular kind of metaphor than is good for representativeness of the entire range of metaphoricity. A more controlled method of sampling may yield a more varied set of metaphors that can reveal more intricate relations than one 'monster factor' and perhaps one additional 'aesthetic factor'.

Furthermore, the use of the label 'aesthetic' by Katz et al. (1985) seems too *ad hoc* to be taken very seriously. My alternative explanation is to regard it as a basically emotive addition to the highly conceptual framework of their entire study. This suggestion is supported by the observation that Katz et al. (1985: 378) have re-interpreted Gentner's richness as an emotional form of richness – see the quotation above. As will have become apparent from the previous discussion, Gentner's main concern did not lie in the emotive side of richness, but in its conceptual nature. That there may be affective correlates involved in richness seems quite plausible, but this is not what Gentner meant by richness.

Finally, difficulties with Katz et al.'s (1985) experimental design prevent any serious comparison between literary and non-literary metaphors. The ratings of the poetic and the constructed metaphors were carried out by two different groups of subjects, so that correspondences and differences in the data may be due either to metaphor effects or subject effects. This will have to be redressed in the envisaged studies of the next chapters.

7.6 Conclusion: literary and non-literary metaphors

This chapter has sketched out a framework for the study of metaphor properties as they can be observed in textual study. The issue of the difference between literary and non-literary metaphors was placed within this framework by postulating a number of basic dimensions for all metaphors and, indeed, all textual entities, for which it is expected that some or all will exhibit typical differences between literary and non-literary metaphors. Hitherto we have discriminated between three relatively cognitive dimensions: those based in linguistic form, conceptual content, and communicative function. I also added two less cognitive dimensions, emotive value and moral position; they are loosely attached to the cognitive dimensions for this moment. A separate aesthetic dimension was not included, on account of the fact that the domain of the aesthetic and the literary are social constructs which receive various concrete realizations in the above-mentioned dimensions of reading. The findings of previous metaphor studies can be interpreted in this framework without difficulty, and new questions for research are generated by this incorporation of previous findings in the theory.

I will now sum up the expectations regarding the difference between literary and non-literary metaphors by discussing each of the postulated dimensions. They served as hypotheses for the empirical research to be reported in Chapter 8.

1. What may be a good metaphor from one *conceptual* point of view, clarity, need not necessarily be a good metaphor from an aesthetic, or literary point of view. Similarly, what may be a good metaphor from another conceptual point of view, richness, may be a useless metaphor if it is to fulfil an explanatory function in scientific discourse. It is an empirical question whether a particular conceptual quality is also experienced as contributing to an aesthetic or literary quality in the discourse-typical sense.

2. *Communicative* function and related metaphor properties such as 'enlightening' or 'suggestive' is another obvious dimension from which metaphors may derive their attribution of good or bad quality regarding literature, journalism, religion and so on. As we have seen, support for this view can be found in Gentner (1982), who revealed correlations between conceptual richness and evocative function for literary metaphors, and between conceptual clarity and explanatory function for scientific ones. There may also be a relation between the metaphor property based in conceptual structure and the one based in communicative function.

3. The final predominantly cognitive dimension is the *linguistic* dimension. Here we may return to the factor of 'interpretability' revealed in the studies of Katz et al. (1985). Their metaphors were always presented in formulaic form, controlling for the effect of differences between the linguistic expression of metaphors. However, the aesthetic appeal of metaphor may also be influenced by linguistic variation: the tenor may be absent, the 'canonical' order of tenor and vehicle may be switched, the metaphor may be condensed into a compound or a phrase rather

than a sentence, or it may be expressed as a related figure of speech, such as simile or analogy. Such variation may affect the 'interpretability' of metaphors in obvious ways, and there may be systematic variation between literary discourse and other types of discourse in the exploitation of such linguistic possibilities. To some extent, the typically literary character of metaphor may also be explicable from this perspective. More variety in experimental materials can take care of this problem.

4. Apart from the cognitive dimensions discussed above, metaphors may also exhibit a general *emotive* aspect that may be more or less noticeable and suitable to the occasion. The relation between such general emotive differences between metaphors and their occurrence in literary discourse is an important aspect that has to be included in an investigation of aesthetic quality.

5. Similarly, the question arises whether the aesthetic appeal by metaphors is affected by such features as political colour, value-ladenness, and so on. Although this is an important – moral – dimension, it is less easy to relate in a specific form to literariness. The extent to which metaphors in literature are characterized by a specific attribute in this area remains an open question at present.

Notes

1. I recently came across Wayne Booth's (1988) chapters on the moral value of metaphor, providing independent support for my approach.

2. The idea that metaphors and analogies can be analysed as propositional networks is not uncommon in present-day psychology. However, the reliability of such analysis may cause some difficulty. There is a good deal of intuitive assessment involved in this sort of exercise, and however ingenious the analyst, additional means will have to be used to ensure the reliability of the analyses. This is a methodological problem which I am sure can be solved by further research, and I am willing to take this for granted in order to continue with the development of the theoretical model. But the presumption of a reliable analytical basis cannot remain unmentioned here.

CHAPTER EIGHT

Literary and journalistic metaphors

Do metaphors exhibit distinct properties that may be related to the various dimensions of discourse which can be derived from the processing of linguistic form, conceptual structure, communicative function, emotive value, and moral purport? And do literary metaphors differ from non-literary metaphors with regard to these discourse properties of metaphors? In this chapter I will present two empirical studies dealing with these two questions.

The first study is based on a sample of ninety-six English-language metaphors, and the second is a follow-up study with 164 Dutch metaphors. The metaphors were investigated by means of the Semantic Differential technique developed by Osgood (1972). In both studies, raters assessed metaphors with respect to a large quantity of properties by filling in a series of rating scales for every metaphor. The rating scales were meant to cover the whole area of the discourse dimensions of metaphors discussed in the previous chapter. Their role was to feed into a factor analysis which reduces the large number of potential properties to just a few underlying factors. It was hoped that the factors were relatable to the postulated discourse dimensions. This would provide an answer to the first of the above-mentioned questions.

The metaphors were sampled in such a manner as to be representative of two types of discourse: literary prose and journalistic prose. Thus, a comparison could be made between these two discourse types regarding the typical properties of metaphors on all emerging underlying dimensions. It was expected that the literary metaphors would show different characteristics regarding their linguistic, conceptual, and possibly other properties than the journalistic metaphors. This would provide an answer to the second of the above-mentioned questions.

8.1 Dimensions and properties of ninety-six English-language metaphors

8.1.1 Introduction

This study took its cue from the work by Katz and his colleagues referred to in the previous chapter. The advantage of using the Semantic Differential technique over their method is that it is less costly in terms of number of raters, because all of the scales were applied to the same subjects rather than to different groups of subjects. Moreover, the procedure of having the same raters judge both literary and non-literary metaphors made it possible to carry out a controlled comparison between the two samples, which was prevented in Katz et al. (1985) because different raters had reacted to different groups of metaphors. Finally, the studies by Katz and his associates appeared to be limited to an investigation of only conceptual attributes of metaphors, whereas the present study included other dimensions of discourse, too. This was the reason for the first prediction tested here, namely that more than 'one monster factor' would be discovered (*pace* Marschark et al. 1983: 38).

This study also owes some of its development to another study, Carroll (1972). He used the Semantic Differential technique for his investigation of 'vectors in prose style'. The original Semantic Differential developed by Osgood used a number of scales which were intended to measure the affective side of meaning, such as 'good-bad', 'hot-cold', and so on. Carroll (1972) developed a number of rating scales that were less metaphorical than the ones commonly associated with Osgood. They involved more traditionally stylistic oppositions, such as 'complex – simple'. Some of his scales correspond with the concerns of the cognitive studies referred to in Chapter 7, like 'clear – hazy', while others could be included without further ado in the scales used below for the measurement of the other discourse aspects of metaphor.

I will not embark on as extensive a methodological discussion of the Semantic Differential as I did with thinking out loud in Chapter 5. Some points cannot remain unmentioned, though. For instance, the fact that it was originally developed to measure the meaning of words could raise some questions about its applicability to the measurement of sentence meaning. However, psychological research practice has given ample precedent for such an extension. Also, the question of which scales to use, and how they may be related to various dimensions, is a tricky one to answer at this moment. I believe it can only be solved by actually doing the research and carrying out piecemeal improvement. And finally, the issue of how one can be sure that it is the metaphors themselves that are being rated, and not, for instance, the contexts in which they are offered for rating, is a very complex problem to tackle in theory. I will deal with it by having the judges in the Dutch follow-up study rate the metaphors of the two experimental texts used in the Dutch underlining experiment reported in Chapter 3 and in the think-aloud experiment reported in Chapter 6. These metaphor rating data can then be related to the metaphor processing data of those earlier studies in order to find out if they actually predict the behaviour of the readers. If they do, then we also have evidence that the Semantic Differential did measure the pertinent phenomena, namely metaphor properties. This issue will be dealt with in Chapter 9.

8.1.2 Method

MATERIALS

Literary metaphors (N = 48) were culled from recent works of fiction in English and American English, every metaphor coming from a different author. Non-literary metaphors (N = 48) were sampled from four different newspapers dated Monday 19 August 1991: *The Herald Tribune*, *The Wall Street Journal Europe*, *The Independent* and *The Times*. The forty-eight most recent writers of both English and American fiction that were in my personal library were evenly divided and ordered by year of first publication.[1] The first metaphor that appeared on the second page was sampled for rating. From the four newspapers twelve metaphors were sampled from each. The total number of pages of each newspaper was divided by twelve, producing a two-page or three-page interval for each newspaper. Metaphors were selected from every second or third page. Analysis of the relevant pages was systematically varied, from top left through top right through bottom right and so on. Advertisements were disregarded. Metaphors were copied and later offered with a small part of their context. However, the sources from which metaphors were taken were not disclosed to the subjects. A selection of the materials is presented in Table 8.1.

SD SCALES

The scales used for the operationalization of the metaphor properties that can be derived from theoretically postulated discourse dimensions of metaphor are presented in Table 8.2 They represent a first attempt at operationalizing the discourse aspects of metaphor discussed in Chapter 7. A distinction is made between relatively pure scales, expected to measure a property related to only one discourse dimension or factor, on the one hand, and a number of complex measuring scales whose objects can be

Table 8.1: Examples of materials used in English-language metaphor rating study

(*a*) *British English fiction*
[Riding home on the last train, I was struck by a black London Transport maintenance man sitting opposite me.] The black was looking at his loosely *cupped* hands: . . .

Alan Hollinghurst, *The Swimming-pool Library*

[I have a terrible red-eye.] I look like *the Hound of the Baskervilles.*

Martin Amis, *London Fields*

[The swimming match is not going to be held in the best pool.] Instead, it's going to be held way down in the south, in some greasy little *puddle.*

Ian McEwan, *The Innocent*

(*b*) *American English fiction*
'For the last month you've been spending every moment you can with her. You're *madly* in love with her, aren't you?'

Kathy Acker, *Blood and Guts in High School Plus Two*

[A party including Carl Jung are on a boat trip across the ocean, when a great midsummer mist descends.] Jung especially was gripped by the conception of this *'prehistoric monster' wallowing through the daylight-darkness towards its objective*, and felt we were slipping back into the primeval past.

D. M. Thomas, *The White Hotel*

The town in the middle of this place was called Deadrock, a modest place of ten thousand souls, originally named for an unresolved battle between the Army and the Assiniboin – Deadlock – but renamed Deadrock out of some sad and irresolute boosterism meant *to cure* an early-day depression.

Thomas McGuane, *Nobody's Angel*

In any event, as I was saying, the night was hectic, as these things always are, and the party was already under way when I arrived, trailing associate professors and graduate students – my face bright red, I imagine, from my long climb up the *icy* flagstone steps.

John Gardner, *Freddy's Book*

(*c*) *Herald Tribune*
Iran's government, using secret intermediaries and shuttle diplomacy, has taken the lead in negotiating the terms and conditions for the release of the 10 remaining Western hostages held in Lebanon by pro-Iranian militants, high-level Western Officials say. The full *mobilization* of Iran's diplomatic corps in the negotiations now under way with Secretary-General Javier Pérez de Cuéllar of the United Nations suggests that President Hashemi Rafsanjani of Iran may have overcome the powerful opposition in his government to forcing a resolution of the hostage crisis, these officials say.

Residents secured their property in North Carolina's coastal resorts Sunday and joined *an exodus of* tourists and beach goers fleeing to higher ground as a hurricane churned northward toward the coast.

Table 8.1 continued

Perhaps the most striking aspects of the case of Donald Leroy Evans are that his claim to be the nation's newest known serial killer has apparently caused few *public shock waves*, and that authorities are taking him quite seriously.

(*d*) *The Independent*

[About Channel Rail link:] In what would amount to its fourth *U-turn* on the funding of the link in as many years, the Department of Transport has asked the construction group Trafalgar House whether it is interested in resurrecting its joint scheme with BR, rejected by the Cabinet a year ago.

A ferret called Cuddles is helping to control the booming rabbit population on thousands of miles of railway embankment. With the failure of myxomatosis, the laboratory-created viral disease that nearly wiped out rabbits in the 1960s, British Rail has turned to this *traditional pest controller*.

A state-funded scheme which has provided training and homes for hundreds of homeless teenagers *faces* closure because of cuts in government grants.

The old peasant women sang joyfully as they marched down the hot and dusty lane of the Hungarian village of Mariapocs. Their traditional costumes *blazed* a trail of bright colours as they held aloft their home-made banners and tiny shrines.

related to several factors on the other. The assignment of properties to discourse dimensions was done on intuitive grounds, taking into consideration as much extant theoretical work as possible. I will not devote discussion to motivating the assignment of every particular scale to the factors in question, trusting that the general approach is transparent: scales measuring linguistic properties make reference to metaphors as expressions; conceptual scales, to metaphors as ideas; communicative scales, to metaphors as parts of illocutionary acts; emotive scales, to metaphors as triggers for particular feelings; and moral scales, to metaphors as signs of a particular value-laden stance.

The large number of scales was motivated by the exploratory nature of this study: if some of the scales would not turn out to be related to the expected factors, others might be, so that the goal of separating the basic dimensions of discourse from each other could still be reached. Given the state of research, this is an inevitable ploy when a first attempt is made to discover whether there is an intelligible relation between a range of scales and a number of postulated underlying factors. Finally, care was taken that every postulated dimension was represented by at least four properties, to facilitate the emergence of distinct factors for every discourse dimension.

RATERS

Judges were participants at the 11th Conference of the Poetics and Linguistics Association, held at Lancaster University in September 1991.

Table 8.2: Metaphor scales used in the semantic differential

(a) Pure scales

Dimension	Scale	Source
Linguistic	original – trite expression	1
	striking – common language	—
Conceptual	complex – simple idea	1–3
	imageable – not imageable	2
	new – old idea	2
	clear – hazy	1–3
	abstract – concrete	1
Communicative	explanatory – confusing	3
	informative – illustrative	—
	persuasive – implausible	—
	entertaining – serious	—
Emotive	beautiful – ugly	—
	funny – serious	1
	subtle – obvious	1
	shocking – touching	—
	pleasant – unpleasant	1
	tasteful – tasteless	—
Moral	opinionated – impartial	1
	political – apolitical	—
	approving – disapproving	—
	earnest – flippant	1

(b) Complex scales

Dimension	Scale	Source
Linguistic + conceptual	difficult – easy to comprehend	2
	precise – vague	1
Conceptual + emotive	appropriate – far-fetched	4
	interesting – boring	1
	profound – superficial	1
Communicative + emotive	intimate – remote	1
	formal – informal	1
	polite – impolite	—
	natural – affected	1

1 = Carroll (1972), 2 = Katz et al. (1988), 3 = Gentner (1982), 4 = Tourangeau and Sternberg (1981)

They were all researchers and teachers of language and literature. The test was distributed among fourteen volunteers. They were asked to return the questionnaires as soon as they had found time to fill them in. Ten questionnaires were returned within six weeks after the conference had ended.

PROCEDURE

The literary and non-literary metaphors were offered in mixed and rand-omized order for rating on thirty seven-point scales. Each of the scales embodied a contrast between two extremes of a potential metaphor characteristic, the middle position indicating equal applicability of both sides or irrelevance of the scale. Instructions for rating were modelled on the example by Osgood and Suci (1972). Care was taken that no more than three metaphors from one domain of discourse (literature or journal-ism), or from British versus American English, followed each other.

8.1.3 Results

METAPHOR SCALES

Apart from one special case, there were thirteen missing values, where subjects had inadvertently missed filling in a particular scale for a particular metaphor. The missing values exhibited no particular pattern of occurrence. They were replaced by the means calculated from the other raters' scores, rounded off to whole figures for simplicity of calculation. However, because one rater declined to fill in the scales for one particular metaphor which he deemed not metaphorical, and because the same judge assigned two neighbouring metaphors only middle values ('4') indicating irrelevance of the scales, this rater was left out of consideration in the calculations.

First, inter-observer agreement was estimated for all scales.[2] Statistical analysis showed that there was great consistency between raters in their assessment of such varied features of metaphors as their presumable linguistic, conceptual, communicative, emotive and moral nature. This facilitated averaging across raters in order to obtain more solid data.

Overall mean scores were calculated for each scale for the two kinds of metaphors. Table 8.3 shows the means and standard deviations for all literary and all journalistic metaphors for every scale. Differences between the literary and the journalistic metaphors were investigated by transform-ing these data by means of a factor analysis into a smaller number of underlying dimensions.[3]

FACTOR ANALYSIS

A principal component analysis (PCA) was attempted on thirty rating scales for ninety-six literary and journalistic metaphors. An automatic computer program warning signalled the potential presence of multi-colline-arity and singularity. This indicates too high correlations between some of

Table 8.3: Means of metaphor-scales (standard deviations in brackets)

	Source of metaphors	
Scale	Literary	Journalistic
original – trite	4.17 (1.58)	5.67 (1.02)
striking – common	4.18 (1.53)	5.57 (1.12)
difficult – easy	5.76 (1.17)	6.48 (0.62)
complex – simple	5.12 (1.36)	6.11 (0.88)
precise – vague	2.96 (1.48)	3.20 (1.08)
imageable – not imageable	3.08 (1.20)	2.42 (0.71)
new – old	4.40 (1.66)	6.01 (1.04)
clear – hazy	2.94 (1.12)	2.30 (0.73)
appropriate – far-fetched	2.57 (0.89)	2.26 (0.61)
interesting – boring	3.45 (1.20)	4.97 (0.95)
abstract – concrete	4.60 (1.45)	4.89 (0.70)
profound – superficial	4.19 (0.91)	5.06 (0.62)
explanatory – confusing	2.80 (0.92)	2.34 (0.55)
informative – illustrative	3.99 (0.86)	2.88 (0.74)
persuasive – implausible	3.01 (0.64)	2.89 (0.41)
entertaining – serious	3.51 (0.87)	4.32 (0.75)
beautiful – ugly	3.72 (0.56)	4.06 (0.29)
funny – serious	4.34 (0.97)	4.79 (0.66)
subtle – obvious	4.26 (1.18)	5.44 (0.69)
shocking – touching	3.96 (0.44)	3.97 (0.20)
pleasant – unpleasant	3.97 (0.66)	4.09 (0.39)
intimate – remote	3.49 (0.66)	4.18 (0.52)
formal – informal	4.26 (0.96)	3.90 (0.72)
natural – affected	3.67 (0.83)	3.63 (0.49)
polite – impolite	4.13 (0.46)	4.05 (0.27)
tasteful – tasteless	3.84 (0.56)	4.09 (0.26)
opinionated – impartial	3.61 (0.71)	3.71 (0.69)
political – apolitical	4.54 (0.52)	4.13 (0.65)
approving – disapproving	4.04 (0.74)	4.16 (0.75)
earnest – flippant	3.47 (1.02)	3.24 (0.69)

N of raters = 9; N of metaphors = 96

the variables subjected to analysis, and presents a mathematical problem for factor analysis. Visual inspection of the correlation matrix revealed that there were many rating scales exhibiting high bivariate correlations. After removing the four rating scales with relatively low reliability coefficients, and seven scales with high bivariate correlations which were expected to measure similar metaphor traits, a PCA with varimax rotation and estimation of factor scores was executed with success.[4]

This PCA on nineteen rating scales extracted five factors, accounting for

Table 8.4: Results of PCA: factor loadings of 19 metaphor scales (loadings < 0.40 are suppressed)

	Factor				
Scale	I	II	III	IV	V
original – trite	0.87	—	—	—	—
precise – vague	—	0.71	—	—	—
appropriate – far-fetched	—	0.82	—	—	—
abstract – concrete	—	− 0.73	—	—	—
profound – superficial	0.85	—	—	—	—
explanatory – confusing	− 0.42	0.82	—	—	—
informative – illustrative	− 0.73	—	—	—	—
persuasive – implausible	—	0.82	—	—	—
beautiful – ugly	0.52	—	0.71	—	—
funny – serious	—	—	—	− 0.91	—
subtle – obvious	0.87	—	—	—	—
shocking – touching	—	—	− 0.90	—	—
pleasant – unpleasant	—	—	0.85	—	—
formal – informal	—	—	—	0.87	—
natural – affected	—	0.72	—	—	—
tasteful – tasteless	—	—	0.82	—	—
opinionated – impartial	—	—	—	− 0.40	0.66
political – apolitical	—	—	—	—	0.80
earnest – flippant	—	—	—	0.91	—
Percentage explained variance:	29.0	20.8	14.9	9.7	6.4
Eigenvalue:	5.51	3.96	2.83	1.84	1.22

80.9 per cent of the total variance in the data. A large proportion of the variance exhibited by every single rating scale is accounted for by the present factor-solution.[5] Table 8.4 shows how the rating scales are related to the factors discovered in the analysis. It reports the so-called 'factor-loadings', or the sizes of the correlations between the rating scales and the factors. A high factor loading indicates that a particular rating scale is closely correlated with a particular factor.[6]

The first factor has high positive loadings from the scales 'subtle – obvious', 'original – trite expression', and 'profound – superficial'. It also has a relatively high negative loading from 'informative – illustrative'. The respective signs of these loadings indicate that the following sides of the scales are related to the factor in question: obvious, trite, superficial, and informative. This factor hence turns out to capture the difference between common or conventional metaphors as opposed to other metaphors that are 'subtle', 'original', 'profound', and 'illustrative'. Common metaphors are also explanatory rather than confusing, and they are not found to be

191

beautiful, as their opposites are. In the present context, conventionality may be taken as being closely related to the linguistic familiarity of many of the metaphors – compare the role of 'trite expression'. Factor I will therefore be labelled 'linguistic conventionality'.

Factor II has high positive loadings from the scales measuring metaphors as 'appropriate – far-fetched', 'explanatory – confusing', 'persuasive – implausible', 'precise – vague', and 'natural – affected'; it has a high negative loading from 'abstract – concrete'. The respective signs of these loadings indicate the lack of conceptual transparency of an idea expressed by a metaphor, because they correspond to the following sides of the scales: far-fetched, confusing, implausible, vague, affected, and abstract. This factor hence pertains to the understandability of metaphors. It is therefore labelled 'conceptual difficulty'.

Factor III has high loadings from the following scales: 'shocking – touching', 'pleasant – unpleasant', 'tasteful – tasteless', and 'beautiful – ugly'. All signs of the loadings indicate that this factor captures the less likeable sides of these scales. It is therefore labelled 'negative value'.

Factor IV is primarily characterized by high loadings from 'funny', 'flippant', and 'informal'. It seems, then, that this factor captures the opposite of the polite (that is, serious, earnest, and formal) interpersonal manner of metaphors. It has to do with their communicative function, and will be labelled 'impolite communicative manners'.

The last factor, Factor V, has markedly fewer scales loading on it: it only has high loadings from 'apolitical' and 'impartial', as opposed to 'political' and 'opinionated'. Both positive loadings suggest a metaphor attribute of 'lacking an ideological position', or neutrality. Factor V may hence be seen as 'unbiased moral position'. However, given its poor definitional structure, this will have to remain a tentative proposal.

LITERARY AND JOURNALISTIC METAPHORS

Having determined that metaphors may be described with reference to more than just one or two factors, and that these factors bear a transparent relation to general dimensions of discourse, the final question to be answered is the one pertaining to differences between literary and journalistic metaphors. We now proceed to a comparison between the mean scores of the two kinds of metaphors on the underlying dimensions. This can be done by computing factor scores. This is a mathematical procedure for deriving the scores for each factor by combining the component variables (rating scales) of that factor according to their relative weights or loadings. Factor scores hence embody a derived set of data which could also have been obtained by direct measurement, had we known the identity of the factors in advance.

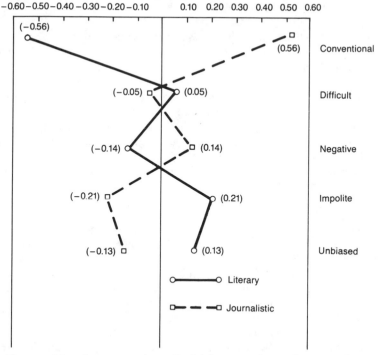

Fig. 8.1: Mean factor scores for 96 English literary and journalistic metaphors

Mean factor scores were computed for both kinds of metaphors by averaging values across metaphors on each of the five factors resulting from the above PCA. The results of this operation are shown in Figure 8.1 It can be observed that the signs of the mean factor scores of the literary metaphors are all opposite to those of the journalistic metaphors. There is also a good deal of variation regarding the distance between the means of the two groups of metaphors.

These data were analysed by means of analysis of variance to test whether the different average values of the literary and the journalistic metaphors on all of these factors were statistically significant.[7] It turned out that there are significant differences between the means of the literary and the journalistic metaphors for Factor I, conventionality, and for Factor IV, impolite manners. In general it may be concluded, then, that there are some differences between the characteristics of literary and non-literary metaphors. In particular, literary metaphors are less conventional in linguistic terms, and less 'comme-il-faut' as to communicative manners, than journalistic metaphors.

8.1.4 Discussion

Differences between metaphors cannot be attributed to one underlying monster-factor, as was argued by Marschark et al. (1983; Katz et al. 1988). Nor can they be explained by just two basic factors, cognitive and aesthetic, as was suggested by Katz et al. (1985). The present study has revealed that no fewer than five psychological dimensions of metaphors may be involved in explaining differences between them. Some of these dimensions are cognitive, and all of them are relatively independent of the domain of the aesthetic because they show up in journalistic metaphors just as clearly as in literary ones.

Moreover, these factors were not found by accident, but derive from the theoretical motivation of the design of the study. In particular, my adoption of a general discourse view of language use and reading led to the expectation that differences between metaphors are to be treated like differences between other aspects of discourse, and hence may be traced back to more than just one or two underlying dimensions of discourse. The nature of these discourse dimensions was formulated independently of the research tradition of Katz and his colleagues. The theoretically motivated operationalization of the postulated dimensions in diverging kinds of scales measuring distinct properties led to the discovery of five intelligible properties of metaphors which can be related to the dimensions. The results of the study show that differences between metaphors can be reduced to their relative (linguistic) conventionality, (conceptual) difficulty, (communicative) manners, (emotive) value, and (moral) position.

Some comments have to be made now in order to make this observation more specific. First there is the matter of the number of the dimensions. The fact that there are five factors in the factor-solution presented in Table 8.4 is encouraging for further research, but does not prove beyond doubt that there are indeed five factors. The fifth factor is too poorly defined for such a conclusion and may be due to mathematical chance. It hence requires further elaboration in the next study. This can be done by adding relevant scales to 'political – apolitical' and 'opinionated – impartial'. Pending this investigation in the next section of this chapter, I will defer until later a further consideration of the nature of the dimensions in terms of discourse, and a comparison with the previous findings of Katz and his colleagues and other researchers.

A second question to be dealt with briefly now is the relation between the factors and the measuring scales. Many of the latter did not seem to tap the dimensions that they were designed to measure. I will give three examples. 'Profound – superficial' was conceived as a conceptual scale, but turned out to be related to linguistic conventionality. 'Explanatory – confusing' and 'persuasive – implausible' were designed as measures of communicative traits (metaphors as parts of illocutionary acts), but instead revealed a relation with conceptual difficulty. And finally, 'funny – serious' was intended as emotive, but appeared to be related to communicative manners. What do these shifts imply?

This question can be better answered if we consider those scales that did behave as predicted. The following scales can be treated as successful marker variables for the factors they were intended to measure: 'original – trite expression' for the linguistic factor; 'appropriate – far-fetched' for the conceptual factor; 'shocking – touching' for the emotive factor; and 'political – apolitical' for the moral factor. However, it should be added that the linguistic factor is filled out by a scale that was intended as emotive, 'subtle – obvious'; and the conceptual factor is filled out by an originally communicative scale, namely 'persuasive'. Perhaps it is not surprising that a particular metaphor trait, such as linguistic conventionality or conceptual difficulty, may also be related to particular communicative or emotive features of metaphors. In general, the idea of distinguishing between dimensions of discourse does not imply that there cannot be a relation between them. On the contrary, it is only natural that there should be mutual relations between a property related to one dimension of discourse and another property related to another dimension. When metaphors are highly conventional (linguistically), they are also highly superficial (conceptually) and highly obvious (emotively). When metaphors are highly appropriate (conceptually), they are also highly persuasive (communicatively) and natural (emotively). Hence it is not contradictory to observe a relation between a purportedly conceptual scale such as 'superficiality' and an allegedly linguistic metaphor trait such as Factor I, conventionality.[8]

The second main question that was posed at the beginning of this chapter pertained to differences between literary and non-literary metaphors. Having found that metaphors in literary texts are not essentially different from metaphors in journalistic texts in that their properties exhibit the same underlying factor structure, the comparison between these two types of metaphors revealed that there are two dimensions upon which literary metaphors are different from journalistic ones. The fact that there is a group of literary metaphors that are original expressions as opposed to the rather more trite nature of some journalistic metaphors is no surprise to anyone familiar with the range of writing in literary prose and serious journalism. Also, part of this picture is the fact that this group of literary metaphors tends to be profound and subtle, whereas the journalistic metaphors are superficial and obvious.

The difference between literary and journalistic metaphors regarding communicative manners was less predictable. But it is not disturbing that some journalistic metaphors are serious, formal, and earnest, as opposed to the funny, informal, and flippant nature of some literary metaphors. A glance at the purport of much journalistic writing corroborates such an impression. This also fits with the theoretical assumption that journalism is a type of discourse that is governed by the fact convention: abiding by the facts involves seriousness, formality, and earnestness, while keeping aloof from humour, informality, and flippancy. The latter aspects of discourse involve communicative manners that are apparently highly compatible with an aesthetic function.

The general conclusion regarding differences between metaphors as revealed in this study, then, is twofold, and conforms with our expectations. First, properties of metaphors are based on more than one general dimension of discourse, and literary as well as journalistic metaphors can be described in the same manner with reference to these dimensions. Second, however, on two of these dimensions it emerged that literary metaphors exhibit a different tendency from journalistic metaphors. Both of these differences between literary and journalistic metaphors are understandable from the point of view of differences between types of discourse.

8.2 A follow-up study with 164 Dutch metaphors

8.2.1 Introduction

The results of the previous study can be taken as the starting-point for a larger study to check our conclusions. Factor analysis is a powerful statistical tool producing results that are often readily interpretable, but it has also been objected that sample size and hence chance play too large a role in the construction of the factors. Because the number of metaphors in the previous study is relatively small, certainly when the two samples of literary and journalistic metaphors are considered separately (N = 48 in each), the factor solution, although intelligible and suggestive, may not be sufficiently solid. Moreover, the weak representation of what I have called the moral factor, which had high loadings from only two scales, may also have distorted the relationship as calculated between the totality of factors. Therefore, a larger sample of metaphors and an additional number of measuring scales were deemed necessary for the purpose of corroboration.

The aim of this study is related to the results of the first study. It was designed to answer the following two questions. First, can differences between metaphors be traced back to the five postulated underlying dimensions? In other words, does the present study yield an identical factor solution, with the moral factor better consolidated? Second, are there differences between literary and journalistic metaphors in their relation to these dimensions? In concrete terms, can differences between literary and journalistic metaphors be reduced to the same dimensions as before, the conventionality dimension and the impolite manners dimension? Do the other dimensions also manifest a difference?

8.2.2 Method

MATERIALS

Literary metaphors (N = 82) were collected from recent novels and short stories by Dutch and Flemish authors, each metaphor deriving from a different author. Non-literary metaphors (N = 82) were selected from three issues each of three different Dutch quality newspapers, published between Thursday 24 October and Saturday 26 October 1991. The papers used were *NRC-Handelsblad*, *Trouw*, and *de Volkskrant*. The methods of sampling and presentation were identical to those of the first study, except that the literary texts were not in my personal possession, but belonged to a bibliophile friend. The materials, being in Dutch, are available on request.

SD SCALES

The scales making up the Semantic Differential were the nineteen scales contributing to the factor solution of the previous study. Two scales expected to tap the moral factor were added: 'critical – conforming', and 'objective – subjective'. Note that 'polite – impolite' was also added; it had been included in the study with the English materials, but was deleted from that factor solution on account of its relatively small reliability. Its renewed inclusion in the present investigation reflects its theoretical importance.

RATERS

Judges were nine volunteer graduates in the Humanities, each of whom was a professional in the field of literature or language as a researcher, editor, publisher, translator, or teacher.

PROCEDURE

Judges took the test in their own time, and were given three weeks to complete it. The test consisted of two parts. In Part A, the total of 164 literary and non-literary metaphors was offered in mixed and randomized order for rating on twenty-two seven-point scales, in the manner of the English study. Judges were instructed not to look at Part B before they had finished Part A. Part B consisted of three sections: in the first section, sixteen metaphors selected at ten-item intervals from Part A were offered for rating for a second time in order to inspect overall reliability by means of test-retest correlations. The second and third sections of Part B contained a series of fifty-three metaphors from two continuous pieces of text: they were the experimental texts of the Dutch underlining and the think aloud studies reported in Chapters 3 and 6. These data were collected for the additional analysis of those processing data. They will be reported in the next chapter and left out of consideration here.

8.2.3 Results

METAPHOR SCALES

There were six isolated missing values, and three subjects inadvertently skipped a (different) entire metaphor each, producing another sixty-six missing values. All missing values were replaced by estimations, computed by averaging the scores of the other subjects on the scale in question, and rounding off to the nearest whole figure.

Intra-rater reliability was examined in order to compare individual stability of scoring throughout the test among the nine raters. Bivariate correlations were calculated for each rater between the data on the 16 test-retest items of Part A and Part B for each of the rating scales. One rater had markedly lower correlation coefficients than the other raters, and was removed.

Inter-rater agreement was estimated among the eight remaining judges for Part A for each of the measuring scales.[9] All scales but one ('objective – subjective') had good reliability co-efficients. This shows that averaging among subjects was a meaningful excercise.

Averaged scores of the eight remaining judges were used to examine overall stability between test and retest. To this end, bivariate correlations between the mean metaphor scores in the test and in the re-test were computed for every scale. There was one extremely low correlation between test and retest, for 'earnest – flippant', and one low correlation for 'pleasant – unpleasant', which led to their removal from the data.[10]

For every metaphor scale, mean scores were computed by averaging across metaphors for each of the two samples; the results are shown in Table 8.5 The difference between the mean scores of the two kinds of metaphors was tested again after data transformation into factor scores.[11]

Table 8.5: Mean scores on scales for literary and journalistic metaphors (standard deviations in brackets)

	Source of metaphors	
Scale	Literary	Journalistic
original – trite	4.11 (1.57)	5.15 (1.21)
precise – vague	3.47 (0.95)	3.21 (0.78)
appropriate – far-fetched	3.36 (0.79)	3.18 (0.63)
abstract – concrete	4.28 (0.92)	4.60 (0.86)
profound – superficial	4.48 (0.92)	5.12 (0.68)
explanatory – confusing	3.25 (0.86)	2.99 (0.62)
informative – illustrative	3.86 (1.13)	2.99 (0.77)
persuasive – implausible	3.38 (0.60)	3.26 (0.48)
natural – affected	3.74 (0.91)	3.55 (0.71)
subtle – obvious	4.57 (0.99)	5.36 (0.76)
polite – impolite	4.06 (0.26)	3.98 (0.32)
formal – informal	4.42 (0.60)	3.90 (0.86)
funny – serious	4.13 (0.81)	4.14 (0.71)
beautiful – ugly	3.91 (0.64)	4.35 (0.42)
shocking – touching	4.12 (0.36)	3.97 (0.21)
tasteful – tasteless	3.75 (0.53)	4.12 (0.33)
critical – comforting	3.97 (0.51)	4.31 (0.51)
objective – subjective	4.49 (0.65)	3.91 (0.74)
opinionated – impartial	4.16 (0.40)	4.13 (0.52)
political – apolitical	4.48 (0.29)	4.12 (0.58)

N of raters = 9; N of metaphors = 164

FACTOR ANALYSIS

Just as before, an initial PCA revealed the presence of potential multicollinearity and singularity. This was solved by the removal of two scales with high bivariate correlations ('explanatory – confusing' and 'natural – affected'). Then another PCA was performed on eighteen rating scales, and factor scores estimated. There were four factors, accounting for 78.8 per cent of the total variance in the data.[12] The factor solution also accounts for a good deal of the variance in every individual rating scale.[13] The relation between the rating scales and the factors is shown in Table 8.6.[14]

Factor I has high loadings from 'far-fetched', 'vague', and 'implausible', and it also has considerable loadings from 'subtle', 'abstract' and 'illustrative'. It may hence be recognized from the previous study as the 'conceptual difficulty' factor. A complication in comparison with that study has been caused by the apparent inclusion of the distinct 'conventionality' factor of the previous study by the difficulty factor of the present one: 'original' and

Table 8.6: Results of PCA: factor loadings of 18 metaphor scales (loadings < 0.40 are suppressed)

Scale	Factor			
	I	II	III	IV
original – trite	− 0.54	0.59	− 0.43	—
precise – vague	0.91	—	—	—
appropriate – far-fetched	0.91	—	—	—
abstract – concrete	− 0.73	—	—	—
profound – superficial	− 0.53	0.74	—	—
informative – illustrative	0.73	− 0.40	—	—
persuasive – implausible	0.87	—	—	—
subtle – obvious	− 0.76	0.55	—	—
polite – impolite	—	—	0.80	—
formal – informal	—	—	0.90	—
funny – serious	—	—	− 0.84	—
beautiful – ugly	—	0.90	—	—
shocking – touching	—	− 0.46	—	0.64
tasteful – tasteless	—	0.86	—	—
critical – conforming	—	0.58	− 0.50	—
objective – subjective	0.53	—	0.58	—
opinionated – impartial	—	—	—	0.63
political – apolitical	—	—	—	0.83
Percentage explained variance:	38.1	18.1	15.6	7.0
Eigenvalue:	6.86	3.25	2.81	1.27

'profound' are related to the difficulty factor in the present case, whereas they were independent and, together with 'subtle', crucially important for the conventionality factor in the first case. We will come back to this point in the discussion below.

Factor II is characterized by high loadings from 'ugly', 'tasteless', and 'superficial'. It is predominantly filled out by 'trite', 'conforming' and 'obvious'. All of these features clearly mark (negative) feelings. The marginal relation of 'shocking' to this factor can also be interpreted in this light. This factor is therefore labelled as the 'negative value' factor. Note that the two conventionality variables of the English study which were included by the difficulty factor above, namely 'trite' and 'superficial', have also been partially incorporated by the present negative value factor.

Factor III captures the informal, funny, and impolite nature of some metaphors. This factor is consequently regarded as the 'impolite manners' factor. It also has considerable loadings from 'subjective' and 'critical', two variables which may be seen to relate negatively to politeness in the light of their opposites, 'objective' and 'conforming'.

The last factor, Factor IV, features high loadings from 'apolitical', 'impartial' and 'touching'. Reversing the perspective, this factor captures the political, partial, and shocking nature of metaphoricity. This makes it into a moral factor pertaining to a metaphor's unbiased or biased position.

COMPARISON WITH THE ENGLISH-LANGUAGE STUDY

All four factors discovered in the Dutch study seem to be related to four of the five factors reported in the English study. If Factor I (conventionality) of the English study is ignored, the other four factors of that study exhibit a suggestive degree of correspondence with Factors I to IV of the present study. However, there is a difference between the identity of the variables included in both investigations. Six scales used in one study were not used in the other, or vice versa; they are 'explanatory − confusing', 'natural − affected', 'pleasant − unpleasant', 'polite − impolite', 'critical − conforming', and 'earnest − flippant'. The removal of six variables out of a total of twenty-one makes a formal comparison too distorted to be valuable: this difference is too large to justify a formal comparison between the two factor solutions by means of correlation or computation of Cattell's Salient Similarity Index − see notes 3 and 11. The relation between the two factor solutions with respect to the remaining variables is shown in Table 8.7, and it provides sufficient informal indication that the factors are comparable.

It can be seen from Table 8.7 that the conceptual difficulty factor has identical loadings from 'precise − vague', 'appropriate − far-fetched', 'abstract − concrete', and 'persuasive − implausible' in the two studies. Four other variables are related to this factor in the Dutch study but not in the English one: 'original − trite', 'profound − superficial', 'informative − illustrative', and 'subtle − obvious'. These variables were all part of the 'conventionality' factor in the first study but were lost in the next. As to the second factor, labelled as 'negative value' in both studies, three variables have equal loadings in the two studies: 'ugly', 'shocking', and 'tasteless'. The scales indicated by 'trite', 'superficial', 'illustrative', and 'obvious' only relate to this factor in the Dutch study. Again, these were all contributors to the separate conventionality factor in the first study. For Factor III, 'impolite manners', two out of four variables perform identically in the two studies: 'formal − informal', and 'funny − serious'. 'Opinionated' loads on this factor in the first study only; and 'original', in the second only. The last factor has the same loadings in the two studies from 'opinionated − impartial' and 'political − apolitical'; but 'shocking − touching' is related to the factor of unbiased position only in the Dutch study.

Table 8.7: Factor loadings of metaphor scales in English and Dutch studies

| | Factor | | | |
| | Conceptual difficulty Engl/Du | Negative value Engl/Du | Impolite manner Engl/Du | Unbiased position Engl/Du |
Scale				
original − trite	0 −	0 +	0 −	
precise − vague	+ +			
appropriate − far-fetched	+ +			
abstract − concrete	− −			
profound − superficial	0 −	0 +		
informative − illustrative	0 +	0 −		
persuasive − implausible	+ +			
subtle − obvious	0 −	0 +		
formal − informal			+ +	
funny − serious			− −	
beautiful − ugly		+ +		
shocking − touching		− −		0 +
tasteful − tasteless		+ +		
opinionated − impartial			− 0	+ +
political − apolitical				+ +

+ positively salient; − negatively salient; 0 no relation

LITERARY AND JOURNALISTIC METAPHORS

Mean factor scores of the two kinds of metaphors resulting from the above PCA are shown in Figure 8.2. The reliability of their difference was examined by performing a multivariate analysis of variance.[15] The results showed a significant difference between literary and non-literary metaphors regarding difficulty, negative value, impolite manners, and unbiased position. It may be concluded that literary metaphors are more difficult, have a greater positive value, are less polite, and less biased than journalistic metaphors.

8.2.4 Discussion

The findings of the present Dutch study are sufficiently similar to those of the previous English study to warrant a comparative discussion of the discourse dimensions of metaphoricity discovered here. With some interesting variations, the basic pattern of the previous study was corroborated by the findings. In particular, the factors produced in the PCA are reasonably interpretable from the point of view of the discourse theory developed in

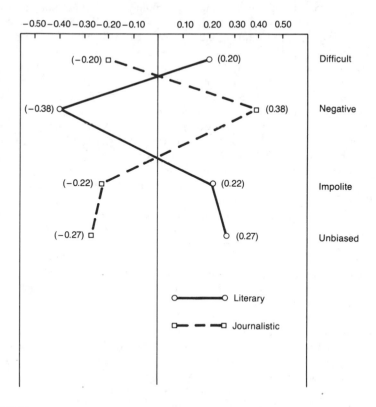

Fig. 8.2:   Mean factor scores of 164 Dutch literary and journalistic metaphors

Chapter 7. However, the full discourse pattern of five distinct dimensions expected from a theoretical point of view was not confirmed by this study.

The most noticeable difference between the two studies is the disappearance of the theoretically important factor of conventionality discovered before. Instead, the scales making up the conventionality factor in the English study have now merged with the scales contributing to the conceptual clarity factor, which was still separate before. (This holds for 'original – trite', 'precise – vague', 'profound – superficial', 'informative – illustrative', and 'subtle – 'obvious'.) At the same time, these very scales, apart from 'precise – vague', also contribute to the second factor in the present study, negative value, but with reversed signs in comparison with their role in the conceptual difficulty factor. How can this difference between the two studies be explained?

It is useful to begin by pointing out a finding reported but not discussed in the first study. Note 6 (section 8.1.3) stated that the factor correlation matrix showed a correlation of 0.25 between Factor I and Factor II. Usually the level of importance for taking into account such factor correlations in the discussion is somewhat higher, for which reason it was omitted from consideration. But in the present context it may be asked whether there was a suggestive tendency there. For it is not at all implausible that there may be a correlation between the factors of conceptual difficulty versus clarity on the one hand, and originality versus conventionality on the other. Perhaps it was due to the limited size of the sample of the first study that this correlation did not reveal itself in its full strength.

This suggestion becomes more plausible when we remember that practically the same scales of the previous conventionality factor also load on the present negative value factor, with reversed signs. Again, it is no wonder that conventional metaphor attributes such as triteness, superficiality, and obviousness go together with the negative value attributes of ugliness, tastelessness, and conformity. Thus the question arises whether the purportedly linguistic factor discovered in the first study is a truly linguistic factor at all. Conventionality and originality may just as well be regarded as part of conceptual clarity on the one hand, and of negative or positive value on the other.

A complex reply to this query is that the conventionality factor in the English study is partly linguistic, and partly not. It may be the case that, in that study, the conventionality factor has captured both a linguistic and a conceptual property of metaphors, which, in more sensitive research designs, may be distinguished more clearly. The apparent success of the first study in identifying the postulated linguistic dimension motivated the maintenance of the scales as they stood, but the findings of the present study now throw a different light on this issue. For it should be noted – with hindsight – that the second study is relatively weak on the number of scales tapping purely linguistic qualities of metaphors. One could think of alternative scales for the linguistic dimension such as 'grammatical – ungrammatical', 'dense – explicit', and 'normal – abnormal language use'. Pending the exploration of such scales, the hypothesis of a linguistic dimension to metaphoricity still awaits an answer.

As a result of the outcome of such an investigation, the factor labelled 'conceptual clarity' may or may not include the aspect of conventionality versus originality. However this may be, the conceptual core of the clarity factor is transparent: it consists of 'precise – vague', 'appropriate – far-fetched', 'abstract – concrete', and 'persuasive – implausible' (both studies). The large size of this factor is, moreover, sound evidence for the general opinion that differences between metaphors crucially depend on their conceptual nature.

Let us now turn to the next factor in the second study, negative value. In both studies, the value of metaphors is characterized by high loadings from 'beautiful – ugly' and 'tasteful – tasteless'. This factor is filled out in the first case by two further obviously emotive scales, 'pleasant – unpleasant' and 'shocking – touching', the latter playing a markedly less important role in the negative value factor in the second case. There, by comparison, we see additional contributions from 'original – trite', 'profound – superficial', 'subtle – obvious', and 'critical – conforming', which are the former (linguistic) 'conventionality' scales. However, as I said above, these attributes may all be regarded as associated with positive or negative emotions about metaphors. The basis of the negative value factor can hence be considered to be fairly well confirmed, but its relation to the potentially linguistic attributes previously linked to the conventionality factor remains an open question.

As to the communicative manners of metaphors, the triad 'formal – informal', 'funny – serious', and 'polite – impolite' is the basis of this factor in the Dutch study. The less important scale of 'opinionated – impartial' belonging to this factor in the English study is replaced by the similar scale of 'critical – conforming' in the Dutch study. This factor is therefore also a relatively clear discourse dimension upon which metaphors differ.

More problematic is the factor pertaining to the moral position of metaphors. True, its basic structure is highly similar in both studies, for the only two variables loading highly on it in the previous case ('opinionated – impartial' and 'political – apolitical') are also the basis for this factor in the second study. Nor is the filling out of this factor in the present study by the scale 'shocking – touching' an insuperable difficulty, for this scale manifestly taps emotions that go with the varying moral positions defined by the two central scales just mentioned. However, it was noted in note 12 (section 8.2.3) that the moral factor lay beyond the break in size of the eigenvalues in the screeplot, suggesting that Factor IV might not be a 'real' factor after all. I had similar suspicions in the discussion of this factor in the previous study on account of its small size and the low number of variables contributing to it. This raises severe doubts.

In defence of a presumable moral factor, however, it may be recalled that the communalities of precisely its two central scales, 'opinionated – impartial' and 'political – apolitical', were relatively low (note 13). This suggests that these scales are relatively isolated from the other factors, and are defined primarily by the postulated moral factor. This turned out to be especially true of the scale 'political – apolitical', for upon inspection it manifested only three significant correlations with all of the other rating scales. However, the question whether this factor for metaphoricity has been consolidated better than in the first study has to be answered negatively: the evidence is still somewhat tenuous, and further research will have to clarify this issue.

The second basic question addressed differences between literary and journalistic metaphors. In this respect, the present study showed that all four discourse dimensions of metaphoricity appeared to be relevant for a discrimination between the two kinds of metaphors. The finding of the previous study indicating a divergence in communicative manners between the two kinds of metaphors was confirmed. The addition of an opposition between literary and journalistic metaphors with regard to negative value is no surprise: that literary metaphors have a more positive value than journalistic ones fits in with our expectations. The role of moral position has to be qualified from the perspective of the tentative nature of this dimension, but it may be understood on the basis of the typical function of a good deal of journalistic metaphors. Finally, the disappearance of the originality vs. conventionality distinction is explicable from the above considerations on the conceptual difficulty factor, which in the second study includes the separate linguistic conventionality factor of the first. This factor, as is evident, also bears on the discrimination between literary and journalistic metaphors, in that literary metaphors are more difficult, or less clear, than journalistic ones.

8.3 Conclusion

The general discourse approach adopted in this book has proved a fruitful guideline for the construction of the Semantic Differentials in these two studies. The idea that language processing involves a number of distinct cognitive aspects, linguistic, conceptual, and communicative, and that it also includes a number of non-cognitive features, such as emotive and moral ones, made me interested in a wider range of properties of metaphors than has been examined hitherto. Indeed, the intention of revealing a number of basic discourse dimensions which underlie differences between metaphors has proved effective in that we have at least obtained a first sight of the above-mentioned conceptual, communicative, emotive, and moral dimensions. Whether there is a linguistic dimension, too, remains unclear, because it seems that the conventionality factor of the first study can also be regarded as an artefact which, in the second study, was resolved between the conceptual difficulty and negative value factors.

Another result of the present studies is that we have discovered relations between metaphor attributes which were located theoretically on different dimensions of discourse. For instance, positive metaphors (emotive dimension) may also be original expressions (linguistic dimension) and they may be apt or far-fetched (conceptual dimension). This result may be compared to the relations reported by Gentner (1982) between richness and literary goodness, and between clarity and scientific goodness of metaphors. Thus the fact that differences between metaphors can be described with reference to the basic discourse dimensions of conceptual difficulty, emotive value, communicative manners, and moral position does not mean that these are the only characteristics with which these groups may be distinguished from each other. On the contrary, conceptual difficulty or clarity has a number of concomitant features in the areas of linguistic form and communicative function, and the same goes for emotive quality, and so on.

This may be illustrated by turning to the main difference between metaphors motivating the present chapter, the one between literary and non-literary metaphors. Table 8.8 provides an overview of the characteristics of the literary and journalistic metaphors included in the last study. As can be seen, the main dimensions of conceptual structure, emotive value, communicative manners, and moral position all attract metaphor attributes from other dimensions than the one they derive from themselves.

By way of conclusion, the difference between the literary and the journalistic metaphors summarized in Table 8.8 can be tentatively connected to the discourse theory of literature developed in the foregoing chapters. The difficult conceptual structure of literary metaphors goes with the possibility for subjective and polyvalent processing characteristic of literature, while the clear conceptual structure of journalistic metaphors ties in with the possibility for intersubjective and monovalent processing. The positive value of literary metaphors, as opposed to the negative value of journalistic metaphors, reflects the familiar division between the aesthetic and the factual domains discourse from which they derive. The polite communicative manners of journalistic metaphors can be understood from the need for pragmatically ('factually') oriented and monovalent discourse in society, while the impolite nature of literary metaphors mirrors the liberation from this need in aesthetic discourse. And finally, the biased position of journalistic metaphors can be regarded as being due to the societal interests that are part and parcel of journalistic discourse, whereas literary metaphors can express a factually more disinterested, aesthetic attitude.

Table 8.8: Properties of literary and journalistic metaphors in Dutch study

Factor	Literary	Journalistic
Conceptual structure	difficult	clear
	original	trite
	vague	precise
	far-fetched	appropriate
	abstract	concrete
	profound	superficial
	illustrative	informative
	implausible	persuasive
	subtle	obvious
	subjective	objective
Emotive value	positive	negative
	original	trite
	profound	superficial
	illustrative	informative
	subtle	obvious
	beautiful	ugly
	touching	shocking
	tasteful	tasteless
	critical	conforming
Communicative manners	impolite	polite
	original	trite
	impolite	polite
	informal	formal
	funny	serious
	critical	conforming
	subjective	objective
Moral position	unbiased	biased
	touching	shocking
	impartial	opinionated
	apolitical	political

Notes

1. 'Personal' in this case does not imply 'idiosyncratic': as can be seen from the examples in Table 8.1, most of these writers are part of the set curriculum at university courses in contemporary literature.
2. Crohnbach's α was calculated for every scale for nine raters over ninety-six metaphors. The bulk of the scales had reliability coefficients ranging between 0.84 and 0.98. The exceptions were 'complex – simple' (0.71), 'intimate – remote' (0.78), 'polite – impolite' (0.80), and 'approving – disapproving' (0.80).

3. Before this could be done, however, it first had to be shown that the two samples could be treated as belonging to the same population. To this end, a comparison between separate factor solutions for both kinds of metaphors was envisaged in order to ascertain whether they had the same number of factors with similar labels and with similar rating scales loading on these factors. Two separate principal components analyses (PCAs) with varimax rotation were performed for the mean scores of every literary and journalistic metaphor on thirty scales. Both PCAs revealed six factors with eigenvalue larger than one, but screeplots indicated the presence of different numbers of factors for the literary and the journalistic metaphors: 3 and 4, respectively. For both groups, it turned out that the first four factors could be labelled in the same way, with the additional note that Factors III and IV had changed position between the two samples, indicating a corresponding shift in the variance they explained for each group of metaphors. Moreover, practically the same rating scales loaded highly on the relevant factors for the literary and the journalistic metaphors. The correlations among the loadings of scales on literary and journalistic factors were 0.90, 0.91, 0.95, and 0.90, respectively, for the first four factors (all significant at $p < 0.001$). To check that these are not inflated correlations, Cattell's Salient Similarity Index was calculated for the factor with the least number of corresponding loadings, Factor I (Tabachnik and Fidell 1989: 642–4). This index compares the number of paired scales that are identically related to the factor with the number of paired scales that are contrarily related to the factor, simultaneously taking into account the number of pairs of scales which do not relate to the factor at all. The s value was 0.80, which exceeded the value expected by chance at $p < 0.001$. The factor structure for literary and journalistic metaphors was hence sufficiently similar for the first four factors (accounting for 76.8 per cent and 71.1 per cent of the variance, respectively) to subject them to a combined PCA.

4. The problems of multicollinearity and singularity are not serious for PCA itself, but only for estimation of factor scores (Tabachnik and Fidell 1989: 604). These problems were hence ignored when the two kinds of metaphors were compared above – see note 3.

5. Communality values ranged from 0.65 to 0.90.

6. Factor loadings were obtained by varimax rotation. Oblique rotation was also requested in order to inspect whether the interpretability of the factors would be enhanced by such a procedure. However, as a result of this kind of rotation, factors are not independent of each other, and correlations between factors have to be examined for interpretation. It turned out that interfactor correlation was low: two bivariate correlations reached the level of $r = 0.25$ (varimax Factor I × Factor II) and $r = -0.25$ (varimax Factor III × Factor IV), the rest was smaller than $r = 0.16$. These co-efficients indicate that there is less than 10 per cent overlap in variance among factors (cf. Tabachnik and Fidell (1989: 637). This suggests that the factors are relatively independent, even when dependence is allowed through non-orthogonal rotation. Moreover, all five factors appeared to be readily interpretable in the orthogonal varimax solution, and only one factor of the oblique solution differed (slightly) from the varimax solution. For

Table VIIIA: Effect of source on mean factor scores (univariate tests of within item effects)

(i) Conventionality

Source of variation	SS	d.f.	MS	F
SOURCE BY FACTOR (1)	29.81	1	29.81	42.99**
WITHIN CELLS	65.19	94	0.69	

(ii) Difficulty

Source of variation	SS	d.f.	MS	F
SOURCE BY FACTOR (2)	0.26	1	0.26	0.26
WITHIN CELLS	94.74	94	1.01	

(iii) Negative value

Source of variation	SS	d.f.	MS	F
SOURCE BY FACTOR (3)	1.86	1	1.86	1.88
WITHIN CELLS	93.14	94	0.99	

(iv) Impolite manners

Source of variation	SS	d.f.	MS	F
SOURCE BY FACTOR (4)	4.20	1	4.20	4.34*
WITHIN CELLS	90.80	94	0.97	

(v) Unbiased position

Source of variation	SS	d.f.	MS	F
SOURCE BY FACTOR (5)	1.70	1	1.70	1.71
WITHIN CELLS	93.30	94	0.99	

$**p < 0.01; *p < 0.05$

these reasons, there was no ground for reporting the oblique results, and the varimax solution was retained.

7. A multivariate analysis of variance was executed on the dependent variables of conventionality, difficulty, negative value, impolite manners, and unbiased position. There was one within-factor of 'factor scores' (with the five levels of Factor I through Factor V) and one between-factor of 'source' (with the two levels 'literary discourse' and 'journalistic discourse'). The results of the univariate F-tests for each dependent variable are reported in Table VIIIA above.

8. This situation also clarifies the large number of variables showing bivariate correlations: they were variants of each other at different dimensions of discourse. It is therefore less drastic than it seems to have discarded so many of

the original measuring scales as we did before executing the factor analysis above.

Another consideration involves the sometimes vague nature of the labels of the scales themselves. Although I believe that there is good reason to regard 'obvious' as an emotive scale, it is also quite understandable that raters have used this scale in a rather more linguistic and conceptual manner. This can only be resolved by conducting further work in order to improve instructions for raters.

9. Reliability co-efficients (Crohnbach's α) ranged between 0.87 and 0.99 for all scales but three. 'Pleasant – unpleasant' and 'tasteful – tasteless' managed a sufficient 0.83 and 0.81, respectively, but the new scale 'objective – subjective' only had 0.68.

10. Correlations ranged between a low $r = 0.70$ for 'abstract – concrete' and 'opinionated – impartial' to a high $r = 0.96$ for 'original – trite'. The scales removed from the data had $r = 0.12$ ('earnest – flippant') and $r = 0.56$ ('pleasant – unpleasant').

11. Following the procedure of the previous study, separate factor analyses were performed on the mean scores of every literary and journalistic metaphor for the 20 scales remaining after the removal of 'earnest – flippant' and 'pleasant – unpleasant' in order to examine whether they may be treated as belonging to the same population. Both Principal Component Analyses with varimax rotation exhibited four factors with eigenvalue larger than one. All four factors seemed recognizable as familiar from the previous study. In the literary sample, the fourth factor was somewhat dubious on account of its occurrence after the break in size of eigenvalues in the screeplot; but its eigenvalue was 1.34, and it bore a good similarity to the fourth factor in the journalistic sample, so it was included in the formal comparison between the factor solutions for the two sets of metaphors. For the literary and the journalistic metaphors, factors could be labelled in the same way, except that Factor II and III in the literary sample corresponded to Factor III and II in the journalistic sample. There was sufficient correspondence between the two samples regarding the loading pattern of the distinct rating scales on these factors. Correlations between the loading patterns were significant for all four factors ($r = 0.99, 0.95, 0.96,$ and $0.88, p < 0.001$, respectively). Cattell's Salient Similarity Index was calculated again for the factor with the smallest number of corresponding loadings, Factor IV. The s value was 0.75, which exceeded the value expected by chance at $p < 0.001$. Thus the two samples were sufficiently similar for all four factors to allow a combined factor analysis.

12. Judging from the screeplot, there was a break in size of the eigenvalues after the third factor, but the fourth factor was readily interpretable, had a large enough eigenvalue (1.27), and explained a reasonable 7 per cent of the total variance. Moreover, when the factor analysis was rerun with predetermined solution of three factors, the residual correlation matrix showed a high number of considerable residuals: this suggests that the fourth factor is indeed useful in accounting for the additional 7 per cent of the total variance (see Tabachnik and Fidell 1989: 636). Therefore it was retained.

13. Communalities ranged from 0.65 to 0.90. Especially the communalities of the variables of Factor IV, namely 'shocking – touching', 'opinionated – impartial' and 'political – apolitical', were relatively low: 0.65, 0.66, and 0.70, respectively.
14. Factor loadings were obtained after varimax rotation. In order to examine whether factors were independent, oblique rotation was also requested. Inspection of the factor correlation matrix showed that factors were sufficiently independent despite non-orthogonal rotation: the highest correlation between factors was $r = 0.25$ for Factor II × Factor III, which is well below the limit of 0.30 advised as a cut-off point by Tabachnik and Fidell (1989: 637). This indicates that maintenance of orthogonal rotation is feasible and does not unduly distort the relation between the factors.
15. A multivariate analysis of variance was performed upon difficulty, negative value, impolite manners, and unbiased position; there was one within-factor of 'factor scores', having the levels of Factor I through Factor IV, and one between-factor of 'source', with the levels 'literary discourse' and 'journalistic discourse'. The results of the univariate F-tests are reported in Table VIIIB.

Table VIIIB: Effect of source on mean factor scores (univariate tests of within item effects)

(i) *Difficulty*

Source of variation	SS	d.f.	MS	F
SOURCE BY FACTOR (1)	6.53	1	6.53	6.76*
WITHIN CELLS	156.47	162	0.97	

(ii) *Negative value*

Source of variation	SS	d.f.	MS	F
SOURCE BY FACTOR (2)	23.16	1	23.16	26.83**
WITHIN CELLS	139.84	162	0.86	

(iii) *Impolite manners*

Source of variation	SS	d.f.	MS	F
SOURCE BY FACTOR (3)	7.72	1	7.72	8.06**
WITHIN CELLS	155.28	162	0.96	

(iv) *Unbiased position*

Source of variation	SS	d.f.	MS	F
SOURCE BY FACTOR (4)	12.11	1	12.11	13.00*
WITHIN CELLS	150.89	162	0.97	

$**p < 0.01; *p < 0.05$

CHAPTER NINE

Properties and processes

The last-topic of this study is the relation between differences among metaphors and their understanding by readers. The findings on metaphor processing presented in Chapters 3 and 6 suggest that the understanding of metaphors in literature and in journalism is affected by the activation of a discourse-typical processing strategy on the part of the reader. However, it may also be the case that differences between metaphors themselves determine the attention readers pay to them. Therefore the question arises as to the relation between metaphor properties and their processing during reception. This question will be at the centre of this final chapter.

It will lead us back to the two processing studies of Chapter 3 and Chapter 6 which used the same literary and journalistic text as experimental materials. As will be recalled, the metaphors in these texts were rated by a group of independent judges in the Dutch rating study discussed in Chapter 8. These data will now be used to investigate whether differences between metaphors affect their processing in literary and non-literary, in this case journalistic, reception. In particular, is there a relation between metaphor qualities on the one hand and underlining for literariness versus journalistic nature on the other in the study of Chapter 3? Second, do metaphor qualities determine the incidence of topic construction, context construction, explicit identification, explicit appreciation, and refunctionalization in the thinking out loud study presented in Chapter 6? To answer these questions, the next section will first report the results of the rating study concerning the properties of the metaphors in the two experimental texts.

9.1 Metaphor properties

9.1.1 Introduction

To what extent are the metaphors of the experimental texts used in the underlining and think-aloud studies comparable to the metaphors of the larger Dutch sample used for rating in Chapter 8? Do the literary and journalistic metaphors of the two texts in question exhibit the same differences as those which were found in the overall rating study? In other words, how representative of the general difference between literary and journalistic metaphors are the metaphors present in the two experimental texts? These are the questions of this section. They will afford a platform from which to continue with our investigation into the relation between metaphor properties and discourse processes in the next sections.

The properties of the metaphors in the experimental texts were determined by collecting rating data of the kind reported in Chapter 8. Data collection was part of that very study, the same raters carrying out the assessment of the metaphors of the experimental texts as an additional task. Separate analysis of these data by means of a factor analysis, however, was not deemed feasible, because of the small number of metaphors (N = 53). Inclusion in the overall factor analysis was not felicitous either, because of the fact that the metaphors we are presently dealing with all come from only two texts. Therefore, another approach to the analysis of the rating data of the metaphors present in the experimental texts was adopted here.

Taking the results of the Dutch rating study as a criterion, I used the rating scores on what may be regarded as the marker variables for the four central factors – difficulty, value, politeness, and moral position – as a first means to examine the properties of the experimental metaphors. The scales are 'appropriate – inappropriate', 'beautiful – ugly', 'formal – informal', and 'political – apolitical', respectively (see Table 8.6). The differences between the literary and journalistic metaphors found in Chapter 8 acting as a guideline, the following questions have to be answered by data analysis (see Figure 8.2):

1. Are the literary metaphors more far-fetched than the journalistic metaphors?
2. Are the literary metaphors more beautiful than the journalistic ones?
3. Are the literary metaphors less formal than the journalistic ones?
4. Are the literary metaphors less political than the journalistic ones?

Table 9.1: Mean scores of metaphors in literary and journalistic text

Scale	Text	
	Literary (*N of metaphors* = 27)	*Journalistic* (*N of metaphors* = 26)
appropriate – far-fetched	2.78 (0.57)	2.88 (0.59)
beautiful – ugly	3.46 (0.58)	4.03 (0.51)
formal – informal	4.00 (0.47)	4.34 (0.82)
political – apolitical	4.13 (0.45)	4.06 (0.45)

9.1.2 Method

Rating data were collected on all twenty-seven literary and twenty-six journalistic metaphors in the manner of the Dutch rating study reported in Chapter 8 (section 2.2). Data collection concerning these metaphor characteristics was a separate, added part of the general data collection for that study. The same rating scales, raters, and procedure were used. An evaluation of the present materials can hence proceed without difficulty against the basis of the findings in that study.

9.1.3 Results

The mean scores of the metaphors in the literary and the journalistic text, averaged across eight raters, are presented in Table 9.1. It can be observed that the mean scores of the metaphors on the scale 'appropriate – far-fetched' are approximately equal. However, the metaphors in the literary text were perceived on average to be more beautiful than those in the journalistic text. Furthermore, the literary metaphors have a lower mean score on 'formal – informal' than the journalistic metaphors: the literary metaphors are more formal. Finally, the political position expressed by the two kinds of metaphors is about the same.

The differences were tested for their statistical reliability by means of a multivariate analysis of variance.[1] The results of the separate tests for each of the dependent variables showed that only one dependent variable manifested a reliable difference between the experimental literary and journalistic metaphors, 'beautiful – ugly'. The metaphors in the literary text are more beautiful than the metaphors in the journalistic text. There also was a tendency for the difference between the literary and journalistic metaphors to become significant with respect to the variable 'formal – informal'. The other metaphor attributes did not show any statistically reliable differences between the two textual conditions.

9.1.4 Discussion

Only one of the differences between literary and journalistic metaphors found in the more representative sample of the Dutch rating study reported in the previous chapter is also present in the experimental materials of the underlining and think aloud studies. The metaphors of the experimental literary text were found to be more beautiful than the metaphors in the experimental journalistic text. The important general difference between the conceptual difficulty or clarity of the literary and journalistic metaphors in the overall rating study is absent from the two texts used for the processing studies. Instead, the metaphors in the literary and the journalistic experimental text are equally appropriate or far-fetched, the property taken as a marker variable for 'difficulty – clarity'. When we turn to the third factor of the previous chapter, manners of communication, the situation is worse. It appears that there is a tendency towards having the reverse situation from the one in the general rating study: the metaphors in the journalistic text are almost more informal than the ones in the literary text. Finally, the metaphors in the experimental texts do not exhibit the expected difference with regard to the least consolidated factor of moral position either: they are equally apolitical.

The conclusion must be that the metaphors in the two experimental texts do not show the same differences as the ones found in Chapter 8 between a large sample of literary and journalistic metaphors. Taking the results of that chapter as a guideline, the metaphors in the experimental texts are less representative of general differences between literary and journalistic metaphors than was hoped beforehand. Therefore I will use only some of the data on the properties of the metaphors in the experimental texts for an investigation of their influence during processing. It is clear that we can use the attribute of value, for that is the only factor manifesting an identical tendency as in the overall study: the literary metaphors were found to be more beautiful than the journalistic ones. However, because of the tendency towards a reverse relation for the factor of communicative manners, and because of the lack of difference between the two kinds of metaphors on the smallest (and dubious) factor of moral position, these two aspects will be left out of consideration. As to the conceptual property of 'appropriate – far-fetched', here the lack of the expected difference between the two kinds of metaphors may still be turned to our advantage for reasons to be explained in the next section.

9.2 Properties and processes in underlining

9.2.1 Introduction

Let us now combine the issue of the metaphor properties of clarity and value on the one hand and reader performance in processing the two experimental texts on the other. I will discuss this in terms of the notion of attention, for both the underlining study and the think-aloud study dealt with metaphor processing in terms of attending to metaphors, either by means of underlining or by means of verbalization. What is the relation between attention to metaphors during processing on the one hand and differences between metaphors regarding their appropriateness (or conceptual clarity) and their beauty (or emotive value) on the other? In this section, we will look at the underlining study.

It will be remembered that the underlining study contained two texts and two experimental conditions. The texts were the originally literary and journalistic text, and the conditions involved two contexts of presentation (section 3.3). Readers were either given the instruction to read the literary text as literary and the journalistic text as journalistic (authentic context group) or the other way around, that is, the literary text as journalistic and the journalistic text as literary (perverse context group). As reported in section 3.3.3., there was an interaction effect between text and context, amounting to an increased attention to metaphors in the originally literary text by the authentic context group, but in the originally journalistic text by the perverse context group. Both of these increases were due to the instruction to read the text as literary. We will now incorporate the role of the metaphor properties of relative clarity and value in this situation.

When metaphors are conceptually unclear, they may be expected to require more attention in comparison with clear metaphors because they constitute a processing problem that has to be solved. In the context of the underlining study, this forces unclear metaphors to the attention of the reader, offering a clear moment to decide whether the unclear metaphor is regarded as typically literary or typically journalistic. I predict that readers should regard relatively unclear metaphors as typically literary because of the expectation that literary texts are complex or polyvalent. Readers should not take unclear metaphors as typically journalistic because they should expect clarity and monovalence there. Clear metaphors should be regarded as typically journalistic. Therefore, unclear metaphors should be underlined less frequently as typically journalistic than clear ones.

The hypothesis to be tested by means of data analysis is that there will be an interaction between metaphor property, text, and context condition: in the authentic context group, unclear metaphors should be underlined more often than clear metaphors in the originally literary text (for literariness), but unclear metaphors should be underlined less often than clear metaphors in the journalistic text (for journalistic nature). The reverse situation should hold for the perverse context condition: unclear metaphors should be underlined less often than clear metaphors in the originally literary text (for journalism), whereas unclear metaphors will be underlined more often than clear metaphors in the originally journalistic text (for literariness).

Now let us turn to the role of emotive value. Metaphors with a positive value may be beautiful and tasteful, among other qualities. This at least suggests that positive metaphors may be underlined more often for literariness during literary reading than for their typical journalistic nature during journalistic reading. There is no generally founded expectation that metaphors in journalism ought to be positive in the above sense. Indeed, according to the tendencies found in the previous chapter, metaphors in journalism are generally found to have a negative value when compared with literary metaphors. In other words, negative metaphors may be underlined more often than positive ones when readers select typically journalistic passages. Therefore, the same situation arises as above with regard to clarity: there should be an interaction between metaphor property, text, and experimental condition.

The predictions are as follows. In the authentic context group, readers should underline positive metaphors more often than negative ones for literariness (in the originally literary text), but negative metaphors more often than positive ones for journalistic nature (in the originally journalistic text). In the perverse context group, readers should underline negative metaphors more often than positive ones for journalism in the originally literary text, but positive metaphors more often than negative ones for literariness in the originally journalistic text. These predictions were tested by additional analysis of the data collected in the experiment reported in Chapter 3.

9.2.2 Method

Procedure, subjects, and *materials* are as in Chapter 3 (section 3.3.2).

METAPHOR PROPERTIES

For the factor of relative clarity, the three most important variables of 'appropriate – far-fetched', 'precise – vague', and 'persuasive – implausible' were averaged. For the factor of negative or positive value, 'beautiful

– ugly' and 'tasteful – tasteless' were averaged. In this way, more solid figures were obtained for the two intended attributes of clarity and value than if only the values of the marker variables used in the previous section had been used.

It should be recalled here that, because of the manipulation of the two texts by means of adding or deleting a 'journalistic' title, two metaphors in the original title of the genuinely journalistic text had to be left aside. This brings the total of literary and journalistic metaphors to twenty-seven and twenty-four, respectively. The two groups of metaphors were next divided into two groups for each of the properties of clarity and value. For clarity, there were fourteen clear and thirteen less clear metaphors in the literary text, and twelve clear and twelve less clear metaphors in the journalistic text. For value, there were fourteen positive and thirteen less positive metaphors in the literary text, and twelve positive and twelve less positive metaphors in the journalistic text.[2]

9.2.3 Results

We will first look at the underlining data with respect to the property of metaphor clarity. Having separated the clear from the less clear metaphors for each text, I counted the number of metaphors underlined by each subject for all four groups of clear versus unclear literary and clear versus unclear journalistic metaphors. Then these four groups of scores were averaged across subjects. Thus I obtained an average underlining score for clear and less clear metaphors in both reading conditions. The results of this preparation of the data are presented in Table 9.2.

At first sight, the idea of an interaction between metaphor property, text, and context seems to be borne out by some of the data. For instance, less clear metaphors were underlined more often than clear metaphors for literariness in the originally literary text in the authentic context condition, and for the originally journalistic text in the perverse context condition. However, the other averages do not lie very far apart or are identical. In order to test whether the differences between the various conditions were statistically reliable, a multivariate analysis of variance was performed.[3]

There was a clear main effect for the contextual conditions of presentation: more metaphors were underlined in the authentic condition than in the perverse condition. However, this main effect has to be interpreted with reference to the significant interaction effect. This is a variant of the situation discussed in Chapter 3 (section 3.3). The test statistics show that context interacts with metaphor type in both texts. This is according to the prediction. I will now look at each of the interactions between context and textual condition separately. Because we are interested in the differen-

Table 9.2: Mean proportional incidence (and standard deviation) of metaphor inclusion in underlining divided by degree of clarity

	Text			
	Literary		*Journalistic*	
Context	Clear mets	Less clear	Clear mets	Less clear
Authentic	0.43 (0.20)	0.51 (0.23)	0.26 (0.14)	0.26 (0.13)
Perverse	0.11 (0.16)	0.09 (0.15)	0.24 (0.16)	0.34 (0.12)

tial effect of metaphor properties within texts, this is best done by taking the texts as the point of reference.

In the *originally literary text*, the interaction is due to the fact that less clear metaphors were selected more often than clear ones by the authentic context group, but not by the perverse context group. This agrees with the prediction, for the authentic context group read the literary text as literary, whereas the perverse context group read it as journalistic. The interaction shows that there is a relation between less clear metaphors and literariness. However, it does not show that there is a relation between clear metaphors and journalistic reading. Apparently, the interaction does not go so far as to promote the clear metaphors to the status of typically journalistic passages.

In the *originally journalistic text*, less clear metaphors were also selected more often than clear ones for literariness, namely by the group of readers in the perverse context condition, who were offered the originally journalistic text as literary. However, there is no difference again between the two types of metaphor regarding the selection of typically journalistic passages (authentic context condition). There is an additional significance of the within-subjects effect of metaphor type within text, which can now be explained as also being due to the interaction effect: on average, less clear metaphors are underlined more often by groups of subjects because of the large difference in the perverse condition, for there is no difference between the clear and unclear metaphors in the experimental condition. In other words, the same relation obtains in the originally journalistic text as in the originally literary text: there is a striking relation between relative metaphor unclarity and literary reading, but there is no relation between metaphor clarity and journalistic reading. The prediction of an interaction between metaphor property, text, and context has been confirmed only for the relation between the metaphor property of relative unclarity and the instruction for literary reading.

Now we will consider the results regarding the property of value. The data were prepared in the same manner as with clarity. They are shown in Table 9.3.

To test whether value differences between metaphors affected the

Table 9.3: Mean proportional incidence (and standard deviation) of metaphor inclusion in underlining divided by degree of value

	Text			
	Literary		*Journalistic*	
Context	Positive mets	Less positive	Positive mets	Less positive
Authentic	0.57 (0.22)	0.37 (0.22)	0.31 (0.16)	0.20 (0.11)
Perverse	0.07 (0.11)	0.12 (0.19)	0.32 (0.18)	0.27 (0.14)

underlining of passages for literary and journalistic nature, the same statistical analysis of the data was performed as with the property of clarity.[4] The results of the analysis tell almost the same story as was the case with clarity. There was a significant overall context effect, but it had to be interpreted with reference to the interactions. Therefore we will discuss each of the textual conditions separately again.

For the *originally literary text,* positive metaphors were underlined more often than less positive ones by the authentic context group, that is, as typically literary passages. However, the subjects in the perverse context condition, whose task for the originally literary text was to select typically journalistic passages, underlined less positive metaphors more often than positive ones. In other words, there is an inverse relation between metaphor type in the literary text and reading instruction: in the originally literary text, positive metaphors were regarded more often as literary than less positive metaphors, while relatively negative metaphors were regarded as journalistic more often than positive ones. This is according to the predictions.

In the *originally journalistic text,* there is a lack of interaction between metaphor type within text on the one hand and context of presentation on the other. In both of the context conditions, less positive metaphors were underlined less often than positive metaphors. In other words, the positive metaphors in the originally journalistic text were relatively frequently selected as literary (perverse context group); this corresponds with the tendency in the originally literary text, and with the prediction. But positive metaphors were also selected quite frequently as typically journalistic passages (authentic context group). This result differs from the finding with the originally literary text, where less positive metaphors were selected as typically journalistic. Moreover, this finding goes against our prediction that journalism corresponds with relatively negative metaphors rather than positive ones. In sum, the interaction of metaphor property with journalism does not fall out as clearly as predicted.

9.2.4 Discussion

There is a relation between metaphor property and discourse-typical reading. The hypothesis that there is an interaction between the metaphor properties of clarity and value on the one hand and literary versus journalistic reading on the other has received encouraging support from the data. However, there were also some unexpected findings, which have to be accounted for. I will begin with clarity.

The prediction that less clear metaphors would be underlined more often than clear ones as typically literary was confirmed by both conditions. In the authentic context group, this meant that subjects underlined less clear metaphors more frequently than clear metaphors in an originally literary text. But in the control group, the same tendency could be observed for less clear metaphors in what was originally a journalistic text. This is strong evidence for the power of a literary reading strategy which interacts with relatively unclear metaphors.

The reverse of this thesis was not confirmed by the data. It was expected that clear metaphors would be underlined more often than less clear metaphors as typically journalistic passages. This was expected on the grounds of the relation between clarity and monovalence. However, it turned out that the clear and less clear metaphors were selected equally frequently as typically journalistic. Relatively unclear metaphors were apparently not avoided when readers were selecting typically journalistic passages. They may have been interesting, for instance, or informative, and could have been selected as typically journalistic on those grounds.

When we consider the findings for the positive and less positive metaphors, a comparable situation can be observed. The predicted interaction between positive metaphors and literary reading was observed in both conditions. Again, the fact that this interaction was found in a non-literary text which was offered as literary constitutes strong evidence for a reading strategy which relates literary reception to positive metaphors. However, the predicted interaction between relatively negative value and journalistic reading was found in only one of the two conditions. In the other condition, positive metaphors were selected more frequently than less positive ones as typically journalistic. This finding can be explained by relativizing our view of the relation between relatively negative metaphors and journalism. Journalism does not only have less positive metaphors; it may also have quite positive ones which are also experienced as typically journalistic. It can be seen, then, that I was too hasty in postulating a relation between negative metaphors and journalism. The relation is more complex, and may involve both positive and less positive metaphors.

9.3 Properties and processes in thinking out loud

9.3.1 Introduction

I will now turn to the implications of the metaphor properties for reader performance in thinking out loud. The think-aloud study reported in Chapter 6, it will be remembered, contained two factors. First, there was the factor of reading condition, subjects being offered the literary and journalistic experimental texts discussed in the previous sections for literary and journalistic reception, respectively. Second, there was the factor of literary socialization, with one group of experts, namely academics from Dutch departments of modern literature, and one group of controls, namely academics from one Dutch department of anthropology. Both groups had to think aloud about both texts. It was found that the metaphors in the literary text were accorded more attention than the ones in the journalistic text for all five different processing categories included in the analysis, and that there was no reliable difference between the two groups. We will now investigate to what extent different metaphor properties may have affected these findings.

When metaphors are conceptually less clear, they may be expected to require more focus processing because they constitute a processing problem that has to be solved. Moreover, readers may often return to less clear metaphors at later stages of reading, because such metaphors may need reconsideration or re-incorporation after the initially more problematic stage of processing. The greater amount of processing initially spent on less clear metaphors may also increase their availability for retrieval from memory at later moments of processing, where additional metaphor processing may become possible as a result of developments in the text. Finally, relatively unclear metaphors may invite more frequent context construction, identification, and appreciation than clear ones: because of their relative unclarity, readers may be sooner disposed to evaluate whether all their processing effort has been worth the trouble; to provide a name for the obstacle to processing; and to consider what authors may have intended to say by them. In other words, less clear metaphors may trigger focus processing, refunctionalization, context construction, identification, and explicit appreciation more frequently than clear metaphors. In principle, this kind of effect can be expected for all kinds of discourse, for clear and unclear metaphors occur everywhere.

However, the think-aloud study reported in Chapter 6 showed that the metaphors in the literary text were accorded more attention than the metaphors in the journalistic text. Because the metaphors were equally (un)clear in both texts, as was shown at the beginning of this chapter, the question arises how this can be explained. Is it a matter of a larger overall attention to metaphors in literature, which has led to an increase in attention to both clear and less clear metaphors in the literary text? Or, alternatively, do the clearer metaphors profit more from the increased attention to metaphors in literature than the less clear ones, because the unclear ones are accorded enough attention on account of their relative unclarity anyway? Or, a third possibility, are the clearer metaphors not prominent enough to be included in the increased attention to metaphors in literature, and does this kind of attention induce even more attention to the unclear metaphors than they provoke on account of their own unclarity in the first place?

The expectations in this connection can be based on the findings of the underlining study in the previous section. It turned out there that it was the unclear metaphors which were accorded more attention than the clear ones in the literary reading conditions, but that this was not the case in the journalistic reading conditions. Therefore, it seems that the third scenario listed above is the most likely. In other words, it is predicted that the less clear metaphors are accorded relatively more attention than the clear ones in literary reading, but that this need not hold for journalistic reading.

Let us now consider the role of emotive value. The findings in the underlining study showed that positive metaphors were underlined for literariness much more often than less positive ones. This suggests that they should also be used for literary text processing more often than the less positive ones in thinking out loud. We would expect, in literary reading, metaphors with a positive value to be explicitly appreciated more often than more negative metaphors. Identification and context construction may be stimulated along with this process. When such positive metaphors are indeed positively valued by readers, then we may also expect that they will be refunctionalized more often than the less positive metaphors. As to focus processing, no prediction can be formulated regarding its relation to emotive value. However, the general expectation that metaphors are accorded more attention in literary reading may also include more frequent focus processing regarding metaphors that are felt to have a positive value in one of the senses enumerated above. In sum, positive metaphors should play a stimulating role with regard to the incidence of all five metaphor processes in the literary reading condition.

I will now consider the relation between the role of emotive value differences between metaphors and journalistic reading. The underlining study showed conflicting evidence for this relation: in one condition, less positive metaphors were underlined for journalism more often than positive ones, and in the other condition, it was the other way around. The general underlining and think aloud data have shown that metaphors are regarded as a typical ingredient in literary reading, but that they are accorded less attention in journalistic reading. However, when metaphors become less positive and more prominently negative in journalism, we might expect them to be experienced as relatively obtrusive. This might increase the attention readers assign them. Negative prominence of metaphors in journalism is not likely to be associated with good journalistic writing. In other words, these metaphors do not have to be regarded as 'typically journalistic' during underlining – quite the opposite – for readers to accord attention to them in the thinking out loud task as prominently negative. Hence we can expect that relatively negative metaphors will be accorded more attention than positive ones in journalistic reading.

9.3.2 Method

Procedure, subjects, and *materials* are as described in Chapter 6. *Metaphor attributes* were established as in the previous section for the underlining study. The two metaphors appearing in the title of the journalistic text and omitted from analysis in the underlining study were re-included.

9.3.3 Results

To investigate the effect upon processing of the aspects of metaphors, all metaphors were divided into two groups, namely those with a low score for clarity and value and those with a high score (note that this has to be done separately for each text). Next, mean scores for the experts and the controls on the incidence of the five metaphor processing operations for all metaphors were cross-classified by this binary classification of metaphors in the two texts. The results of this exercise are shown in Table 9.4 for clarity.

It can be seen from Table 9.4 that the means for less clear metaphors tend to be higher than those for clear ones in the literary condition for both the experts and the controls. However, this pattern is less obvious in the journalistic condition. In order to test whether degree of clarity affected the processing of metaphors in literary and journalistic reading, the processes of focus processing, context construction, identification, appreciation, and refunctionalization were analysed as dependent variables in a separate analysis of variance for each. The structure of these analyses is identical to the ones performed in Chapter 6, with the additional factor of metaphor type.[5]

There was a notable overall effect for the metaphor attribute of clarity upon the incidence of four of the five metaphor processes in question. There was a lack of a statistically significant effect for explicit identification, but there was a tendency for this to be significant. It is only on account of the large number of tests that this result cannot be reported as actually

Table 9.4: Mean proportional incidence (and standard deviations) of metaphor-processes in literary and journalistic reading for metaphors divided by degree of clarity

(a) Experts

| | Reading | | | |
| | Literary | | Journalistic | |
Process	Less clear	Clear	Less clear	Clear
Focus processing	0.24 (0.23)	0.16 (0.16)	0.19 (0.17)	0.22 (0.21)
Context construction	0.20 (0.17)	0.12 (0.14)	0.16 (0.14)	0.15 (0.12)
Identification	0.20 (0.16)	0.14 (0.11)	0.16 (0.12)	0.18 (0.13)
Appreciation	0.21 (0.13)	0.15 (0.11)	0.19 (0.13)	0.18 (0.13)
Refunctionalization	0.12 (0.07)	0.08 (0.08)	0.12 (0.07)	0.09 (0.09)

(b) Controls

| | Reading | | | |
| | Literary | | Journalistic | |
Process	Less clear	Clear	Less clear	Clear
Focus processing	0.19 (0.12)	0.08 (0.07)	0.14 (0.09)	0.14 (0.10)
Context construction	0.15 (0.12)	0.05 (0.06)	0.12 (0.09)	0.08 (0.08)
Identification	0.13 (0.16)	0.07 (0.07)	0.13 (0.15)	0.09 (0.09)
Appreciation	0.25 (0.15)	0.12 (0.12)	0.25 (0.15)	0.15 (0.13)
Refunctionalization	0.10 (0.12)	0.04 (0.05)	0.08 (0.09)	0.07 (0.08)

significant, but it does fall in with the general pattern. By contrast, there was no overall interaction effect for metaphor attribute by literary socialization. Only for the process of appreciation do we observe a result which is tendentially significant. However, these overall effects have to be interpreted with reference to their interaction with reading condition, for an inspection of the data and the test statistics shows that they are only due to the literary reading condition. So there is an interaction between literary reading and metaphor attribute, just as was expected. Literary reading strategies boost the attention paid to less clear metaphors for all five processes except identification. There was a tendency for this process, again, to be significant in the literary condition. However, inspection of the relevant statistics shows that these findings cannot be generalized beyond the present materials: replication with other metaphors is necessary.

These findings go for both groups of readers, for there is no interaction with literary socialization.[6] In other words, both groups of readers pay

Table 9.5: Mean incidence (and standard deviations) of metaphor processes in literary and journalistic reading for metaphors divided by degree of value

(a) Experts

| | Reading | | | |
| | Literary | | Journalistic | |
Process	Positive	Less pos	Positive	Less pos
Focus processing	0.24 (0.22)	0.17 (0.17)	0.16 (0.16)	0.25 (0.23)
Context construction	0.21 (0.17)	0.12 (0.12)	0.14 (0.13)	0.17 (0.14)
Identification	0.25 (0.21)	0.09 (0.06)	0.16 (0.13)	0.18 (0.13)
Appreciation	0.28 (0.20)	0.09 (0.08)	0.16 (0.12)	0.22 (0.16)
Refunctionalization	0.14 (0.09)	0.07 (0.07)	0.05 (0.06)	0.16 (0.08)

(b) Controls

| | Reading | | | |
| | Literary | | Journalistic | |
Process	Positive	Less pos	Positive	Less pos
Focus processing	0.20 (0.12)	0.08 (0.07)	0.10 (0.08)	0.18 (0.11)
Context construction	0.14 (0.13)	0.05 (0.05)	0.06 (0.07)	0.14 (0.11)
Identification	0.17 (0.19)	0.04 (0.05)	0.06 (0.09)	0.16 (0.17)
Appreciation	0.32 (0.19)	0.07 (0.07)	0.12 (0.12)	0.27 (0.17)
Refunctionalization	0.12 (0.13)	0.03 (0.04)	0.04 (0.06)	0.11 (0.11)

more attention to the less clear metaphors than the clear ones in the literary text only. The only exception to this general picture is the fact that unclear metaphors are also appreciated more often than clear ones in the journalistic reading condition.

Now we have to look at the analysis of the influence of emotive value. Table 9.5 summarizes the mean scores for both groups of subjects regarding focus processing, context construction, identification, appreciation, and refunctionalization for metaphors with a higher or lower positive value in the literary and the journalistic reading condition. It is immediately apparent from Table 9.5 that the results for the effect of emotive value on metaphor processing are markedly different from the results for clarity. The prediction that metaphors with a positive value are accorded more attention than metaphors with a less positive value in the literary reading condition seems to be borne out by the mean scores of the five processes in both groups of readers. Furthermore, the difference between the two reading conditions assumes the form expected: there seems to be an inverse relation between the function of positive and less positive metaphors in literary and journalistic reading. In literary reading, it is the positive metaphors that are dealt with more frequently by the readers, whereas in the journalistic reading condition, it is the less positive metaphors which receive this extensive treatment. These impressions are confirmed by statistical analysis of the data.[7]

A series of analyses of variance was performed upon each of the dependent variables of focus processing, context construction, identification, and appreciation – refunctionalization had to be dropped for technical reasons.[8] The hypothesis that positive metaphors are accorded more attention than less positive metaphors in the literary reading condition was confirmed for all four metaphor processing categories. These findings may be generalized beyond the present materials for explicit appreciation, and there is a similar tendency for focus processing. However, simultaneous generalization beyond subjects *and* materials is not allowed. There was no main effect of literary socialization, nor an interaction effect of literary socialization and metaphor type, which suggests that both groups of readers manifested this tendency in equal measure.

The interesting additional finding is the role of emotive value differences between metaphors in journalistic reading. Metaphors with a less positive emotive value were processed more frequently in explicit terms in this kind of reading than metaphors with a more positive value. There was a tendency for identification to be significant in this context, too. This result agrees with our hypothesis. In this case, too, there was no interaction with literary socialization.

9.3.4 Discussion

In thinking out loud during text processing, metaphor attributes interact with reading strategies. Less clear metaphors and positive metaphors play different roles in literary reading and non-literary reading, attracting more attention in literary reading. This can be understood on the basis of the general idea that literary reading boosts the attention paid to metaphors in reception, while non-literary reading does not do so. Thus, more prominent metaphors such as unclear or positive ones are allowed to play a more important role in reception during literary reading than during non-literary reading.

This may be further clarified with reference to the idea that there may be a link between relative unclarity and polyvalent processing, and positive value and subjective processing. If literary reading is subjective and polyvalent, then relatively unclear and positive metaphors provide an opportunity to apply the reading strategies going with these qualities. This does not hold for journalistic reading, which is presumed to be intersubjective and monovalent. From this perspective it can also be explained why less positive and negative metaphors are accorded more attention in journalistic reading. If journalistic reading aims at monovalence and intersubjectivity, then negative metaphors may become a hindrance for this goal. They are hence accorded more explicit attention than less negative and positive metaphors. In other words, there is also an interaction effect for metaphor attribute and reading attitude here, but in the reverse direction.

The fact that this finding does not correspond with a similar one regarding clarity can be explained as follows. If journalistic reading is set towards monovalence and pays less attention to style, then readers are generally less biased towards attending to metaphors. The fact that unclear metaphors were accorded so much attention in journalistic reading can be explained from the point of view of their dysfunctionality in this respect. In terms of clarity, unclear metaphors are dysfunctional. Therefore, it could well be that both clear and unclear metaphors are accorded equal attention in journalistic reading, for opposite reasons: the clear ones are used because they are functional, while the unclear ones are used because they are dysfunctional. This might be an explanation for the equal incidence of metaphor processing for clear and unclear metaphors in journalistic reading.

The fact that there was no difference between the literary experts and the controls falls into a pattern which was already established in Chapter 6. The mean scores of the two groups do occasionally show some conspicuous differences. There may be a question of statistical power here.[9] But it should also be noted that the difference between the literary experts and the controls was simply not as large as we had expected. Further work will have to follow this up.

9.4 Conclusion

This chapter has investigated the relation between metaphor properties and literary versus journalistic reading. The question was raised whether particular metaphor properties exhibited a special relation with one or the other kind of reading. This issue was examined by a further analysis of the underlining and think-aloud data reported earlier in the book. After analysis of the metaphors in the experimental texts, two aspects were chosen for further investigation, namely the conceptual property of relative clarity and the emotive one of relative value. These two metaphor attributes were used to investigate whether metaphors with a different degree of clarity or positive value had a differential effect upon the underlining and thinking out loud data. It turns out that there are well-observable and understandable relations between distinct metaphor properties on the one hand and literary and journalistic reading on the other. Indeed, the findings in the two studies manifest a remarkable similarity, while their differences are also revealing.

First, there is the metaphor aspect of clarity. In both the underlining and the think aloud study, it appeared that there was a relation between relatively unclear metaphors and literary reading. In both of the studies, the less clear metaphors were accorded more attention than the clearer ones: they were underlined more often as typically literary, and they were processed more often in terms of focus meaning, context construction, identification, appreciation, and refunctionalization. These phenomena did not occur in journalistic reading. They can be understood with reference to the general view of literary reading propounded in Chapter 2. Unclear metaphors, by their very nature, offer possibilities for subjective and polyvalent processing. These possibilities will be realized sooner when readers have adopted a generally subjective and polyvalent processing attitude to the text because they know that text is literary. This explains why the relatively unclear metaphors were accorded more attention than the clearer ones in literary reading than in journalistic reading. When it is remembered that the metaphors in the two texts were equally (un)clear, then the results of this study show that it is the attitude of the reader which has boosted the attention to the less clear metaphors in the literary reading process. Although differences between metaphors evidently play a role, because clear and unclear metaphors serve different functions when they are approached as literary or journalistic (underlining study), they seem to be overruled by attitude of reading (thinking out loud).

Literary reading should be contrasted with non-literary reading in which metaphors are approached from a general need for factuality and monovalence. The relation between this type of reading and relative clarity proved to be slightly more complex than predicted. In the underlining study, it was expected that clear metaphors would emerge as typically journalistic more often than unclear ones, but this did not prove to be the case. In the think aloud study, less clear metaphors were expected to receive some attention on account of their difficulty for processing, while clear metaphors were expected to receive attention for their useful discourse function in terms of monovalence and intersubjectivity. The evidence in this chapter shows that, indeed, there was no difference between the attention readers pay to clear and less clear metaphors in journalism, except for one case, namely the fact that unclear metaphors are appreciated more often than clear ones. The latter exception is a fact which stands to reason: unclear metaphors in journalism stand out for dysfunctionality, and will be judged as obstacles to factuality and monovalence.

The property of emotive value showed a similar pattern. In the underlining study, positive value was related to literary reading in that readers underlined positive metaphors more frequently than less positive ones for typical literariness. However, the prediction that there was a relation between journalistic reading and less positive and negative value proved wrong for the underlining study. In one case, such a relation could be observed, but in the other, it was positive metaphors that were underlined as typically journalistic. The expectation that relatively negative metaphors are typically journalistic had to be revised. In retrospect, it is a matter of course that journalistic texts can contain many positive metaphors which are clear and therefore typically journalistic. The same may still be held of the reverse of this statement: some negative metaphors may also be regarded as typically journalistic. This is why the relation between metaphor value and journalism fell out as ambivalently as it did in the underlining study.

In the think aloud study, the metaphor attribute of positive value was seen to exert an influence upon the number of times attention was paid to a metaphor in literary reception by the subjects during thinking out loud. In the literary condition, metaphors with a high positive value were identified and appreciated explicitly more often than metaphors with a lower positive value. They also received more attention in terms of their focus meaning and their presumed intentions or effect. Finally, they were also refunctionalized at later stages of the reading process more often than the metaphors with a less high positive value. None of these phenomena took place in journalistic reading. This agrees with the theoretical expectations: positive metaphors afford readers with an opportunity to exercise their subjective appraisal of style, for instance.

The role of value in relation to type of discourse becomes more complex when we include the role of metaphors with a less positive value in journalistic reading. The findings for relatively negative value in relation to journalism differed in an interesting manner from those of the underlining study, where we had found an ambivalent relation. In thinking out loud, however, for all five kinds of metaphor processing, metaphors with a relatively negative value received more attention than metaphors that were less negative, that is, more positive in journalistic reading. Metaphors with a negative value were identified and appreciated more often, and their focus meanings and author intentions were constructed more often than metaphors with a less pronounced negative value. This is precisely the opposite of the literary reading condition, where all of these processes were triggered more often by metaphors with a relatively positive value. It seems, then, that this can be seen as evidence *ex negativo* for the special relation between metaphors and literary reception: if metaphors become too obtrusively negative in non-literary reading, they will be noted as being out of place.

This brings to a conclusion our exploration of the relation between metaphor properties and discourse processes. It turns out that there are very fine effects upon text processing when it comes to differences between metaphors. The same metaphor attributes serve different functions in two kinds of reading. This was established for two distinct kinds of metaphor properties, namely the conceptual one of clarity and the emotive one of positive or negative value. Moreover, this was observed by means of two different tasks and methods, and in three different groups of readers: students of literature, academic researchers of literature, and academic researchers of another discipline (anthropology). The tendencies revealed in the present chapter are quite solid. They cry for further development with reference to other texts, metaphor properties, types of reading, and types of texts. But these are research issues for the future.

Notes

1. A multivariate analysis of variance was performed upon the four dependent variables of appropriateness, beauty, formality, and political nature. There was one within factor of 'scales', with the four levels of appropriateness, beauty, formality, and political nature, and one between factor of 'text', with the levels of literature and journalism. The results of the univariate F-tests are reported in Table IXA below.
2. It should also be noted that metaphors are nested under text: the comparison between clear versus unclear, and positive versus negative metaphors involves a different set of metaphors in the two textual conditions. This will have to be taken into account in the statistical design.
3. Having determined that the data did not present fundamental problems for the assumptions of analysis of variance, a multivariate analysis of variance was executed upon the dependent variables of metaphor type within text. There was one between-subjects factor of context with two levels (authentic and perverse) and two within-subject factors of text (originally literary and originally journalistic) and metaphor type (clear and unclear), the latter within-subject factor of metaphor type being nested within the former of text. Note that $\alpha = 0.025$, because we are running two analyses (with regard to clarity and value) on the same set of data. Thus, an experiment-wise α of 0.05 is retained. The main results of the analysis are laid out in Table IXB.
4. A multivariate analysis with one between-subject factor of context (authentic and perverse) and two within-subject factors of text (originally literary and originally journalistic) and metaphor type within text (positive and negative, nested under text) yielded the results presented in Table IXC.

Table IXA: Effect of source on mean scale scores (univariate tests of within item effects)

(i) Appropriate

Source of variation	SS	d.f.	MS	F
SOURCE BY FACTOR (1)	0.13	1	0.13	0.37
WITHIN CELLS	17.31	51	0.34	

(ii) Beautiful

Source of variation	SS	d.f.	MS	F
SOURCE BY FACTOR (2)	4.38	1	4.38	14.86**
WITHIN CELLS	15.05	51	0.30	

(iii) Formal

Source of variation	SS	d.f.	MS	F
SOURCE BY FACTOR (3)	1.54	1	1.54	3.51
WITHIN CELLS	22.42	51	0.44	

(iv) Political

Source of variation	SS	d.f.	MS	F
SOURCE BY FACTOR (4)	0.07	1	0.07	0.34
WITHIN CELLS	10.16	51	0.20	

$**p < 0.01$

5. Prior to testing, screening of the data revealed one subject among the controls who was a multivariate outlier — this subject was removed. In the literary expert group, one subject had a univariate outlier on metaphor identification: for conceptual clarity, his score was reduced so that z-score < 3.0.

Each of the dependent variables of focus processing, context construction, identification, appreciation, and refunctionalization was tested in a separate multivariate analysis of variance. Independent variables were the between-subject factor of literary socialization (experts vs. controls) and the within-subject factors of text (literary vs. journalistic) and metaphor type (clear vs. unclear, nested within texts). Each of the analyses was performed twice: once treating subjects as a random factor while collapsing over materials (*F1*), and once treating materials as a random factor while collapsing over subjects (*F2*). Note that the design for *F2* is slightly different from *F1*, because in the design for *F2*, it is the scores of the two groups of readers which become a 'within-subject' factor in relation to the metaphors: every metaphor is processed once by the experts and once by the controls. To retain an overall α of 0.05, every test was executed at $\alpha = 0.005$: two metaphor attributes were tested as to their effect upon five dependent variables. The results of the analyses are laid out in Table IXD.

6. Tendencies for an effect of literary socialization are found in the analysis of *F2*, producing the same situation as in Chapter 6.

Table IXB: Tests and parameter estimates of effect of metaphor clarity on underlining

(i) *Tests of context, metaphor type (clarity) within text, and their interaction*

	Source of variation	SS	d.f.	MS	F
Between subject	CONTEXT	0.80	1	0.80	12.77**
	WITHIN CELLS	1.76	28	0.06	
Within subject effects	METTYPE IN TEXT	0.05	2	0.03	4.28*
	CONTEXT BY METTYPE IN TEXT	0.07	2	0.04	5.97*
	WITHIN CELLS	0.34	56	0.01	

(ii) *Parameter estimates for literary and journalistic text*

		Literary text t	Journalistic text t
Metaphor type within text		-1.72	$-2.28!$
Context by metaphor type within text	$-$	$2.67*$	$-2.28!$

$\alpha = 0.025; **p < 0.005; *p < 0.025; !0.025 < p < 0.05$

Table IXC: Tests and parameter estimates of effect of metaphor value on underlining

(i) *Tests of context, metaphor type (value) within text, and their interaction*

	Source of variation	SS	d.f.	MS	F
Between subject	CONTEXT	0.83	1	0.83	13.29**
	WITHIN CELLS	1.76	28	0.06	
Within subject effects	METTYPE IN TEXT	0.18	2	0.09	8.55**
	CONTEXT BY METTYPE IN TEXT	0.25	2	0.12	11.42**
	WITHIN CELLS	0.60	56	0.01	

(ii) *Parameter estimates for literary and journalistic text*

	Literary text t	Journalistic text t
Metaphor type within text	$3.01**$	$2.86**$
Context by metaphor type within text	$5.17**$	0.95

$\alpha = 0.025; **p < 0.005$

7. Recall that, due to prior data screening, one adjustment was made of an identification score for value. Moreover, in one case, singularity was found while carrying out the analysis: this happened for refunctionalization in the case of 'value'. Hence this analysis was not pursued any further.

Table IXD: Tests and parameter estimates of effect of metaphor clarity and literary socialization on thinking out loud

(i) Tests of literary socialization, metaphor type (clarity) within text, and their interaction

Independent variable	Dependent variable	F1	df	F2	df	minF' (df)
Literary socialization	Focus processing	1.98	1/31	22.04*	1/49	1.82 (1/37)
	Context construction	2.66	1/31	5.88	1/49	1.83 (1/58)
	Identification	2.27	1/31	16.37*	1/49	1.99 (1/40)
	Appreciation	0.03	1/31	0.96	1/49	
	Refunctionalization	2.12	1/31	11.76*	1/49	1.80 (1/42)
Metaphor type within text	Focus processing	8.67*	2/62	1.15	2/49	1.02 (2/62)
	Context construction	9.66*	2/62	1.44	2/49	1.25 (2/64)
	Identification	5.05!	2/62	2.88	2/49	1.83 (2/96)
	Appreciation	17.75*	2/62	1.77	2/49	1.61 (2/59)
	Refunctionalization	6.56*	2/62	2.54	2/49	1.83 (2/84)
Literary socialization by metaphor type within text	Focus processing	0.47	2/62	0.35	2/49	
	Context construction	0.37	2/62	0.85	2/49	
	Identification	1.60	2/62	0.19	2/49	
	Appreciation	5.16!	2/62	1.10	2/49	0.91 (2/70)
	Refunctionalization	0.47	2/62	0.12	2/49	

(ii) Parameter estimates for literary and journalistic text, F1

		Literary t	Journalistic t
Metaphor type within text	Focus processing	− 3.77*	0.73
	Context construction	− 3.48*	− 1.50
	Identification	− 2.75!	− 0.76
	Appreciation	− 5.21*	− 3.05*
	Refunctionalization	− 3.13*	− 1.51
Literary socialization by metaphor type within text	Focus processing	0.47	0.92
	Context construction	0.49	0.86
	Identification	0.19	2.09
	Appreciation	1.98	2.51
	Refunctionalization	0.66	− 0.73

$\alpha = 0.005;$ *$p < 0.005;$!$p < 0.01$

8. Each of the dependent variables of focus processing, context construction, identification, appreciation, and refunctionalization was tested in a separate multivariate analysis of variance. Independent variables were the between-subject factor of literary socialization (experts vs. controls) and the within-subject factors of text (literary vs. journalistic) and metaphor type (positive vs. less positive,

Table IXE: Tests and parameter estimates of effect of metaphor value and literary socialization on thinking out loud

(i) *Tests of literary socialization, metaphor type (value) within text, and their interaction*

Independent variable	Dependent variable	F1	df	F2	df	minF' (df)
Literary socialization	Focus processing	2.00	1/31	23.43*	1/49	1.84 (1/36)
	Context construction	2.74	1/31	5.75	1/49	1.86 (1/59)
	Identification	2.33	1/31	18.13*	1/49	2.07 (1/39)
	Appreciation	0.02	1/31	0.83	1/49	—
Metaphor type within text	Focus processing	13.70*	2/62	9.97*	2/49	5.77 (2/103)
	Context construction	14.11*	2/62	2.02	2/49	1.77 (2/63)
	Identification	17.96*	2/62	2.91	2/49	2.50 (2/65)
	Appreciation	39.86*	2/62	12.99*	2/49	9.80 (2/79)!
Literary socialization by metaphor type within text	Focus processing	0.48	2/62	1.12	2/49	
	Context construction	0.46	2/62	0.15	2/49	
	Identification	1.64	2/62	2.34	2/49	
	Appreciation	1.70	2/62	0.92	2/49	

(ii) *Parameter estimates for literary and journalistic reading, F1*

		Literary t	Journalistic t
Metaphor type within text	Focus processing	3.83*	− 3.56*
	Context construction	4.08*	− 3.11*
	Identification	4.92*	− 2.73!
	Appreciation	7.48*	− 4.05*
Literary socialization by metaphor type within text	Focus processing	− 0.95	− 0.13
	Context construction	0.04	1.12
	Identification	0.46	2.01
	Appreciation	− 0.90	1.73

$\alpha = 0.005$; *$p < 0.005$; !$p < 0.01$

nested within texts). Each of the analyses was performed twice: once treating subjects as a random factor while collapsing over materials (*F1*), and once treating materials as a random factor while collapsing over subjects (*F2*). Note that the design for *F2* is slightly different from *F1*, because in the design for *F2*, it is the scores of the two groups of readers which become a 'within-subject' factor in relation to the metaphors: every metaphor is processed once by the experts and once by the controls. To retain an overall α of 0.05, every test was executed at $\alpha = 0.005$: two metaphor attributes were tested as to their effect upon four dependent variables. The results of the analyses are laid out in Table IXE.

9. Tendencies of an effect of literary socialization were found in the *F2* analyses.

Conclusion

CHAPTER TEN

Understanding metaphor in literature

There is something special about understanding metaphor in literature. If literature is a kind of discourse which permits maximal subjective involvement to the reader, understanding metaphor in literature may be the epitome of this kind of reading experience. Its basis in non-literal analogy can trigger fantasies, rich ideas, and pleasure in language which few other literary signs may be able to equal. This study has shown that metaphors have a function of enhancement regarding the literary reading experience which can be observed empirically in the various kinds of mental representations readers construct for metaphors during literary reception. These facts can be explained as due to two contextual effects of literature as a distinct kind of discourse on the act of reception: as a product of literary production, literary metaphors exhibit typical properties in comparison with non-literary metaphors and, during reception itself, readers pay special attention to metaphors in literature as opposed to non-literary discourse.

In a way it is strange that this highly characteristic phenomenon has not received this kind of study before. It seems to me that this says a lot about literary criticism. Indeed, the assumption that the study of literature involves an act of *criticism* is quite telling: the literary scholar often engages literature at the level of cultural participation, not scientific observation. And if the discipline dealing with literature is designated as literary *theory*, another typical feature is placed in the forefront: literary theorists tend to speculate about their object, and may end up with modelling an aspect of it, but their strength has not lain in empirical testing. The present study was partly begun on the assumption that there are no insuperable obstacles which prevent us doing empirical research on understanding metaphor in literature, and that criticism is an activity which belongs to the object of investigation, literary discourse. I have attempted to demonstrate that holding these premises nevertheless allows the conduct of fundamental research on literature without having to retreat to marginal areas of investigation.

Current fashions in literary theory emphasize that there are no data or observations without theory, proclaiming a theoretization of all literary studies. I would like to stress that this claim can be turned round with just as much legitimacy: there is no theory without observation and data either. Although the label *empirical* studies of literature may seem paradoxical, it should be regarded as pleonastic. The scientific study of literature is both theoretical and empirical.

But I do not believe that the quarrel about the primacy of theory or data is very fruitful. The *interaction between theory and data* is what good science is about. My book has been an attempt to boost this interaction for the study of understanding metaphor in literature. Because of the historical situation in literary studies, the book has acquired the character of a psycholinguistic study, but I regard this as an epiphenomenon. The study of understanding metaphor in literature requires an *interdisciplinary* approach, involving attention to aspects psychological, linguistic, and literary. As long as the general approach aims for the fruitful and critical interaction between theory and data it is immaterial if it is labelled as literary, linguistic, or psychological.

This is not to deny the relevance of differences between disciplines. Indeed, it has only been possible to perform this study because of the availability since the beginning of the 1980s of three theories rooted in the three disciplines with which we are concerned here: Lakoff and Johnson's (1980) cognitive linguistic theory of metaphor, Van Dijk and Kintsch's (1983) psychology of discourse processing, and Schmidt's (1980) social systems theory of literature. My study of understanding metaphor in literature has required an integration of these three theories which has led to adaptations and elaborations in each. In this conclusion I will point out some of the most important issues which have been more or less implicated by my study. Understanding metaphor in literature can thus also be regarded as a specific case whose study may have fruitful repercussions on more general approaches to metaphor, understanding, and literature.

The study of metaphor was radically subverted by the cognitive turn, but the most interesting implications for linguistics can be found in the work by George Lakoff. If it has become *bon ton* to speak of metaphor as belonging to the realm of cognition, Lakoff and his collaborators have taken the bull by the horns and attempted to spell out what this means for metaphor as a form of linguistic expression. The relation they have revealed between conceptual metaphors and linguistic expressions of various rhetorical kinds – including metaphors, analogies, similes, and so on – has provided linguistics with a new source of inspiration, especially in the area of semantics. Any definition of linguistic metaphor, or metaphor as a textual entity, has to begin with a consideration of these views.

However, it is one thing to analyse the semantics of non-literal language patterns and explain them with reference to conceptual metaphors and cultural experience; and it is something quite different to conclude that conceptual metaphors do not only motivate language patterns, but also trigger understanding processes of linguistic metaphors in each and every individual mind. I have emphasized that what can be *analysed* as a linguistic metaphor does not always have to be *realized* as one. There are various cognitive scenarios which can be imagined as being instantiated from one language user to another, and their use still has to be investigated with reference to different conditions of language use. That the difference between literary and non-literary metaphor understanding is one of the relevant parameters in this connection has been shown by this study. Indeed, metaphors are realized as metaphors in various ways more frequently in literature than outside it.

Although all or most linguistic metaphors could have a conceptual basis in the minds of individual language users, this is not very likely. When one considers data of various kinds, it turns out that there are interesting differences among metaphors when it comes to their cognitive processing: some are not noticed as non-literal, others are used figuratively without difficulty, and still others give rise to highly complex conceptualizations. My findings about the varying incidence of explicit identification in and outside literature raises the interesting issue whether implicit identification can be revealed to behave in a similar way. Other techniques than thinking out loud and underlining will have to be applied for this kind of research.

As a result, Lakoff's (1986a) definition of 'literal' and 'metaphorical' language has been adjusted to take account of the difference between linguistic or semantic analysis on the one hand, and pragmatic observation on the other. I have related the weakness of Lakoff's new definition of linguistic metaphor to his analytic method. This is not to say that analysis is useless. However, what I do wish to maintain is that the analysis of general language patterns is useless if one wants to use them for drawing *conclusions* about individual language usage. They can act as *predictions* and hence *explanations* of *some* individual behaviours, i.e. the ones which have been observed when the data about the language patterns were collected. But structural language analysis can never prove that all individuals use metaphors in a certain way. This is where empirical work comes in.

I am aware that I have not carried out any extensive linguistic analysis of metaphors myself. For instance, the data collected and analysed in Chapter 8 can be subjected to further investigation by relating them to a number of analytic properties of the metaphors in question. It can be imagined that a property such as metaphor difficulty is associated with such analytic variables as word order, presence of tenor or ground, grammatical level of expression of the metaphor, and so on. These are issues which I have left aside for future research. They could explain the behaviour of readers just as well as the empirically collected data about metaphor properties which I have reported here. My preference for the empirical method was strategic rather than anything else. What I wanted to do was to show how there is a respectable alternative to the traditional method in linguistics and literary studies of language analysis and text interpretation. Since there may be a methodological question of reliability in these analysis-oriented disciplines, I would advocate a pluriform approach in which analytic data about language and texts are complemented by empirical ones. One manner in which this can be done was that used in Chapter 8.

I will now move on from a consideration of metaphor to the more complex phenomenon of understanding metaphor. My main aim here has been to connect the more limited view of metaphor processing in psycholinguistics to a more broadly oriented theory of reading. This was necessary because I intended to develop a theory of understanding metaphor *in literature*. I have used Van Dijk and Kintsch's (1983) multi-faceted model of discourse processing for this purpose, because it provides sufficient links for building connections with both metaphor processing research in psycholinguistics and text comprehension research in the empirical study of literature. Most psycholinguistic metaphor processing research turns out to deal with the levels of decoding and conceptualization, while some interesting empirical research on literary text comprehension has to do with the reader's construction of a communicative context model.

There are two important aspects which have featured in my discussion of Van Dijk and Kintsch (1983), constituting relatively specific elaborations of their model. The first is the role of communicative processing, leading to the reader's construction of a communicative context model. What is interesting about the communicative context model is that it can fulfil a function in both time-limited and leisurely metaphor processing. For instance, the construction of a communicative context model during time-limited comprehension enables readers to understand ironic metaphors by relating those metaphors to the apparent aims of their authors. But context models are also fundamental for the leisurely comprehension. I have argued that leisurely comprehension includes such typically literary processes as explicit identification and appreciation, and I believe that these processes are facilitated by the availability of a context model. In a context model, readers can develop a model of the text-as-message, and metaphors can be represented as a particular kind of expression as part of that model. A context model also affords representations of presumably intended effects of the text on the reader, allowing for the construction of an implicit response to the metaphor by the reader. Both of these kinds of information in the context model can form the basis of explicit metaphor identification and appreciation during leisurely comprehension.

Indeed, it seems that there is a grey area between the two kinds of comprehension, in which the context model can perform a bridging function. This can be imagined best when we take into account the varying difficulty of metaphors: some metaphors require much more extended and attentive focus processing than others, so that it becomes hard to say when the click of comprehension has occurred. Before it has occurred, processes which might be expected to belong to leisurely comprehension such as identification and appreciation may occur before focus processing has been successfully completed, leading to an intermingling of time-limited and leisurely processes. Indeed, 'time-limited' focus processing may be affected by such intervening 'leisurely' explicit identification in that it may trigger or stimulate relatively conscious metaphor processing strategies related to analogical reasoning. This is where the labels begin to need scare-quotes, and these speculations require much further research.

The second important aspect regarding the model of Van Dijk and Kintsch (1983) is my highlighting of the effect of the factor of context on discourse processing. I have emphasized that there may be discourse-typical conventions which guide the construction of linguistic, conceptual, and intentional representations of texts, and that literary reading can be fruitfully approached in this manner. The source of such discourse-typical conventions is social, but they do have an effect on the psychological processes of decoding, conceptualization, and communication. This had been demonstrated for literary reception in general before, but it turns out that these ideas can also explain the typical nature of understanding metaphor in literature. The relation between the social origin and nature of these conventions and their psychological correlate is one of the most fascinating objects of research for discourse theorists.

This leads us on from the theory of Van Dijk and Kintsch (1983) to Schmidt (1980). The conclusion about the psychology of reading is that more attention to communicative processing and the role of context variables can increase our view of the variable nature of text comprehension, both in terms of time-span, and depth and content of processing.

Chapter 2 emphasized the hypothetical nature of my definition of literature by means of subjectivity, fictionality, polyvalence, and form-orientation. However, the theoretical basis of that proposal lies in a well-motivated view of literature as a specific social domain of communicative action by means of words. The most exhaustive description of that domain has been put forward by Schmidt (1980), and I have elaborated his ideas of the typically literary discourse conventions of aestheticity and polyvalence. I know that Schmidt's conventions have received a good deal of criticism, but I still believe that they can be used as a source of inspiration for empirical work about literary reception. In other words, I am not concerned about the theoretical status and elaboration of these conventions; what I advocate is their use for the operationalization of literary reading processes in the context of empirical research on literary reception.

This is not a strategy of immunization against critique. On the contrary, the implementation of the notions of subjectivity, fictionality, polyvalence, and form-orientation enables the conducting of empirical research which can test implications of the general view formulated by Schmidt. I do not claim that mine are the only operationalizations, implementations, and implications that can be looked at; nor do I claim that I have performed my research without flaw. What I do claim, however, is that it is possible to evaluate this research and its bearings on the theory, in order to judge whether further progress can be made by following the present course. I feel that the evidence put forth in this study is interesting enough to warrant such further research, because the notions of subjectivity, fictionality, polyvalence, and form-orientation have played an intelligible role in the explanation of the incidence of particular processes and properties regarding metaphor in literary discourse as opposed to non-literary discourse. The next step which should be taken is to include these notions more explicitly in the empirical research itself.

Successful examples of such inclusion in the previous chapters relate to the processes of explicit identification and appreciation. The former was defined by the occurrence of a metalingual term indicating the rhetorical status of a metaphor as a figure of speech. This is usually regarded as a matter of language form. Appreciation was defined as the occurrence of a personal judgement on the part of the reader about the nature or quality of the metaphor. This is a manifestation of subjective involvement. But other direct relations between features of literary reception and metaphor can also be envisaged. In particular, the content of focus processing, vehicle construction, metaphor construction, and functionalization can all be subjected to analysis regarding their degree of subjectivity and polyvalence. Although such research will not be easy to carry out, it will be worth the effort. The condition for such an analysis, that we have reliable analyses of these processes as distinct phenomena during reading, is on the agenda for research in the more immediate future.

Another direct application of the features of subjectivity, fictionality, polyvalence, and form orientation lies in the area of metaphor structures. The fact that literary metaphors are on average more difficult than journalistic ones may be related to their triggering of subjective and polyvalent processes during reception, but can these metaphors also be described as subjective and polyvalent themselves? In other words, do literary metaphors stage non-literal analogies which are more subjective, that is, less generally shared between members of our culture, than non-literary metaphors? And do literary metaphors mean more than one thing more often than non-literary metaphors? This would amount to a further investigation of the ideas put forth in section 2.3 Can these questions be investigated by means of additional metaphor analysis in order to validate any kind of rating data, somewhat in the manner of Gentner's approach to the difference between scientific and literary metaphors? These are natural extensions of the research reported in this book. They would also pull back into the centre of attention the text and its features, an object which seems to have suffered unjustly from 'the cognitive turn' in literary studies.

Apart from such extensions, further precision will also be required. When I speak of literary metaphors, I take it that metaphors occurring in narrative fiction are sufficiently representative of all literature as opposed to non-literary types of discourse to be able to use the general label 'literary'. But this is a gross simplification. Even though it may be true that this class of metaphors is sufficiently subjective and polyvalent, or difficult and positive, for it to be distinct from journalistic metaphors, this does not mean that their properties illustrate all literary metaphors to the same degree. I do not doubt that there is variation between metaphors in different genres, periods, languages, and cultures, and these dimensions all need to be examined. My findings may be limited to the particular genre and period from which my textual materials derive, but this is no great difficulty: it only means that more research is needed before more fine-grained conclusions can be drawn about the special nature of understanding metaphor in literature.

Bibliography

Alverson, H. (1991) Metaphor and experience: looking over the notion of image schema. In Fernandez, J. (ed.) *Beyond Metaphor: The Theory of Tropes in Anthropology*. Stanford University Press, Stanford, pp. 94–117.

Anderson, R.C. and **Pichert, J.W.** (1978) Recall of previously unrecallable information following a shift in perspective, *Journal of Verbal Learning and Verbal Behavior* **17**: 1–12.

Andringa, E. (1990) Verbal data on literary understanding: a proposal for protocol analysis on two levels, *Poetics* **19**: 231–57.

Ballstaedt, S.-P. and **Mandl, H.** (1984) Elaborations: assessment and analysis. In Mandl, H., Stein, N.L. and Trabasso, T. (eds) *Learning and Comprehension of Text*. Lawrence Erlbaum, Hillsdale, NJ, pp. 331–52.

Beardsley, M.C. (1958) *Aesthetics*. Harcourt, Brace Co, New York.

Beaugrande, de, R. (1989) Toward the empirical study of literature: a synoptic sketch of a new society, *Poetics* **18**: 7–28.

Black, E. (1993) Metaphor, simile and cognition in Golding's *The Inheritors*, *Language and Literature* **2**: 37–48.

Black, M. (1962) *Models and Metaphors*. Cornell University Press, Ithaca.

Black, M. (1979) More about metaphor. In Ortony, A. (ed.) *Metaphor and Thought*. Cambridge University Press, Cambridge, pp. 19–43.

Booth, W.C. (1988) *The Company We Keep: An Ethics of Fiction*. University of California Press, Berkeley.

Bransford, J.D. and **Johnson, M.K.** (1972) Contextual prerequisites for understanding: some investigations of comprehension and recall, *Journal of Verbal Learning and Verbal Behavior* **11**: 717–26.

Brunner, E.J. (1982) Interpretative Auswertung. In Huber, G.L. and Mandl, H. (eds) *Verbale Daten. Eine Einführung in die Grundlagen und Methoden der Erhebung und Auswertung*. Belz, Weinheim and Basel, pp. 197–219.

Camac, M.K., and **Glucksberg, S.** (1984) Metaphors do not use associations between concepts, they are used to create them, *Journal of Psycholinguistic Research* **13**: 443–55.

Carroll, J.B. (1972) Vectors of prose style. In Snider J.G. and Osgood, C.E. (eds) *Semantic Differential Technique: A Sourcebook*. Aldine, Chicago, pp. 593–602.

Clark, H.H. (1973) The language-as-fixed-effect fallacy: a critique of language statistics in psychological research, *Journal of Verbal Learning and Verbal Behavior* **12**: 335–59.

Clement, J. (1988) Observed methods for generating analogies in scientific problem solving, *Cognitive Science* **12**: 563–586.

Culler, J. (1981a) Beyond interpretation. In Culler, J., *The Pursuit of Signs: Semiotics, Literature, Deconstruction*. Cornell University Press, Ithaca, pp. 3–17.

Culler, J. (1981b) Semiotics as theory of reading. In Culler, J., *The Pursuit of Signs: Semiotics, Literature, Deconstruction*. Cornell University Press, Ithaca, pp. 47–79.

Culler, J. (1981c) The turns of metaphor. In Culler, J., *The Pursuit of Signs: Semiotics, Literature, Deconstruction*. Cornell University Press, Ithaca, pp. 188–209.

Culler, J. (1988) *Framing the Sign: Criticism and Its Institutions*. University of Oklahoma Press, Norman and London.

Dascal, M. (1987) Defending literal meaning, *Cognitive Science* **11**: 259–81.

Dascal, M. (1989) On the roles of context and literal meaning in understanding, *Cognitive Science* **13**: 253–7.

Dawson, M. (1982) *Multidimensional Responses to Metaphor*. Unpublished master's thesis, University of Western Ontario.

Deffner, G. (1984) *Lautes Denken – Untersuchung zur Qualität eines Datenerhebungsverfahrens*. Peter Lang, Frankfurt/M.

Deffner, G. (1988) Concurrent thinking aloud: an on-line tool for studying representations used in text understanding, *Text* **8**: 351–67.

Dirven, R. (1985) Metaphor as a basic means for extending the lexicon. In Paprotté, W. and Dirven, R. (eds) *The Ubiquity of Metaphor: Metaphor in Language and Thought*. John Benjamins, Amsterdam, pp. 85–119.

Dirven, R. and Paprotté, W. (1985) Introduction. In Paprotté, W. and Dirven, R. (eds) *The Ubiquity of Metaphor: Metaphor in Language and Thought*. John Benjamins, Amsterdam, pp. *vii–xix*.

Ericsson, K.A. (1988) Concurrent verbal reports on text comprehension: a review, *Text* **8**: 295–325.

Ericsson, K.A. and Oliver, W.L. (1988) Methodology for laboratory research on thinking: task selection, collection of observations, and data analysis. In Sternberg, R.J. and Smith, E.E. (eds) *The Psychology of Human Thought*. Cambridge University Press, Cambridge, pp. 392–428.

Ericsson, K.A. and Simon, H.A. (1984) *Protocol Analysis: Verbal Reports As Data*. MIT Press, Cambridge.

Fernandez, J.W. (1991a) *Beyond Metaphor: The Theory of Tropes in Anthropology*. Stanford University Press, Stanford.

Fernandez, J.W. (1991b) Introduction: confluents of inquiry. In Fernandez, J.W. (ed.) *Beyond Metaphor: The Theory of Tropes in Anthropology*. Stanford University Press, Stanford, pp. 1–13.

Fischer, P.M. (1982) Inhaltsanalytische Auswertung von Verbaldaten. In Huber, G.L. and Mandl, H. (eds) *Verbale Daten. Eine Einführung in die Grundlagen und Methoden der Erhebung und Auswertung*. Belz, Weinheim and Basel, pp. 179–96.

Fish, S. (1980) *Is There A Text In This Class?* Harvard University Press, Cambridge, Mass.

Flower, L. (1987) Interpretive acts: cognition and the construction of discourse, *Poetics* **16**: 109–30.

Fokkema, D.W. and **Kunne-Ibsch, E.** (1977) *Theories of Literature in the Twentieth Century: Structuralism, Marxism, Aesthetics of Reception, Semiotics.* C. Hurst, London.

Freeman, D.C. (1993) 'According to my bond': *King Lear* and re-cognition, *Language and Literature* **2**: 1–18.

Freund, E. (1987) *The Return of the Reader: Reader-Response Criticism.* Methuen, London.

Friedrich, P. (1991) Polytrope. In Fernandez, J.W. (ed.) *Beyond Metaphor: The Theory of Tropes in Anthropology.* Stanford University Press, Stanford, pp. 17–55.

Gentner, D. (1982) Are scientific analogies metaphors? In Miall, D.S. (ed) *Metaphor: Problems and Perspectives.* Harvester, Brighton, pp. 106–32.

Gentner, D. (1983) Structure mapping: a theoretical framework for analogy, *Cognitive Science* **7**: 155–70.

Gentner, D. (1989) The mechanisms of analogical learning. In Vosniadou, S. and Ortony, A. (eds) *Similarity and Analogical Reasoning.* Cambridge University Press, Cambridge, pp. 199–241.

Gerrig, R.J. (1989) Empirical constraints on computational theories of metaphor: comments on Indurkhya, *Cognitive Science* **13**: 235–41.

Gerrig, R.J. and **Healy, A.** (1983) Dual processes in metaphor understanding: comprehension and appreciation, *Journal of Experimental Psychology: Learning, Memory, and Cognition* **9**: 667–75.

Gibbs, R.W. (1984) Literal meaning and psychological theory, *Cognitive Science* **8**: 275–304.

Gibbs, R.W. (1987) What does it mean for a metaphor to be understood? In Haskell, R. (ed.) *Cognition and Symbolic Structure: The Psychology of Metaphoric Transformation.* Ablex, Norwood, NJ, pp. 31–48.

Gibbs, R.W. (1989) Understanding and literal meaning, *Cognitive Science* **13**: 243–51.

Gibbs, R.W. (1990) The process of understanding literary metaphor, *Journal of Literary Semantics* **XIX**: 65–79.

Gibbs, R.W. (1992) Categorization and metaphor understanding, *Psychological Review* **99**: 572–7.

Gibbs, R.W. and **Gerrig, R. J.** (1989) How context makes metaphor comprehension seem 'special', *Metaphor And Symbolic Activity* **4**: 154–8.

Gick, M.L. and **Holyoak, K.J.** (1980) Analogical problem solving, *Cognitive Psychology* **12**: 306–55.

Glucksberg, S. (1986) How people use context to resolve ambiguity: implications for an interactive model of language understanding. In Kurcz, I., Shugar, G.W. and Danks, J.H. (eds) *Knowledge and Language.* North Holland, Amsterdam, pp. 303–25.

Glucksberg, S., Brown, M. and **McGlone, M.S.** (1992) Conceptual knowledge is not automatically accessed during idiom comprehension. Paper presented at conference on 'Art and cognition', Tel Aviv, 1992.

Glucksberg, S. and **Keysar, B.** (1990) Understanding metaphorical comparisons: beyond similarity. *Psychological Review* **97**: 3–18.

Glucksberg, S. and **Keysar, B.** (forthcoming) How metaphors work. In Ortony, A. (ed.) *Metaphor and Thought,* 2nd edition.

Glucksberg, S., Keysar, B. and McGlone, M.S. (1992) Metaphor understanding and accessing conceptual schema: reply to Gibbs (1992), *Psychological Review* **99**: 578–81.

Graesser, A.C., Mio, J. and Millis, K.K. (1989) Metaphors in persuasive communication. In Meutsch, D. and Viehoff, R. (eds) *Comprehension of Literary Discourse: Results and Problems of Interdisciplinary Approaches.* De Gruyter, Berlin, pp. 131–154.

Graves, B. and Frederiksen, C.H. (1991) Literary expertise in the description of a fictional narrative, *Poetics* **20**: 1–26.

Grice, H.P. (1975) Logic and conversation. In Cole, P. and Morgan, J.L. (eds) *Syntax and Semantics.* Academic Press, New York, pp. 41–58.

Groeben, N. (1977) *Rezeptionsforschung als empirische Literaturwissenschaft. Paradigma- durch Methodendiskussion an Untersuchungsbeispielen.* Kronberg, Tübingen.

Groeben, N. (1982) *Leserpsychologie: Textverständnis – Textverständlichkeit.* Aschendorff, Münster.

Groeben, N. and Schreier, M. (1992) The hypothesis of the polyvalence convention: a systematic survey of the research development from a historical perspective, *Poetics* **21**: 5–32.

Groeben, N. and Vorderer, P. (1988) *Leserpsychologie: Lesemotivation – Lektürewirkung.* Aschendorff, Münster.

Haskell, R.E. (ed.) (1987) *Cognition and Symbolic Structures: The Psychology of Metaphoric Transformation.* Ablex, Norwood, NJ.

Hesse, M.B. (1966) *Models and Analogies in Science.* University of Notre Dame Press, Notre Dame, Indiana.

Hintzenberg, D., Schmidt, S.J. and Zobel, R. (1980) *Zum Literaturbegriff in der Bundesrepublik Deutschland.* Vieweg, Braunschweig/Wiesbaden.

Hoffman, R.R. (1985) Some implications of metaphor for philosophy and psychology of science. In Paprotté, W. and Dirven, R. (eds) *The Ubiquity of Metaphor.* John Benjamins, Amsterdam, pp. 327–80.

Hoffman, R.R. and Kemper, S. (1987) What could reaction-time studies be telling us about metaphor comprehension? *Metaphor And Symbolic Activity* **2**: 149–86.

Hoffstaedter, P. (1986) *Poetizität aus der Sicht des Lesers.* Buske, Hamburg.

Holyoak, K.J. (1982) An analogical framework for literary interpretation, *Poetics* **11**: 105–26.

Holyoak, K.J. and Thagard, P.R. (1989) A computational model of analogical problem solving. In Vosniadou, S. and Ortony, A. (eds) *Similarity and Analogical Reasoning.* Cambridge University Press, Cambridge, pp. 242–66.

Honeck, R.P. and Hoffman, R.R. (eds) (1980) *Cognition and Figurative Language.* Lawrence Erlbaum Associates, Hillsdale, NJ.

Huber, G.L. and Mandl, H. (1982) Verbalisationsmethoden zur Erfassung von Kognitionen im Handlungszusammenhang. In Huber, G.L. and Mandl, H. (eds) *Verbale Daten. Eine Einführung in die Grundlagen und Methoden der Erhebung und Auswertung.* Belz, Weinheim and Basel, pp 11–42.

Ibsch, E. and Schram, D.H. (eds) (1987) *Rezeptionsforschung Zwischen Hermeneutik und Empirik. Amsterdammer Beiträge zur Neueren Germanistik Band 23.* Rodopi, Amsterdam.

Ibsch, E., Schram, D.H. and Steen, G.J. (eds) (1991) *Empirical Studies in Literature: Proceedings of the Second International Conference, Amsterdam 1989.* Rodopi, Amsterdam.

Inhoff, A. W., Lima, S.D. and Carroll, P.J. (1984) Contextual effects on metaphor comprehension in reading, *Memory and Cognition* 12: 558–567.

Janus, R.A. and Bever, T.G. (1985) Processing metaphoric language: an investigation of the three-stage model of metaphor comprehension, *Journal of Psycholinguistic Research* 14: 473–87.

Johnson, M. (1988) *The Body in the Mind: The Bodily Basis of Reason and Imagination.* Chicago University Press, Chicago.

Johnson-Laird, P.N. (1989) Analogy and the excercise of creativity. In Vosniadou, S. and Ortony, A. (eds) *Similarity and Analogical Reasoning.* Cambridge University Press, Cambridge, pp. 313–331.

Jongen, R. (1985) Polysemy, tropes and cognition or the non-magrittian art of closing curtains whilst opening them. In Paprotté, W. and Dirven, R. (eds) *The Ubiquity of Metaphor.* John Benjamins, Amsterdam, pp. 85–119.

Just, M.A. and Carpenter, P.A. (1980) A theory of reading: from eye fixations to comprehension, *Psychological Review* 87: 329–354.

Just, M.A. and Carpenter, P.A. (1984) Using eye fixations to study reading comprehension. In Kieras, D.E. and Just M.A. (eds) *New Methods in Reading Comprehension Research.* Lawrence Erlbaum Associates, Hillsdale, NJ, pp. 151–82.

Just, M.A. and Carpenter, P.A. (1987) *The Psychology of Reading and Language Comprehension.* Allyn and Bacon, Boston.

Katz, A.N., Paivio, A. and Marschark, M. (1985) Poetic comparisons: psychological dimensions of metaphoric processing, *Journal of Psycholinguistic Research* 14: 365–383.

Katz, A.N., Paivio, A., Marschark, M. and Clark, J.M. (1988) Norms for 204 literary and 260 nonliterary metaphors on psychological dimensions, *Metaphor And Symbolic Activity* 3: 191–214.

Kennedy, J.M. (1990) Metaphor – its intellectual basis, *Metaphor And Symbolic Activity* 5: 115–23.

Kintgen, E.R. (1983) *The Perception of Poetry.* Indiana University Press, Bloomington.

Kintsch, W. (1988) The role of knowledge in discourse comprehension: a construction-integration model, *Psychological Review* 95: 163–82.

Kittay, E.F. (1987) *Metaphor: Its Cognitive Force and Linguistic Structure.* Clarendon Press, Oxford.

Kövecses, Z. (1988) *The Language of Love: The Semantics of Passion in Conversational English.* Associated University Presses, London and Toronto.

Kreuz, R. and MacNealy, M.S. (eds) (1993) *Empirical Approaches to Literature and Aesthetics.* Ablex, Norwood, NJ.

Lakoff, G. (1986a) A figure of thought, *Metaphor And Symbolic Activity* 1: 215–25.

Lakoff, G. (1986b) The meanings of literal, *Metaphor And Symbolic Activity* 1: 291–96.

Lakoff, G. (1987a) *Women, Fire, and Dangerous Things.* University of Chicago Press, Chicago.

Lakoff, G. (1987b) The death of dead metaphor, *Metaphor And Symbolic Activity* **2**: 143–7.

Lakoff, G. and Johnson, M. (1980) *Metaphors We Live By*. University of Chicago Press, Chicago.

Lakoff, G. and Turner, M. (1989) *More Than Cool Reason: A Field Guide to Poetic Metaphor*. Chicago University Press, Chicago.

Langacker, R.W. (1988) A usage-based model. In Rudzka-Ostyn, B. (ed.) *Topics in Cognitive Linguistics*. John Benjamins, Amsterdam, 127–61.

Larsen, S.F. and Seilman, U. (1988) Personal remindings while reading literature, *Text* **8**: 411–29.

László, J., Meutsch, D. and Viehoff, R. (1988) Verbal reports as data in text comprehension research: an introduction, *Text* **8**: 283–94.

Levin, S.R. (1988) *Metaphoric Worlds: Conceptions of a Romantic Nature*. Yale University Press, New Haven and London.

Levinson, S.C. (1983) *Pragmatics*. Cambridge University Press, Cambridge.

Loewenberg, I. (1975) Identifying metaphors, *Foundations of Language* **12**: 315–38.

MacCormac, E.R. (1985) *A Cognitive Theory of Metaphor*. MIT Press, Cambridge, Mass.

Marschark, M. and Hunt, R.R. (1986) On memory for metaphor, *Memory and Cognition* **13**: 413–24.

Marschark, M., Katz, A.N. and Paivio, A. (1983) Dimensions of metaphor, *Journal of Psycholinguistic Research* **12**: 17–40.

McCabe, A. (1984) Conceptual similarity and the quality of metaphor in isolated sentences versus extended contexts, *Journal of Psycholinguistic Research* **12**: 41–68.

Medin, D. and Ortony, A. (1989) Psychological essentialism. In Vosniadou, S.and Ortony, A. (eds) *Similarity and Analogical Reasoning*. Cambridge University Press, Cambridge, pp. 179–95.

Meutsch, D. (1987) *Literatur verstehen. Eine empirische Studie*. Vieweg, Braunschweig/Wiesbaden.

Meutsch, D. (1989) How to do thoughts with words II: degrees of explicitness in think-aloud during the comprehension of literary and expository texts with different types of readers, *Poetics* **18**: 45–71.

Meutsch, D. and Schmidt, S.J. (1985) On the role of conventions in understanding literary texts, *Poetics* **14**: 551–74.

Miller, G.A. (1979) Similes and metaphors. In Ortony, A. (ed.) *Metaphor and Thought*. Cambridge University Press, Cambridge, pp. 202–50.

Mooij, J.J.A. (1976) *A Study of Metaphor: On the Nature of Metaphorical Expressions, With Special Reference to their Reference*. North Holland: Amsterdam.

Olson, G.M., Duffy, S.A. and Mack, R.L. (1984) Thinking-out-loud as a method for studying real-time comprehension processes. In Kieras, D.E. and Just, M.A. (eds) *New Methods in Reading Comprehension Research*. Lawrence Erlbaum, Hillsdale, NJ, pp 253–86.

Ortony, A. (ed.) (1979a) *Metaphor and Thought*. Cambridge University Press, Cambridge.

Ortony, A. (1979b) The role of similarity in similes and metaphors. In Ortony, A.

(ed.) *Metaphor and Thought.* Cambridge University Press, Cambridge, pp. 186–201.

Ortony, A., Reynolds, R.E. and **Arter, J.A.** (1978) Metaphor: theoretical and empirical research, *Psychological Bulletin* **85**: 919–43.

Ortony, A., Schallert, D.L., Reynolds, R.E. and **Antos, S.J.** (1978) Interpreting metaphors and idioms: some effects of context on comprehension, *Journal of Verbal Learning and Verbal Behaviour* **17**: 465–77.

Osgood, C.E. (1972). The nature and measurement of meaning. In Snider, J.G. and Osgood, C.E. (eds) *Semantic Differential Technique: A Sourcebook.* Aldine, Chicago, pp. 1–41.

Osgood, C.E. and **Suci, G.J.** (1972) Factor analysis of meaning. In Snider, J.G. and Osgood, C.E. (eds) *Semantic Differential Technique: A Sourcebook.* Aldine, Chicago, pp. 42–55.

Palmer, S.E. (1989) Levels of description in information-processing theories of analogy. In Vosniadou, S. and Ortony, A. (eds) *Similarity and Analogical Reasoning.* Cambridge University Press, Cambridge, pp. 332–45.

Paprotté, W. and **Dirven, R.** (eds) (1985) *The Ubiquity of Metaphor.* John Benjamins, Amsterdam.

Pilkington, A. (1991a) Poetic effects: a relevance perspective. In Sell, R.D. (ed.) *Literary Pragmatics.* Routledge, London, pp. 44–61.

Pilkington, A. (1991b) The literary reading process: a relevance theory perspective. In Ibsch, E., Schram D.H. and Steen, G.J. (eds) *Empirical Studies in Literature: Proceedings of the Second International Conference, Amsterdam 1989.* Rodopi, Amsterdam, pp. 117–24.

Quinn, N. (1991) The cultural basis of metaphor. In Fernandez, J. (ed.) *Beyond Metaphor: The Theory of Tropes in Anthropology.* Stanford University Press, Stanford, pp. 56–93.

Quinn, N. and **Holland, D.** (1987) Culture and cognition. In Holland, D. and Quinn, N. (eds) *Cultural Models in Language and Thought.* Cambridge University Press, Cambridge, pp. 3–48.

Reinhart, T. (1976) On understanding poetic metaphor, *Poetics* **5**: 383–402.

Richards, I.A. (1936) *The Philosophy of Rhetoric.* Oxford University Press, London.

Ricoeur, P. (1974) Metaphor and the main problem of hermeneutics, *New Literary History* **6**: 95–110.

Ricoeur, P. (1979) *The Rule of Metaphor: Multi-Disciplinary Studies of the Creation of Meaning in Language.* Routledge and Kegan Paul: London.

Rumelhart, D.E. (1989) Toward a microstructural account of human reasoning. In Vosniadou, S.and Ortony, A. (eds) *Similarity and Analogical Reasoning.* Cambridge University Press, Cambridge, 298–312.

Russell, D.A. and **Winterbottom, M.** (1972) *Ancient Literary Criticism: The Principal Texts in New Translations.* Clarendon Press, Oxford.

Sampson, G. (1981) The resurgence of metaphor, *Lingua* **54**: 211–26.

Schmidt, S.J. (1980) *Grundriss der empirischen Literaturwissenschaft, [Vol. 1]: Der gesellschaftliche Handlungsbereich Literatur.* Vieweg, Braunschweig/Wiesbaden.

Schmidt, S.J. (1985) On writing histories of literature: some remarks from a constructivist point of view, *Poetics* **14**: 279–301.

Schnotz, W., Ballstaedt, S.-P. and **Mandl, H.** (1981) Kognitive Prozesse beim

Zusammenfassen von Lehrtexten. In Mandl, H. (ed.) *Zur Psychologie der Textverarbeitung: Ansätze, Befunde, Probleme.* Urban and Schwarzenberg, Munich, pp. 108–67.

Schram, D.H. (1985) *Norm en normdoorbreking. Empirisch onderzoek naar de receptie van literaire teksten voorafgegaan door een overzicht van theoretische opvattingen met betrekking tot de funktie van literatuur.* VU Uitgeverij, Amsterdam.

Schram, D.H. and Steen, G.J. (1992) 'But what *is* literature?' A programmatic answer from the empirical study of literature, *SPIEL* **11**: 239–58.

Searle, J. (1979) Metaphor. In Ortony, A. (ed.) *Metaphor and Thought.* Cambridge University Press, Cambridge, pp. 92–23.

Sell, R.D. (1991) Literary pragmatics: an introduction. In Sell, R.D. (ed.) *Literary Pragmatics.* Routledge, London, pp. *xi–xxiii.*

Shen, Y. (ed.) (1992) Special issue of *Poetics Today* **13** (4), *Aspects of Metaphor Comprehension.*

Shibles, W. (1971) *Metaphor: An Annotated Bibliography and History.* Language Press, Whitewater WI.

Simpson, G.B. (ed.) (1991) *Understanding Word and Sentence. Advances in Psychology,* Vol. 77. North Holland, Amsterdam.

Soskice, J.M. (1988) *Metaphor and Religious Language.* Clarendon, Oxford.

Sperber, D. and Wilson, D. (1986) *Relevance: Communication and Cognition.* Basil Blackwell, Oxford.

Steen, G.J. (1989) Metaphor and literary comprehension: towards a discourse theory of metaphor in literature, *Poetics* **18**: 113–41.

Steen, G.J. (1990) How to do things with metaphor in literature, *Revue Belge de Philologie et d'Histoire* **68**: 658–71.

Steen, G.J. (1991a) Understanding metaphor in literature: towards an empirical study. In Sell, R.D. (ed.) *Literary Pragmatics.* Routledge, London, pp. 110–26.

Steen, G.J. (1991b) The empirical study of literary reading: methods of data collection, *Poetics* **20**: 559–75.

Steen, G.J. (1992) Literary and nonliterary aspects of metaphor, *Poetics Today* **13**: 687–704.

Steen, G.J. and Schram, D.H. (forthcoming) Literary aspects of reading in thinking out loud. In Kreuz, R. and MacNealy, M.S. (eds) *Empirical Approaches to Literature and Aesthetics.* Ablex, Norwood, NJ.

Sternberg, R.J. and Nigro, G. (1983) Interaction and analogy in the comprehension and appreciation of metaphors, *Quarterly Journal of Experimental Psychology* **35A**: 17–38.

Sternberg, R.J., Tourangeau, R. and Nigro, G. (1979) Metaphor, induction, and social policy: the convergence of macroscopic and microscopic views. In Ortony, A. (ed.) *Metaphor and Thought.* Cambridge University Press, Cambridge, pp. 325–53.

Tabachnik, B.G. and Fidell, L.S. (1989) *Using Multivariate Statistics.* Harper and Row, New York.

Tabossi, P. (1986) Words in context. In Kurcz, I., Shugar, G.W. and Danks, J.H. (eds) *Knowledge and Language.* North Holland, Amsterdam, pp. 277–302.

Thompson, A. and Thompson, J.O. (1987) *Shakespeare, Meaning and Metaphor.* Harvester, Brighton.

Tourangeau, R. (1982) Metaphor and cognitive structure. In Miall D.S. (ed.) *Metaphor: Problems and Perspectives.* Harvester, Brighton, pp. 14–35.

Tourangeau, R. and **Sternberg, R.J.** (1981) Aptness in metaphor, *Cognitive Psychology* **13**: 27–55.

Tourangeau, R. and **Sternberg, R.J.** (1982) Understanding and appreciating metaphors, *Cognition* **11**: 203–44.

Trick, L. and **Katz, A.N.** (1986) The domain-interaction approach to metaphor processing: relating individual differences and metaphor characteristics, *Metaphor and Symbolic Activity* **1**: 185–214.

Tsur, R. (1987) *On Metaphoring.* Israel Science Publishers, Jerusalem.

Turbayne, C.M. (1963) *The Myth of Metaphor.* Yale University Press, New Haven.

Turner, M. (1987) *Death is the Mother of Beauty.* University of Chicago Press, Chicago.

Van Assche, A. (1991) Content analysis and 'experimental' methods in literary study: scientific twins or opponents? In Ibsch, E., Schram, D.H. and Steen, G.J. (eds) *Empirical Studies in Literature: Proceedings of the Second International Conference, Amsterdam 1989.* Rodopi, Amsterdam, pp. 374–53.

Van Dijk, T.A. and **Kintsch, W.** (1983) *Strategies of Discourse Comprehension.* Academic Press, New York.

Van Noppen, J.-P. (ed) (1990) Special issue *Revue Belge de Philologie et d'Histoire* **68**, *How To Do Things With Metaphor.*

Van Noppen, J.-P., De Knop, S. and **Jongen, R.** (compilers) (1985) *Metaphor: A Bibliography of Post-1970 Publications.* Benjamins, Amsterdam.

Van Noppen, J.-P. and **Hols, E.** (compilers) (1991) *Metaphor II: A Classified Bibliography of Publications from 1985–1990.* Benjamins, Amsterdam.

Van Peer, W. (1986) *Stylistics and Psychology: Investigations of Foregrounding.* Croom Helm, London.

Verdaasdonk, H. and **Van Rees, K.** (1992) The narrow margin of innovation in literary research: Siegfried J. Schmidt's proposal for the empirical study of literature, *Poetics* **21**: 141–52.

Vipond, D. and **Hunt, R.A.** (1984) Point-driven understanding: pragmatic and cognitive dimensions of literary reading, *Poetics* **13**: 261–77.

Vipond, D. and **Hunt, R.A.** (1989) Literary processing and response as transaction: evidence for the contribution of readers, texts, and situations. In Viehoff, R. and Meutsch, D. (eds) *Comprehension of Literary Discourse: Results and Problems of Interdisciplinary Approaches.* De Gruyter, Berlin, pp 155–74.

Vosniadou, S. and **Ortony, A.** (1989) Similarity and analogical reasoning: a synthesis. In Vosniadou, S. and Ortony, A. (eds) *Similarity and Analogical Reasoning.* Cambridge University Press, Cambridge, pp. 1–17.

Waern, Y. (1988) Thoughts on text in context: applying the think-aloud method to text processing, *Text* **8**: 327–50.

Wellek, R. and **Warren, A.** (1949) *Theory of Literature.* Penguin, Harmondsworth.

Winner, E. (1988) *The Point of Words: Children's Understanding of Metaphor and Irony.* Harvard University Press, Cambridge, Mass.

Zwaan, R.A. (1993) *Aspects of Literary Comprehension: A Cognitive Approach.* John Benjamins, Amsterdam.

Name Index

Schreier, M., 33
Searle, J., 90
Seilman, U., 11, 128, 129
Sell, R.D., 164, 165
Shakespeare, W., 3, 38, 39, 78n
Shen, Y., 4
Shibles, W., 4
Simon H.A., 109, 112, 115, 116, 118
Simpson G.B., 85, 96
Soskice, J.B.,4
Sperber, D., 49n
Steen, G.J., 33, 65, 66, 72, 75, 89, 101,
    104, 109, 165, 170
Sternberg, R.J., 11, 18, 49n, 171, 178,
    188
Suci, G.J., 189

Tabachnik, B.G., 138, 155n, 209n, 212n
Tabossi, P., 93, 96
Thagard, P.R., 13
Thomas, D.M., 186
Thompson, A., 38
Thompson, J.O., 38
Tourangeau, R., 18, 171, 178, 188
Trick, L., 11, 13, 18
Tsur, R., 38

Turbayne, C.M., 4
Turner, M., 4, 16, 27, 37–41

Van Assche, A., 29, 51, 166
Van der Heijden, A.F.Th., 66, 67
Van Dijk, T.A., 83, 84, 88, 89, 93, 101,
    242, 244–5
Van Noppen, J.-P., 4
Van Peer, W., 50
Van Rees, K., 166
Verdaasdonk, H., 166
Vipond, D., 32, 43, 50, 52, 84, 85, 114,
    120
Vorderer, P., 87
Vosniadou, S., 12

Waern, Y., 110
Warren, A., 31, 32, 45, 49n
Wellek, R., 31, 32, 45, 49n
Wilson, D., 49n
Winner, E., 4, 10
Winterbottom, M., 27

Zoon, C.,66, 67
Zwaan, R., 32, 85, 89, 103

Subject Index